C000301729

A JOURNAL OF CONTEMPORARY WRITING

IRISH PAGES

IRISH PAGES is a biannual journal (Spring-Summer, Autumn-Winter), edited in Belfast and publishing, in equal measure, writing from Ireland and overseas. It appears at the end of each six-month period.

Its policy is to publish poetry, short fiction, essays, creative non-fiction, memoir, essay reviews, nature-writing, translated work, literary journalism, and other autobiographical, historical, religious and scientific writing of literary distinction. There are no standard reviews or narrowly academic articles. Irish language and Ulster Scots writing are published in the original, with English translations or glosses.

IRISH PAGES is a non-partisan, non-sectarian, culturally ecumenical, and wholly independent journal. It endorses no political outlook or cultural tradition, and has no editorial position on the constitutional question. Its title refers to the island of Ireland in a purely apolitical and geographic sense, in the same manner of The Church of Ireland or the Irish Sea.

The sole criteria for inclusion in the journal are the distinction of the writing and the integrity of the individual voice. Equal editorial attention will be given to established, emergent and new writers.

The views expressed in IRISH PAGES are not necessarily those of the Editors. The magazine has no editorial or financial connection to the Linen Hall Library or its Directors.

Submissions are welcome but must be accompanied by a stamped addressed envelope or an international reply coupon. Reporting time is six months. If work is accepted, a copy on disk may be requested.

Your subscription is essential to the independence and survival of the journal. Subscription rates are £16stg/€26/$24 for one year, or £24/€39/$36 for two years. For postage outside Ireland and Britain, add £4/€6/$5 per year for Europe, or £6/€9/$8 per year for the rest of the world. Visit our website at www.irishpages.org for a subscription form. Credit cards are welcome.

IRISH PAGES
The Linen Hall Library
17 Donegall Square North
Belfast BT1 5GB

Advisory Board
Jonathan Allison
John Gray
Maureen Mackin
Bernard O'Donoghue
Daniel Tobin

Legal Advice
Campbell Stafford & Co

IRISH PAGES is designed by Tonic and set in 11.5/12.5 Monotype Perpetua.
It is printed in Belfast by Nicholson & Bass.

This issue has been generously asssisted by the Arts Council of Northern Ireland.

Copyright remains with the authors.

ISBN 0-9544257-4-X

ARTS
COUNCIL
of Northern Ireland

A JOURNAL OF CONTEMPORARY WRITING

IRISH PAGES

CHRIS AGEE, *Editor*

CATHAL Ó SEARCAIGH, *Irish Language Editor*

SEÁN MAC AINDREASA, *Managing Editor*

EDITED AT THE LINEN HALL LIBRARY IN BELFAST

AUTUMN / WINTER 2004

IRISH PAGES

—

VOLUME 2, NUMBER 2, AUTUMN / WINTER 2004

CONTENTS

Machine-cut Turf, Donegal
by Rachel Giese Brown

THE VIEW FROM THE LINEN HALL

Unnatural selection.

In his 1989 essay, "The Hero as Demolition Man," the German poet Hans Magnus Enzensberger describes an anti-heroic paradigm for the future of liberal democracy in the aftermath of the twentieth century's totalitarian dictatorships. Recalling Clausewitz's dictum that retreat under fire is the most difficult of all manoeuvres in war, he continues:

> It is the same in politics. The ultimate act in the art of the possible is being able to surrender an untenable position. If the greatness of a hero is measured by the difficulty of the task he faces, we must not only revise our notion of heroism, but reverse it. Any cretin can throw a bomb. It is a thousand times more difficult to disarm one.

The new breed of political "hero" – if the term can still be used – will be a protagonist of the art of retreat who represents "not victory, conquest, or triumph, but resignation, withdrawal, and devolution". This is the politician of renunciation, the demolition expert who understands that progress *is* retreat wherever the instruments of a system have got the better of our humanity. Among Enzensberger's examples are Khrushchev after Stalin; Suarez after Franco; and, above all, Gorbachev as the driving force that dismantled the Soviet empire. Thus the hero of retreat, by undermining the system supporting him, is typically cast aside, defeated by his own success.

For Enzensberger, this new breed of political protagonist is already mustering inside our own all-conquering – if ecologically commensal – polity. The West too, even in its Cold War triumph, must face up sooner or later to the task of demolition:

> A German philosopher once said that by the end of this century we will want not to have improved the world but to have saved it. This applies not only to those dictatorships that have been scrapped, peacefully or not, before our eyes, but also those Western democracies that face an impending and unprecedented disarmament. Military disengagement is only one of the forms of retreat to consider. Other untenable positions have to be abandoned in our economic war against the Third World, and the most difficult of all our retreats will take place in the war we have been waging against our biosphere since the Industrial Revolution.

Long before 1989, the tenor of that final observation was more commonsense than prophetic insight. Century's end has come, and it does seem we are contemplating not only Lilliputian contexts of improvement-as-usual, but a race to avert a still-more grotesque, baroque and (in the worst scientific scenarios) metaphorically apocalyptic plateau in the degradation of the biosphere, in which man's ecological footprint first outpaces, then overwhelms, the natural phenomena that govern our world. In the coming century, what Casey Walker calls, in this issue, a "world-historical debate" (p.137) between globalists and localists will hinge on this challenge of ecological retreat. If there is to be a withdrawal from elements of our technosphere, leaving a rubble of obsolete ideas and discarded forms, then the localists will need many protagonists of demolition – and fast.

Inveterate beachcombers in Ireland (like this writer) will be aware that there is not a strand on the island free of the escalating flotsam and jetsam of industrial products. Indeed, remote beaches, in furthest Donegal or Mayo, are often the worse, notwithstanding their spectacular setting of cliff, cove and sea-stack. Left to its own devices, a crescent of remote shingle can accumulate on its tidemark a harlequin of plastics dating back decades. All of these have come into existence in living memory, since the fifties – the decade, tellingly, when "environmentalism" went global with the writings of Rachel Carson – even though some of these petrochemical derivatives can last, undisturbed, for 50,000 years. In retrospect, the intersection of Carson's early warnings and the postwar surge in the petrochemical economy seems to mark the moment when the balance between the biosphere and the technosphere tipped precipitously towards the latter.

It cannot be gainsaid: the world is being filled up with human things and influences, and at an astonishingly rapid rate in historical and geophysical terms. There are too many of us by half and our technohive is packing the finite planetary space with unsustainable surfeits of created stuff. A kind of Malthusian mathematics now characterizes our production of artefacts, structures, emissions, effluents, impacts of every stripe. In New York City alone, for instance, five billion beverage containers must be "disposed of" every year. Peter Matthiessen, the great chronicler of the natural world, who grew up on the other end of Long Island, describes how the waters of its Sound have morphed from pristine clarity to clouded degradation in a single lifetime. Whatever the counter-currents of good news, and there are some, that is an apt metaphor for the overall direction of the globe's ecology over the past century.

So too is the human debris on the world's coasts, whereupon last century's explosion of technosphere into biosphere can be read in vivid microcosm. The global tidemark is a vast palimpsest of our monumental ecological impact on the largest and most immemorial wilderness, the sea. What lies out of sight and mind in terrestrial dumps, landfills and fly-tips arrives as an open book on the ebb and flow of the intertidal zone. Three decades ago, I could still be surprised by a moonlit Andalusian shore littered with the debris of rapid industrialization, or a beer can in a pristine cove in circumpolar Labrador. Not long ago, in a national park on a remote Mediterranean island, along the utterly isolated shoreline of a saltwater lake, I studied a tidal scum of oil-globs and small bits of plastic. Nowhere, it seemed, was beyond the anabasis of our exponential waste.

To the technosphere's Brobdingnagian scale and extension must added the escalating durability of its components. In turn-of-the-century London, then the world's largest megapolis, about 85% of waste was cinders and charcoal, easily returned to the soil cycle, and much of the rest was biodegradable, like wood, paper and compost. Now the contemporary economy produces a juggernaut of plastics and other synthetic products that are not subject to the natural timescales of decay, fragmentation or metallic disintegration.

Take, for instance, the proverbial wine bottle. For centuries, the rich ecology of the Iberian cork groves has served wine-makers well. In recent years, however, a variant plastic stopper has begun to make its appearance in the bottles of certain brands. Which means, probably, tens of millions of new non-biodegradable objects of indeterminate persistence being poured onto the globe each year. No doubt the flipchart marketeers will yammer on about their innovative reasons, but this sort of artefact cries out for direct banning – pre-emptive, without concession – as a salutary instance of ecological retreat in miniature.

It gets worse on a myriad of fronts. The ownership of automobiles, with their evolving kaleidoscope of materials, is expected to rise from 900 million to 1.5 billion on the next three decades. Computers were billed as the immaterial end of "the paper office" (forlorn hope!), but, in a blink of ecological time, the IT revolution has actually created a huge waste-mountain of plastics, precious metals, wires, disks, chips and assorted infrastructures that is proving highly difficult to recycle economically. Much of the outdated technology is gathering dust in backrooms and attics, uncertain of its destination, and has yet to reach the dump (in the US) or the recycling depot (in Europe, as of this year). In an unregulated and supremely toxic trade, discarded CDs are being exported to impoverished villages in China, to be smelted for trace elements of precious metals, before ending in Dali-esque slag-heaps: one small piece in the jigsaw of national ecological calamity unleashed by the surging Chinese amalgam of economy and repression.

In the military sphere especially, new generations of quasi-indestructible fabrics and materiel are being devised for widespread application. Like all these examples, no one seems to know, or care, what will happen to these things when they come to be "thrown away". They must languish somewhere, unable to decay, impossible to re-use, difficult to burn, improbable for re-cycling: a quintessential piece of short-termism mandated by the cult of "growth" *per se*. Clearly, if the scale and nature of the technosphere continues in this unbridled fashion, the globe will be swamped everywhere by the geophysical impact of humanity.

All this constitutes what might be called "the waste-space crisis". Our global bind is not, however, merely a complex second-order issue of waste collection, management and elimination, essential as these are. No doubt the ecological way forward here will be "closed-loop systems" (such as those pioneered in a number of German *Länder*) in which all recyclables are extracted; the waste residue used for fuel in power stations and construction; and nothing returned to landfill. In this way, one can imagine the waste stream gradually becoming its own closed and homeostatic system contained increasingly within the production cycles of the technosphere, rather than being flushed back, as is the default norm, into the beleaguered biosphere. If this kind of self-fuelling sustainability could be combined with a general cessation in the war on the biosphere, one might even permit oneself the Chekhovian hope that the future may yet be "unspeakably, amazingly lovely".

No, in the present dire ecological circumstances, the Waste-Space Crisis is an altogether more profound geophysical-cum-anthropological axiom: the visible precipitate of our ravening consumption of the biosphere. "Waste" is our slug's trail through the natural world; "space," the smothering quilt of all our trails. In a "waste" sense, the emblematic impact is climate change; in a "space" sense, the trinity of habitat destruction, loss of biodiversity and mass extinction. For humanity in its own right has now become a colossal geophysical force. In a speech after his dismissal as Environment Minister, Michael Meacher memorably distilled years of Whitehall briefings:

> Our biological carbon activity is now exceeded only by the krill in
> the oceans. Our civil engineering works shift more soil each year than
> all the world's rivers bring to the seas. Our industrial emissions
> eclipse the total emissions from all the world's volcanoes. We are

bringing about species loss on a scale of some of the massive natural extinctions of palaeohistory. We are altering the nitrogen cycle …Some 420 million people live in countries that no longer have enough crop land to grow their own food. Half a billion people live in regions prone to chronic drought. By 2025 that number is likely to have increased fivefold. Marine ecosystems are at risk, including salt-water marshes, mangroves, coastal wetlands and coral reefs. In 1998, the hottest year on record, large areas of forest burned down after prolonged drought. By 2050 it is projected that the Amazon will have died back.

On top of this, alterations in the shimmering disequilibrium of our biosphere will unlock changes that must interact with the original shifts and may grossly magnify their effects. And chaos theory suggests that, for the same methodological reason we cannot exactly predict the weather more than two weeks in advance (i.e., the knock-on effects of the impossibility of perfect measurement), we will never be able to anticipate fully the unfolding of our own geophysical influences.

Politically, one of the more revolutionary pieces of science in recent years must be the concept of "the ecological footprint" trail-blazed by the distinguished biologist E.O. Wilson. Unlike his understanding of humanity's feeling for other life ("biophilia") or of the convergence between science and the arts ("consilience"), this formulation is underpinned by hard empirical numbers. It expresses the average appropriation of productive land and shallow sea by each person in bits and pieces from around the world for food, water, housing, energy, transportation, commerce and waste absorption.

   The ecological footprint ranges from one hectare (2.5 acres) in the developing world to 9.6 hectares (24 acres) in the US, with the global average for the total human population at 2.1 hectares (5.2 acres). *For every person now in the world to reach present American levels of consumption would require four more planet Earths.* With the current global population predicted by the UN to rise and possibly peak at nine-to-ten billion by 2050 (i.e., an addition of 200,000 people per week for the next half century), two further Earths would be needed. A recent study exploring this concept calculates that the human population outstripped the Earth's sustainable capacity in the late seventies. In the decade after the 1992 Summit on the Environment, world GNP has increased by half, even as the global pattern of wealth's ancient dichotomy has deepened.

This eco-equation – comprising the three variables, *economy*, *democracy*, *environment* – has deep political ramifications. Firstly, it makes plain that global growth alone, without massive North-South redistribution, will not lead in the overall direction of social justice, even if the five billion people of the developing world never aspire to levels of American and Western European profligacy. Secondly, and consequently, the spread of real democracy across the less developed nations, echoing Europe's own history, would perforce come to challenge the powers and privileges husbanded by the developed world's ecological footprint.

Lastly, there is a close practical and ethical connection between the population bottleneck, genuine democracy and the necessary stewardship of the natural world on behalf of the common good. Consider, for example, ancient forests, 80% of which have now been consumed or degraded. The staggering rapidity of their destruction – largely for and by the developed world in league with authoritarian local elites – represents a one-off realization of an ancient ecological asset mainly for the benefit of the wealthy footprint. Tribal forest people universally oppose such rapaciousness, understanding well the link between long-term stewardship and self-interest. At the heart of the issues of social justice and ecological defence, then, is the same *imperium* of economy waging war against the global poor and the biosphere. Thus, the common good and the wild commons are naturally democratic allies.

A kind of global political triangulation is emerging, whose three points are the variables listed above. It is, however, an inverted pyramid, with the vertex of environment sustaining the other two. If the balance of this triangulation is not shifted from the current unbridled sovereignty of economy, the gross inequities of the North-South divide will come into intractable contradiction with the spread of global democracy; indeed, in this not-improbable scenario, the power of economy and technoscience will become more and more inimical to the claims of real democracy and a sustainable environment. Already the relations between the three points are literally "ruled" in the interests of a brutalist economy by the *de facto* global government known as the World Trade Organization. "The race is now on between the technoscientific forces that are destroying the living environment and those that can be harnessed to save it," writes Wilson in *The Future of Life* (2001). "We are inside a bottleneck of overpopulation and wasteful consumption. If the race is won, humanity can emerge in far better condition than when it entered, and with most of the diversity of life still intact."

Throughout the twentieth century, the various ideological struggles and systems were united in their prodigal war on the biosphere. Crusoe-like, humanity built up its stockade of creature comforts with, in the main, blithe disregard for the gathering ecological perils. There were intimations and warnings and even eco-battles, but the overall anthropological momentum has not been trammelled, only slowed and questioned, with little sign of the necessary retreats. Now the ecological footprint is Man Friday's warning that the splendid isolation of our hubris is gone forever.

The contemporary technosphere, then, is no less than an *evolutionary* threat to the biosphere. Our cultural evolution is a far twig on a branch of a branch of a branch of the great beech of evolution, but one that is hacking away madly at the whole tree. We risk making our own small berth a monstrous outgrowth compared to the radically deformed rest. Mass disasters, social as well as natural, might then, like storms, devastate parts of our branch's ecological exposure.

With many of our creations, such as mega-dams and agricultural monocultures, technological occupation of the globe is increasingly the long-term problem *per se*; though to say this is still treated as major heresy in much of the political and media worlds. Our technosphere, ramped up by the Industrial Revolution, has become a mobile machine in itself, expanding unstoppably until, perhaps, something judders it to slowdown, or even retreat. Some scientists suggest that our elimination of biodiversity and ecosystems that do not serve our immediate requirements could provoke a total system collapse in the biosphere. What is certain – as the debate over climate change already illustrates – is that the ecological worldview will move from the margins to the centre of historical consciousness in the coming century.

On some level, of course, every technology is destructive geophysically: this is part of the meaning of culture. Nor, of course, is there anything new about our clearing of primeval forests or annihilation of large mammals, both which have been in train, respectively, since Neolithic and Paleolithic times. In one of W.G. Sebald's *omnium gatherum* novels there is a darkly vivid page describing the clearing of forests from pre-historic Europe through to contemporary Brazil and Borneo, a brief history of civilization as combustion:

> Our spread over the earth was fuelled by reducing the higher species of vegetation to charcoal, by incessantly burning whatever would burn … Combustion is the hidden principle behind every artefact … Like our bodies and our desires, the machines we have devised are possessed of a heart that is slowly reduced to embers. From earliest times, human civilization has been no more than a strange

luminescence growing more intense by the hour, of which no one can say when it will begin to wane and when it will fade away. For the time being, our cities still shine through the night, and our fires still spread. (*The Rings of Saturn*, 1998)

Millennia of fearful and exploitative struggle with the natural world: this is the deep-time backdrop to the contemporary consumption of the biosphere.

Yet, against this archaic human pattern, the ecological perspective institutes the equivalent of a Copernican revolution, in which the dependency of economy and social progress on the fixed constraints of the biosphere assumes its centrality. As with the death of the Ptolemaic theory, it is the very antiquity of the worldview overturned that vouchsafes the conceptual power of the insurgent paradigm. Ideas like the ecological footprint are not so much "environmentalism" as a real-world intrusion into the still-ascendant "cornucopian" worldview, our contemporary equivalent of flat-earthers, astrolabes and alchemical quest. In this delirium of anthropomorphism, Earth's horn is (or can be made) perpetually fruitful; growth is, therefore, boundless; and human ingenuity allied to technology can ultimately solve whatever problems the detritus of progress throws up.

Integral to much environmental thinking over recent decades is the implicit aspiration for a restoration. If the war against the biosphere could be decisively limited, if the essentially "chemical" nature of pollution and waste could be rectified, if ecosystems could be spared and/or allowed to regenerate – and so on – nature's own healing powers would be given a powerful breathing space. The momentum of the contemporary technosphere, sustained by what Andrew Kimbrell aptly calls "the technological imagination" (p.195), might be checked and, by implication, reversed in favour of the new paradigm of Earth's human stewardship.

For many of us touched by the environmentalism of the sixties and seventies, this aspiration was undoubtedly influenced by the perception, or actual experience, of a world more commodious than now to the wild spaces of pristine biota. Call it the *Born Free* effect. No doubt, like that filmic kitsch, this feature of the zeitgeist partook of old urban traditions of romanticized nature; no doubt, too, the situation was more dire even then than imagined. But the feeling in the historical air of a globe not wholly spoilt, and the aspiration to defend that, if necessary by self-imposed limits and hard retreat, was and is a truth worth cherishing. It may also be, as one scholar of wilderness has ruefully contemplated, an older passing consciousness at the moment when the full-spectrum global dominance of the technosphere came into sight. Looming over the future of ecological thinking and the biosphere generally is the possibility that most people in a still-more crowded and technologized future will not share, or be able to share, or even care about, this firsthand feeling of a globe still partly unspoilt, and the concomitant desire to protect it. If so, something incomparably rare and precious will have vanished from the common geography of human life.

Alas, worldviews die hard. Though challenged, there is little sign of the technological imagination relinquishing its firm grip on the psychic sceptre. On the contrary, far from being chastised by the waste-space crisis *et al*, one of the salient features of our technosphere over the last two decades is the emergence of a wholly new order of assault on the biosphere. This is the overarching theme of the suite of essays and interviews that follows under the rubric "The Genetic Nightmare".

Having spent millennia bending the biosphere to its will, humanity is now poised to begin re-designing it through the agency of bio- and nano-technology in what is, essentially, a new evolutionary process of "unnatural selection". With biotechnology, life itself will be increasingly engineered and thus technologized, and the wild thoroughly endangered; with nano-technology, matter will be refabricated on sub-atomic and molecular levels, often involving the insertion of micro-computers. To our mass chemical pollution since the Industrial Revolution, we have begun to add two qualitatively different types of contamination: the biological and the genetic (pp.192-193), *both of which are irreversible*.

In this new outcrop of the cornucopian universe, nothing has been learnt from our war on the biosphere. Problems with the sustainability of the biosphere? Let us redesign it in the interests of the technosphere, with no chance of a restoration of the natural *status quo ante*. The biosphere must not merely bend, but conform, to the technosphere and its empire of patents and endless commodification. Billions of years of natural selection must be turned to the topical ends of unnatural selection. It is the supreme hubris of the technological imagination.

As the four scientific critics here make plain (p.155), there is a strongly totalitarian flavour to the "inevitabilities" of the biotech enterprise. This was first borne home to me in a 2000 passage by Wendell Berry about the tyranny of technological and genetic monocultures: "Monsanto's aptly named 'Terminator Gene' – which, implanted in seed sold by Monsanto, would cause the next generation of seed to be sterile – is as grave an indicator of totalitarian purpose as a concentration camp." Armed with genetic irreversibility, the new totalitarians of the technosphere mean to impose their unnatural selection in a unilateral override both of the fabric of evolution (the non-anthropomorphic angle) and of centuries of democratic practice (the anthropomorphic angle). They are, in a real sense, our era's *infidels* (from the Latin *infidelis*: unfaithful), in their radical and cumulatively reckless assault on the given world of evolutionary time.

Unnatural selection's non-compatibility in principle with the whole Darwinian biosphere will be the long-term circle that cannot be squared. If the pollen of GM maize devastates the reproduction of the Monarch butterfly – one of the glories of the North American continent – so be it: the organic and wild must be suborned to the cornucopian, the given biosphere to the fallibly human imprint. The technology is totalitarian because it is a kind of permanent biological legislation in favour of its own premises, ending forever what the opposition defends. Between organic pollen and GM pollen, between the butterfly and its non-existence, there really is no half-way house, no compromise, no long-term coexistence (flowing, in this case, from inevitable cross-fertilization). Life increasingly technologized, or life increasingly preserved: the anthropomorphic reordering of the biosphere, or the preservation of its immemorial and sustaining integrity: this is the long-term ecological, and philosophical, conflict that simply cannot be dodged.

Should any of this surprise us? For a long time the developed world's forte has been an extreme devotion to the technological imagination, its handmaiden technoscience, rampant commodification, and the power of the modern corporation. It is hardly an historical coincidence that the totalitarian impulse has now surfaced obliquely in their biotech interaction.

Not long after the Fall of the Berlin Wall, Vaclav Havel remarked that the now-ascendant West might not be immune to the totalitarian siren-call. Things change: the contemporary balance between an older liberal democracy and late capitalism globalized is not immutable. All power without serious self-restraint or opposition is a formula for the authoritarian turn. It is interesting that the proponent of "the end of history" thesis, in the sense of the end of real ideological struggle, Francis Fukuyama, has turned his apologist's attentions to the future of biotechnology. He has correctly apprehended that it is not ideology, but technology, that will be this century's battlefield of futures.

The epicentre of these totalitarian enchantments is twofold: the corporate or university lab, and the patent office. The biotech lab has become an unacknowledged legislator of immense social power: largely unregulated in spirit, highly secretive vis-à-vis premises and ends, and quite a-democratic. For those familiar with its often bizarre research culture, it is apparent that this vast alliance of academic ego, "lab fever"(i.e., overstatement of results), money, the corporation and the state is continually attempting to create as much *fait accompli* as can be possibly sneaked under the ethical radar of wider society.

The locus of the lab is instigating a dizzying array of ethical issues with which civil society cannot keep up. What happens if GM techniques go DIY for the general population? Given chaos theory applied to the totality of Earth's ecology, can we be sure how even *one* genetic modification may impact or evolve in the long-term? Will widespread genetic modification interact unpredictably with climate change? Can whole ecosystems, such as the soil (and this is already being worked on), now be modified and patented? Will it become impossible over time for evolutionary biologists to correctly interpret natural selection due to widespread genetic modification infilitrating the whole biosphere? Not to mention the Brave New World of designer babies, cloning, and the truly explosive possibilities of germline (human stem cell) genetic engineering, "the single most portentous technological threshold in history" (pp.178-188). Darwin, who surely would have been aghast by much of this, remarks in *Origin of Species*: "No one ought to feel surprise at much remaining as yet unexplained in regard to the origin of species and varieties, if he makes due allowance for our profound ignorance in regard to the mutual relations of all the beings which live around us." That is hardly less true today.

Nothing is inevitable. Biotechnology might be compared to the medieval system of indulgences, by which the Church commodified souls. Likewise, for sceptics and opponents, some collective ecological equivalent of Luther's 95 *Theses* needs to set its face against the biotech simonry. The symbolic first of these should be a fundamental moral opposition to the ownership and release of the stuff of life by dint of its genetic modification, however many patents and principalities may claim this right. History shows over and again that disempowered ideas, meeting with changed circumstances, can seize the Chorus of social values. The symbolic last of these should concern the utter defence of the line whose crossing would constitute a full-scale ecological declaration of war: the design of lifeforms from scratch, which must now be judged a real possibility in the foreseeable future.

If the art of ecological retreat is to take hold, a sea-change in the law's understanding and treatment of nature is required: a migration of legal sensibility not unlike that in antiquity described by Seamus Heaney in "A

Veteran Awareness" (p.101). The right to patent genetically-modified life stems, in the first instance, from a single decision of the Supreme Court in 1980. That is an illustration of both the power and the fragility of legal precedent. In this light, probably the single most important step that could be taken would be the establishment of a World Environment Court, a framework of international law that would place the operation of free trade and competition within parameters safeguarding the biosphere. It would need to be based on a global environment charter; have the power to enforce the many multilateral environmental agreements that already exist between states; and operate on a legal par with the World Trade Organization. The right to bring cases could be extended to NGOs and other public bodies, and the Court might have specialist staffs to investigate environmental damage, inflicted or threatened. Serious thought should also be given to endowing parts of the natural world with legal "personhood" of the sort now enjoyed by corporations. A mountain gorilla is certainly closer to a "person" than the blue oval of the Ford Motor Company.

In time the very existence of the threat of collective and individual responsibility would act as a major brake on our war with the biosphere. Without a legal spur to retreat, one can imagine the ominous direction biotech, in particular, might take. After centuries of modifying and patenting the biosphere, (so reminiscent of seventeenth-century enclosures in England), would not the organic and wild themselves come to be seen as unwelcome "competition"? After all, if you own all the patents to engineered wheat or GM forests (both already widely planted in the US), it might be in your interest to see the social and natural demise of the last "independent" varieties of these species. It would be time to become "terminator" to one part of the old organic order.

Yet great powers have their Achilles heel. With gene and nano, this is the patent system itself, allied to the extreme sensitivity of markets and a consequent need for full political control. The inevitable calamities – a virus escaped, a GM organism running amok like rhododendron, a nano-chip wreaking havoc on its host – will prove a field day for salutary pursuit. For the patent not only confers ownership, but attributes responsibility. Call it the Thermopylae effect. If the terrain is well-chosen, even a small band of localists can hold the pass against the ambitions of a Xerxes.

Chris Agee

ECOLOGY, LITERATURE
AND THE NEW WORLD DISORDER

Gary Snyder

The problem species.

I

Gathered on Okinawa

Writers, scholars, naturalists, and students from all over Japan, from the US, and from Korea and Taiwan are gathered here. The main island of the Ryukyu chair, Okinawa, is at an old cultural crossroads. There is a long history of trade in goods and songs with Taiwan and Korea, and a record of highly respectful formal relations with mainland China still well remembered in Okinawa. In prehistoric times Pacific and Southeast Asian coastal cultural influences met and mingled with influences that came across from the Korean peninsula. Truly this is where the Oceanic and the Continental cultures have long met and where the Northern and the Southern aspects of East Asia came together.

Naha, the largest city on Okinawa and the old capital of the Ryukyu Kingdom, is a city rich in craft and art. The inscription on the sign at the big gate to Shuri Castle says in Chinese characters, "A Nation that Preserves Ceremony" – which I understand in its ancient spiritual meaning of "good manners toward the whole world."

Old Okinawa had a society that became famous for its hospitality, its music (especially the songs and melodies of the *sanshin*, the Okinawan prototype to the *shamisen*), its dance, and performance, its cheerful hardiness, and its self-sufficiency in art and culture. In recent decades the Ryukyus have also absorbed influence from the United States as part of the aftermath of WW II. The presence of the huge military airbase has been very difficult for the island – but many Okinawans also feel that Hawai'ian and mainland American cultural movements have had creative and broadening effects on the ongoing culture.

I would like to call on the spirits of the whole East Asian region and ask them to welcome us here. Our audience and allies for the next four days include ocean currents, volcanoes, Siberian breezes, Pacific storms, the orca of the deep sea, the brown bear of the inner mountains, the tiger of the marshes, the rhesus monkeys of the forests, the red-capped cranes (tancho tsuru) of Siberia, Korea, China, and Japan, the spirits of rice and sweet potato, and as always, the Goddess of Dance and Song.

II

This New World Disorder

We all know that the "post-Cold War" era has suddenly and rudely ended, and we have entered a period in which global relations are defined by new nationalisms, religious fundamentalism, Developed World hubris, stepped up environmental damage everywhere, and expanding problems of health and poverty. What was to have been a "New World Order" is revealed as a greater disorder, much of it coming from the top down.

Disorder is nothing new in the human world. East Asia, the Indian subcontinent, the Middle East, the Mediterranean, and Europe have all gone through cycle after cycle of violent warfare. Much of it has been driven by various combinations of fanatic ideological belief, whipped-up by nationalism, and institutionalized greed. The great civilizations have had moments of peace and marvelous cultural and artistic accomplishments, but then eruptions of hysteria and outbreaks of violence, war after war, have put better projects and values aside, sometimes forever.

The destruction of the World Trade Towers and the sudden loss of thousands of lives is, realistically, not a historical anomaly. There is never a time when a little wisdom, patience, and reflection, will not serve to improve decision-making. The George W. Bush clique that was and is in power in the USA has no sense of history, and no patience. With the war on Iraq we have all been drawn into what Jonathan Schell calls "An American Tragedy." The shredding of international trust, the deceptions practiced on the people of the US and Britain, and the unresolved chaos in the lives of Iraqis, Israelis, and Palestinians make it a world-scale tragedy.

We are gathered to focus on questions regarding the natural world and its presence in the literary arts. In most of the world now the outlook for the environment is not good. Initially the Bush Administration's retreat from environmental priorities was presented as being simply "pro-business." The aftermath of September 11, 2003 then enabled the Bush/Rumsfeld/Cheney forces to cloak their anti-environmentalism in the rhetoric of patriotism. There are corporations and government agencies that enthusiastically welcome this. The post-Nine-Eleven world of research universities is also changing directions. My own school, the University of California at Davis, suddenly had hopes to build a "bio-containment laboratory" to study deadly viruses and bacteria, as a service to the new "anti-terrorist" priorities. "The Environmental Initiative" which was a leading University commitment during the late nineties may now be quietly fading away.

As for literature, in the Modern Language Department, there are probably Eurocentric scholars who always thought "nature literature" was just a shallow trend, and who have begun to hope that things like the recent emergence of eco-criticism – or the study of "the environmental imagination", or concerns for "environmental ethics" and "nature literacy", and the idea that we might all learn to live by "the practice of the wild" – will now pack up and head back to the hills.

But it won't happen. A huge number of contemporary people realize that we can no longer think that the fate of humanity and that of the non-human natural world are independent of each other. A society that treats its natural surroundings in a harsh and exploitative way will do much the same with "other" people. Nature and human ethics are not unconnected. The growing expansion of ecological consciousness translates into a deeper understanding of interconnectedness in both nature and history, and a far more sophisticated grasp of cause-and-effect relationships. The lively recent discipline of Environmental History is constantly enlarging how we understand both nature and culture worldwide. Politically there is a constituency for the environment in every nation. Every one of the world religions has examined its own relation to the environment and is hoping to improve it. In a number of societies, the reverence and care for nature has been deep in the culture from the beginning. In the case of Japan we can see how a long-established care for nature withers in the face of extreme urbanization and aggressive economic expansion.

However, over the last forty years a body of fresh creative (but not fictional) work has been written that remakes the field. A small number of critics and scholars have responded to this with admirable energy, and we are in the midst of the emergence of a distinguished territory of literature that calls for further analysis and for expanded teaching. I am thinking of people who come after Rachel Carson and Aldo Leopold in the zone of literary/ecological theory. Consider the critical and social insights in the writings of Tom Lyon, Sherman Paul, John Elder, Stephanie Mills, Lawrence Buell, Cheryll Glotfelty, David Abram, Scott Slovic and most recently Jed Rasula. Or the hands-on creative non-fiction and "natural history" writings of Gary Paul Nabhan, Peter Matthiessen, David Rains Wallace, David Quammen, Douglas Chadwick, Rick Bass, Barry Lopez, Richard Nelson. Then there is the towering oeuvre of John McPhee, who writes out of the magic of sheer fact. And I'm not even mentioning the recent advances in the ecological and earth sciences, or the committed and engaging research writings of environmental activist writers and groups, with their contribution to shaping public policy and a growth of grassroots American connection with the land.

What we call the "environment" is our endangered habitat and home and we are its problem-species. It is the ultimate source of life and energy, and living in it well, together with each other, is our ancient challenge. In this era of new further disorder, nature is scarcely irrelevant. We can take heart from the fact that the actual physical world sets conditions that are some of the strongest guards against ignorant extremism and fanaticism. "Get real! Get a life!" is the daily message of Mother Nature.

Stay the course, my friends.

III
The Opening of the Field

A poem of this title by Robert Duncan opens with the lines

> Often I am permitted to return to a meadow
> as if it were a given property of the mind
> that certain bounds hold against chaos.

In our field of Literature and the Environment, we are permitted to return to this meadow, this forest, this desert, as a given property of the deeply natural human mind. Here are the bounds that – in ways too complex for us to grasp – hold against chaos. Remembering that chaos is a human invention.

I'd like to take a moment to go over some definitions: the Anglo word *nature* is from Latin *natura* – "birth, constitution, character, course of things" – ultimately from *nasci*, to be born. It connects with the root *nat* which is connected with birth, so we have *nation*, *natal*, and *native*. The Chinese word for nature is *zi-ran* (in Japanese *shizen*), meaning "self-thus." The English word nature is commonly used in its practical science sense, referring to the material universe and its rules. In other words, nature means, "everything" except perhaps the "supernatural". So our conference title, "Wild, Rural, Urban Nature," has no tricks in it. The rural and the urban are part of the phenomenal world.

Wild nature is that part of the physical world that is largely free of human agency. Biological wild nature is that aspect most endangered by human greed or carelessness. *Wild* is a valuable word. It refers to the process or condition of nature on its own: without human intervention. It is a process, a condition, not a place. *The wilds* is a place where wild process dominates.

The word *environment* is, in English, that which "surrounds" – from the Old French *viron*, encircle. In Japanese the term *kankyo* has much the same set of meanings. The weight of feeling between *nature* and *environment*, though, is different. We can relate instantly to a "nature-lover" but an "environment-lover" sounds slightly odd and clumsy. But the word is useful, because it highlights the point that all entities are members of each other's environment. I am part of your surroundings just as you are part of mine. This sort of mutuality is acknowledged in Buddhist philosophy, and highly developed in ecological thought.

As for "literature," we need to remind ourselves that it does not require a writing system to exist. Before writing was invented there were many literary traditions that flourished entirely in the oral mode. These oral literary traditions, some of which are still vibrant, contain huge numbers of riddles, proverbs, myths, rhythmic epic narratives, secular songs and religious chants, and oceans of stories. Many deal in great depth with natural world, and yet often seem unlike what we might think of as "nature writing" today. That is, they are never distanced from their subject matter. They clearly reflect the bio-region of the society, whether arid lands or moist tropical jungle, and do not speak of nature in the abstract. They reflect the mode of subsistence, and so may be largely agrarian in their interests, or they might be engaged with hunting and gathering, and explore interactions with a wide range of animals. They might sing "Night Herding Songs." They give us acute observation and a sense of deep identification with the non-human. If agrarian, the line between the life of the fields and that of the village is not hard and fast. In any case, wilderness, in the sense of being the most inaccessible part of a given territory, is seen as a shared space that is both dangerous and magical, and a place to go for spiritual as well as economic reasons. The study of archaic and oral nature-literature is constantly enlarging the body of lore that all of us are heir to.

Ecology, another key term, has Greek *oikos* as its main root, with the simple meaning of "household." It referred originally to the study of biological interrelationships and the flow of energy through organisms and inorganic matter. It later became virtually a synonym for nature in popular usage. I prefer to use it closer to its earlier scientific meaning.

I have already mentioned the "new world disorder." And what is order? "Wild nature" is the ultimate source of order. The whole phenomenal world and the mathematics that might be said to underlie it are all creatively and freely orderly. Art, architecture, philosophy, agriculture are, from the human standpoint, models of orderliness. There is much that humans find disorderly. But in the non-human universe, not a single leaf that falls from a tree is ever out of place.

IV

East Asia Teaches Us All

The remarkably coherent and persistent cultures of East Asia are in a class by themselves. The literature of these societies (Japan, Korea, Taiwan, and China) is unmatched in the matter of representing nature in art and writing.

All art and song everywhere begins in folk culture: celebration, dance, music, storytelling, song, and poem. In a way the greatest of the original five Chinese classics is the fifth-century BC *Shih Ching*, *Shikyo* in Japanese, the "Book of Song." It is, for East Asian poetry, the "mother of poems." It is also possibly (I love this idea) the "mother of Confucius." It has roots clearly in a folksong tradition that is easily a thousand years older than the written text. Is it about nature? Not exactly. It is poetry of an agrarian society, so there are few "wild landscapes." There are many poems of people going about their daily life in nature, which includes work in the fields and orchards, love and courting, and occasional ceremony and feasting. It names many plants both wild and domestic. East Asian civilizations have never made the sharp separation between the human and the rest of biological nature that is formalized in "The religions of Abraham" – Judaism, Christianity, and Islam. This Abrahamic dichotomy persists in contemporary monotheisms, and is severely with us yet today. Most educated Occidental people who profess to be secularists are still often in thrall to such dualism. In East Asia, from earliest folk religion through Daoism and Confucian teachings, and on into the practices and philosophy of Mahayana Buddhism and folk Shinto in Japan, humans have been seen as part of nature and most likely kin with the higher vertebrates. In all the high schools of Japan, Korea, China, Taiwan, and Vietnam, they teach Darwinian evolution as the model of biological being on earth. They are amazed that schoolboards in the United States might try to ban this.

Paradoxically, because East Asians so easily feel part of nature, it has been thought that whatever humans did was perfectly natural – not a bad assumption in its way – and so deforestation and extinction of species in earlier centuries did not usually alarm people. It was just nature beating up on nature, like elephants I saw smashing and ripping the twigs and limbs off *mopane* trees, their favorite food, in the forests of Botswana. The songs of the *Shih Ching* are benign, practical, sweet, and innocent. The founding anthology of Japanese poetry, the *Manyoshu*, has a morning-of-the-world feeling, too. There is love and loneliness, and there are long solitary travels through what were wild landscapes in the early Heian era. These are the wild grassy fields and reed marshes of lowlands that had not yet been converted to farming. These grassland and wetland poems disappear from later Japanese poetry – the changes in a landscape reflected in poems over the centuries could be a study in itself.

Hsieh Ling-yun, or Setus reium in Japanese (385-433 AD), is considered the first self-conscious poet of larger landscapes. He was a bold mountain explorer in the steep hills of south China. He also wrote a very long prose-poem on the matter of dwelling in the mountains. English-speakers are indebted to the Australian scholar J. D. Frodsham for making his lyric poems available in translation. From the T'ang Dynasty onward, some of China's finest poets were writing lyrics of nature. David Hinton recently compiled an anthology of English translations of what he calls "Chinese wilderness poems," which was published as *Mountain Home* by Counterpoint Press in New York. It contains poems by Wang Wei (Oi), Tu Fu (Toho), Li Po (Rihaku), and Po Chu-I (known as Hakurakuten in Japan), Su Shih (Soshi), and many others. This is the prime list of Chinese poets! They don't really qualify as "wilderness poets" (the Chinese themselves would call some of them "Field and Garden" poets). I like the term "mind/nature poets." Hinton or his publisher is simply making use of the buzz around the word "wilderness" in some American circles. But it's also true that the "mind/nature" axis reaches deeply into the interior wildness, and so these poets deserve our great regard. In Chinese prose writings there are also remarkable travel journals, geographical and geological essays, land-use surveys, and many other sorts of works that deserve closer attention. Most of these Chinese writers are well-known in Korea and Japan, and some have had a profound influence.

In later Japanese literature, the nature-poetry lineage that first comes to mind is the haiku tradition. It is truly a "nature tradition," but a sharply focused one. The vocabulary of the seasons and the symbolic implications of different plants are codified. Social Construction meets poetic landscape! There are thousands of insightful and precious little poems in the tradition. In spite of its limits, it helps people pay attention to botany, the many facets of the seasons, and countless other tiny details of the natural daily world. In America the recent book by Haruo Shimane, *Traces of Dreams: Landscape, Cultural Memory, and the Poetry of Basho* (Stanford), provides fascinating new detail as to the daily social and economic lives of the haiku poets, and their interactions with each other.

The Korean poet Ko Un, though very much a contemporary, is also a kind of bridge from the ancient *Book of Songs* (though his knowledge of both Chinese literature and Korean folksong), into twentieth-century modernism; and then a strong influence of Zen practice. The poems in his English-language anthology called *The Sound of My Waves* are richly human, often village-based, funny and sweet. Another English-language collection, *Beyond Self* (with an astute foreword by Allen Ginsberg), can be called Zen poems, though better than most poems called such, because of their genuine inventiveness and gritty joy. Ko Un is another of what I call "mind/nature" poets.

Many of the best-known East Asian poets were touched by, or even deeply engaged with, the teachings of the Ch'an or Zen or (Korean) Son school of Buddhism. A sly Zen influence can be seen almost everywhere in East Asian art. In terms of the environment, the Buddhist ethical teaching that we should "avoid harm to all beings" as far as reasonably possible, which is the Buddhist teaching of *ahimsa* or non-harming/non-violence/*fusessho*, has had a profound effect. It is not always an easy precept to follow, especially for a modern industrial nation with a developing economy. East Asian industries and expansion have severely damaged the environment, including forests of the Third World countries, in recent years. We study the great writings of the Asian past so that we might surpass them today and hope to create a deeply grounded contemporary literature of nature that celebrates the wonder of our natural world, draws on and makes beauty of the incredibly rich knowledge gained from Science, and then confronts the terrible damage being done today in the name of progress and the world economy.

V

Ecological Imperatives

Nature and *environment* are words that basically refer to "that which is." As such, they are bland terms – colourless, or a shade of light green. (The colour of the environment could just as well be blood red, or sap amber, or sky blue.) Nature, and environment, as terms, feel like "places." *Ecology* is a term, like *wild*, for "process."

Ecology refers to a dynamic process always in flux. It moves us away from the old sense of the world as something created in time that might now be running and getting worn out; away from the idea of the world as a clock or a machine or a computer, to "world as process" – a creation happening constantly in each moment. A close term in East Asian philosophy is the word *Dao*, the Way, *do* in Japanese.

When we come to the field of ecology we are looking at population dynamics, plant and animal succession, predator-prey relationships, competition and cooperation, feeding levels, food chains, whole ecosystems, and the flow of energy through ecosystems – and this is just the beginning. I have learned a great deal in my work on western American forest issues over the last few years from Forest Ecology (with the help of my older son Kai Snyder, who is a professional in the field) – to better understand the constant dynamism of natural systems, the continuous role of disturbance and the unremitting effects of climactic fluctuations.

We might ask what sort of poem or story can draw from the inner energy of an ecosystem? If our kind of literature were parallel to the history of fiction, I'd say we have now reached the point where we're tired of stock figures and charming plots, and want to get into the inner lives and psyches of our characters, with their obsessions, kinkiness, and secrets as well. We will necessarily be exploring the dark side of nature – nocturnal, parasitic, the energies of decomposition, and their human parallels. Also, the term ecology, which includes energy-exchange and interconnection, can be metaphorically extended to other realms. We speak of "the ecology of the imagination" or even of language, with justification; ecology is a valuable shorthand term for complexity in motion.

I've enjoyed, and learned a lot, from a very recent book, Jed Rasula's *This Compost: Ecological Imperatives in American Poetry* from the University of Georgia Press.

In terms of literature-and-nature, it picks up where Lawrence Buell's instructive book, *The Environmental Imagination*, left off and goes way into the territory of both ecology (in the most precise sense) and the adventurous side of contemporary poetics. It does so without needless nature-piety, getting right down to the metaphors of decay and fertility, of mulch and nutrition, as singularly critical to the nature of language and art – and demonstrates this with (for starters) Walt Whitman (who wrote a poem called "This Compost"), Emily Dickinson, Henry Thoreau, and George Santayana. Thoreau once wrote in his *Journals*, "decayed literature makes the richest of all soils."

Rasula moves it right on into Ezra Pound, Charles Olson and the Black Mountain poets, and the Beats with their wild and scientifically informed energy – in particular Michael McClure, Rothenberg's ethnopoetics, Clayton Eshleman's *Deep History*, Paul Shepherd's *Coming Home to the Pleistocene*, Gregory Bateson's *Steps to an Ecology of Mind*, and some contributions from my own thinking as in *The Practice of the Wild* and *A Place in Space*. My own most cogent contribution to Rasula's book, however, is not from those two works but from an earlier essay, "Poetry, Community, and Climax." I will quote a section (edited by me) from it here:

> Detritus cycle energy is liberated by fungi and lots of insects. I would then suggest: as climax forest is to biome, and fungus is to the recycling of energy, so "enlightened mind" is to daily ego mind, and Art to the recycling of neglected inner potential. When we deepen ourselves, looking within, understanding ourselves, we come closer to being like a mature ecosystem. Turning away from grazing on the "immediate biomass" of perception, sensation and thrill; and re-viewing memory…blocks of stored inner energies, the flux of dreams, the detritus of day-to-day consciousness, liberates the energy of our own mind-compost. Art is an assimilator of unfelt experience, perception, sensation, and memory for the whole society. It comes not as a flower, but – to complete the metaphor – as a mushroom: the fruiting body of the buried threads of mycelia that run widely through the soil, intricately married to the root hairs of all the trees. "Fruiting" – at that point – is the completion of the work of the poet, and the point where the artist re-enters the cycle: gives what she or he has re-created through reflection, returning a "thought of enlightenment" to community.

Human history with its languages, migrations, and vast passage of time is also like an old forest floor detritus, of old and new mingled together, old resentments recycled, of ancient recipes rediscovered and perennial mythologies strutting shamelessly on the stage of the moment. The "ecological imperative" must be that we try to see whatever current crisis we are in as part of an older larger pattern. But it also is an imperative to honor diversity whether of species or of languages and customs.

Scholarship continually spades and turns the deep compost of language and memory; and creative writing does much the same but adding more imagination, direct experience, and the ineluctable "present moment" as well. Our work as writers and scholars is not just "about" the environment, not just "speaking for" nature, but manifesting in ourselves the integrity of the wild.

And, here's a delightful turn, the complexity of a working metropolis, with its energy, sewage treatment, transportation, public auditoriums, parks, water, and solid waste systems, is rather like a climax ecosystem. Making these links into song and story is a work for an artist – a chance for somebody to write some great super-urban haiku.

VI

Performance Is Currency

The name of the peerless traditional Japanese drama type called *Noh*, one of the world's greatest art forms, means "accomplishment." Zeami, the founder of *Noh*, wrote dozens of essays on what it took to be accomplished: background learning and reading, attention and much attendance at the performances of others, and practice, practice, practice. Further, he suggests the almost-magical capacity to go beyond years of practice into selfless freedom, again. The ability to yet surprise yourself even years later. Poets and artists who are dedicated to their craft know the importance of skill. And there is one more point: Who is this flower for?

A Zen verse says,

> The moon shines on the river,
> The wind blows through the pines –
> Who is this long, beautiful evening for?
> *(from the Cheng Dao Ke)*

Outwardly the Noh plays were for the dedicated aristocrats and warrior-administrators who supported the arts. Inwardly they are for the tender, deep, true mind-hearts of everyone.

One time in Alaska a young woman asked me, "If we have made such good use of animals, eating them, singing about them, drawing them, riding them, and dreaming about them, what do they get back from us?" An excellent question, directly on the point of etiquette and propriety, and putting it from the animals' side. I told her, "The Ainu say that the deer, salmon, and bear like our music and are fascinated by our languages. So we sing to the fish or the game, speak words to them, say grace. We do ceremonies and rituals. Performance is currency in the deep world's gift economy." I went on to say I felt that non-human nature is basically well-inclined toward humanity and only wishes modern people were more reciprocal, not so bloody. The animals are drawn to us, they see us as good musicians, and they think we have cute ears.

What I was playfully stating is that human contribution to the planetary ecology might be our entertaining craziness, our skills as musicians and performers, our awe-inspiring dignity as ritualists and solemn ceremonialists – because that is what seems to delight the watching wild world.

The critic and writer Ronald Grimes took up this aspect of my curious line of thought – he is a performer himself – and developed it into an actual performance that he called "Performance is Currency in the Deep World's Gift Economy: An Incantatory Riff for a Global Medicine Show." Grimes's background insight as teacher, performer, and student of religion gave him outstanding insight into what I had thrown out as a shamanistic, Mahayanistic intuition and gave it solid footing.

Gift Economy? That might be another perspective on the meaning of ecology. We are living so to speak in the midst of a great potluck at which we are all the invited guests, and we also are eventually the meal. The Ainu, when they had venison for dinner, sang songs aloud to the deer spirits who were hanging about waiting for the performance. In Buddhist spiritual ecology, the first thing to give up is your ego. The ancient Vedic philosophers said that the gods like sacrifices, but of all sacrifices that which they most appreciate is your ego. This critical little point is the foundation of yogic and Buddhist askesis. Dogen famously said, "We study the self to forget the self. When you forget the self you become one with the ten thousand things." (There is only one offering that is greater than the ego, and this is "enlightenment" itself.)

The being who has offered up her enlightenment is called Bodhisattva. In some of the Polynesian societies the Big Person, the most respected and powerful figure in the village, was the one who had nothing – whatever gift came to him or her was promptly given away again. This it the real heart of a Gift Economy, the economy that would save, not devour, the world. (Gandhi once said, "For greed, all of nature is insufficient.") Art takes nothing from the world, it is a gift and an exchange. It leaves the world nourished. The arts, learning, grandmotherly wisdom, a heart of compassion confound the markets, rattle the empires, and open us up to the actually existing human and non-human world. Performance is art in motion; in the moment; enactment and embodiment: which is exactly what nature herself is.

> "Ripples on the surface of the water –
> were silver salmon passing under – different
> from ripples caused by breezes"

> A scudding plume on the wave:
> a humpback whale is
> breaking out in air up
> gulping herring
>   – Nature not a book, but a performance, a
> high old culture

Ever-fresh events
scraped out, rubbed out, and used, used, again –
the braided channels of the rivers
hidden under fields of grass –

The vast wild
    the house alone.
The little house in the wild,
    the wild in the house.
Both forgotten.

No nature

Both together, one big empty house.

This essay is based on a keynote address given at the International Conference of the Association for the Study of Literature and the Environment, held in Naha, Okinawa, in the Ryukyu Archipelago, March 4-6, 2003. It is published courtesy of ASLE and the author.

Gary Snyder's many books of poetry and prose include Turtle Island *(1974),* The Practice of the Wild *(1990),* No Nature: New Selected Poems *(1992),* Mountains and Rivers Without End *(1996) and* The Gary Snyder Reader. *He lives in California.*

THE DEFENCE OF POETRY

Raoul Schrott

Back to the Mediterranean.

Ladies and gentlemen, honourable members of the jury: permit me to preface my plea with a review of the three-thousand-year history of the case hereunder submitted to the Court of Fourth Instance. My aim in so doing is to demonstrate with what malice the indictment is laid, and with what extreme measure of spite, prejudice and ignorance it is drafted. The court is invited to observe how the complaint has focused on varying aspects of the case with each successive appeal. I submit that such circumstance alone will indicate that my learned colleagues have been intent on abusing these proceedings for the purpose of what can only be termed a show-trial! Yes – you have understood me correctly! For literary criticism always begins with the desire to see poetry abolished, and with it my client – whom I consider it my great honour to represent before this court.

The trial in the first instance was characterised by the attempt of Plato, recently called to the bar at that time, to gain in distinction by accusing my client of wilful fraud. According to Plato the meaning of life lay in searching for eternal truth, while my client's poetry offered but imitations of imitations. In his arraignment Plato submitted that poetry was a phantom art: while each thing – a tree, for instance – had an ideal form somewhere in heaven, which not even the best of gardeners could cultivate to perfection, the poet could proffer but a third-hand imitation – consisting of nothing but words. Instead of using words responsibly, however, he manipulated them for the attainment of mere effect. He was thus charged with interfering with the roots of language – by swapping letters: the rootless poet became quite footless mixing his 'g's and 't's, fancy free to traduce the ideal tree to a tree-tease in verse, a curse, and no treat for the reader either. This, according to my learned colleague, constituted reasonable evidence that a poet's lies were contagion to the life of the mind, at the very best turning men into children, at the worst, into women. Plato therefore sought the highest penalty, demanding that my client be prohibited from practising his profession and banished from the Republic, and that his works be publicly burned.

The jury of the day acquitted the defendant in default of evidence – but the prosecution saw fit to lodge an appeal. My client, filing one motion after another, was nonetheless able to stand his ground, and, despite subjection to pressure for centuries and considerable loss of custom, was able to compose a number of startling works. He was not read by many even then, for the common reader was at that time not exactly common – and without the patronage of a Maecenas to fall back on, he was mostly down on his uppers. The difficulty of the situation was compounded by the perennial constraint of seeking some arrangement with the powers-that-be, effectively making him dependent on the political and religious authorities of his age. Take, for example, the republican propaganda he was obliged to disseminate in his *Aeneid*, or again, the virtuous lip-service he has paid to Christianity, whether in the Marian songs of his courtly love poetry, or the *Divina commedia*.

But then came a change of venue: England, 1595; the next major trial was set to commence. The defendant was represented on this occasion by the senior partner of my firm, Sir Philip Sidney. The complaint that my client had done nothing but spread lies had been re-filed, but on this occasion prosecution had refrained from demanding he be banished from society for behaviour injurious to the interests of the state, on the grounds that his profession must be construed too ineffectual to constitute a cultural intervention of any kind, whether negative or positive. Prosecution counsel, a small-minded Puritan by the name of Gosson, noticed, albeit at the eleventh hour, that his argument must, *nolens volens*, lead to the suspension of proceedings. In desperation he chose to play his joker, claiming that my client was guilty in his poetry of the manufacture and distribution of pornography, and I quote: "infecting us with many pestilent desires ... training [men's wit] to wanton sinfulness and lustful love." The fact that this change of strategy, by attributing subversive force to the ineffectual, was in itself contradictory, was of secondary importance. Demanding a verdict was now the least of my learned colleague's concerns; his attentions were directed solely towards ridiculing the defendant in the eyes of society, discrediting him morally. It was, in brief, pure slander.

We gave short shrift to the allegation of obscenity, arguing that it was not poetry which "abuseth man's wit," but that "man's wit abuseth Poetry" – by reading it for its erotic content only. As for that Sword of Damocles forever suspended over our heads in the shape of the count that poetry is without truth and useless, our defence at that time was built on the premise that poetry makes no claim to be factual; that the poet "nothing affirmes, and therefore never lyeth"; that the poet "is not labouring to tell you, what is or is not, but what should or should not be." Returning then to the metaphor of the tree: the poet should be thought of as a gardener sowing the seeds of the possible in the bed of reality, cultivating the image of goodness in the minds of his readers. In this way – and here we have little choice but to extend the analogy with the imaginative restraint imposed by prolonged practise at the bar – thinking about a tree may eventually lead us to define its radical index, which in turn could prompt extraction of both its square and its cubic roots, so that before we know it we may be accelerating through space on said tree-tease, branching into light solids, twigging nano-technological plant, spreading into orbital habitats. Gasps of surprise – followed by the slow crescendo of courtroom applause …

We managed to demonstrate at the time that under the didactic imperative comprehending all imagination the ancient Greek *Eikastike* – "figuring forth good things," according to contemporary etymologists – and the more dissolute *Phantastike* had, like oratio and ratio, language and reason, entered an alliance of their own. Thus the poem could become a "speaking picture," allowing us insights that were entirely novel, or unheard of – epiphanies, proverbial in their transfiguring power. For poetry's use value consisted in its being "the most efficient persuasive force available to human beings." Visible signs of assent on the part of the jury – diminishing now that new questions are mooted as to the actual purpose of poetry. The poet – we took time to explain – was the only mortal whose imagination allowed him access to the various ideals of society. He alone had the strength and the opportunity to portray these in an admirable light for the benefit of his fellow citizens – thereby bringing to the stage a figure who incorporated in his person the ideal intellectual, the ideal politician, the very genius of the age. Virtually speaking, all these qualities were combined in his work.

By this time, we had the jury well on our side. Dame Fortune too, it seemed. For luckily there had been no need to go into my client's personal preferences – in the pursuit of such noble ends – for the manifold masks, disguises and artful gimmicks of coquetry, nor to admit that this meant he was not infrequently taken for some ham actor, dandy or pimp, rather than for the philosopher, soldier and lover he claimed to be.

But take a look for yourselves, ladies and gentlemen, members of the jury! *Ecce homo*: the defendant! Not much left of the grandeur of yesteryear, is there! Not a flicker of fashion about him: his stand-up collar and starched shirt-front look as out of place today as that waxed moustache, those sandals or tartan trousers, the tweed jacket, or the Borsalino under which he imagines he can conceal his thinning, sandy hair. I am perfectly aware, ladies and gentlemen, that he does not create an especially favourable impression, and that the expression of dyspeptic melancholy that has replaced his previously arrogant manner does not render him any the more sympathetic. This, however, can scarcely be attributed to the intervention of the public prosecutor – himself, incidentally, my client's former colleague – when my client was summonsed some thirty years ago to the Court of the Third Instance to attend the most recent trial to date. On that occasion my learned colleague referred to the defendant as a decadent petty-bourgeois, a purveyor of make-believe, with nothing to say for himself and no real interest in changing society. Suddenly a conversation about trees was almost a crime, and even a rhyme was reactionary. And poetry was to be agitprop or nothing! But the greater the enemy, the greater the honour! – as we have already noted. For we were able to dismiss these charges no less elegantly than the earlier actions brought against us, my client this time employing the ruse of simply falling in with them on all counts, penning the required left-wing verse under the pseudonym Pablo Neruda. Until the day came when people grew weary of its leftishness, and my client was once again permitted to display his real talents.

O, yes, my client is ever the opportunist! No harm in admitting that! If we still look somewhat perplexed, however, it is because having first been dubbed "Junge Wilde" and then "yesterday's people," after being vilified as anarchists, demagogues and pornographers, after being asked to prove the truth of our work and after being taken to task for its uselessness, after all that and all that – people now seem to think they can simply ignore us. They declare us mentally unfit. As evidence they point out that we have lost the majority of our audience and all of the social standing we once had; and that these days not even the most trivial broadsheet rag considers us worth the mention. And this, they submit, is our last ditch manoeuvre: instigating a trial in the hope of finding someone to listen to a defence speech.

Admittedly, my client has not always been his own best friend in these matters. I volunteer to submit that we should not be standing here today had his vanity been marginally less, and his inclination to recognize the many illegitimate offspring he has fathered in the course of his chequered career had been marginally greater. Think whom we might summons to testify on his behalf – George Brassens and Jacques Brel, Fabrizio de André and Ivano Fossati, Chico Buarque and Caetano Veloso, Leonard Cohen, Patti Smith and Bob Dylan … indeed even the most commercial pop-singers, the *chansonniers* and hip-hop artistes – especially the latter, since their occupation is nothing but poetry in the classical Greek sense. Even bestseller authors and novelists, headliners and copywriters, all of them cashing in on the high art inherited by my client, treading it underfoot, twisting it this way and that, until it fits their own requirements. Which, on beginning his own career, was exactly what my client did. He is simply too vain to admit it.

And it is here we draw close to the root of the problem, one which – I beg leave to submit – has been overlooked in all the course of our three thousand-year-old proceedings. For the divers complaints brought against my client have derived solely from the fact that he fell foul of a media revolution which drowned the Mediterranean poetic legacy in a whirlpool of oblivion, stranding my client as a living anachronism. The only question remaining is whether his work therewith forfeited its truth and use value.

The German word *Dichtung* (poetry) derives from *diktion*, the *diction* that defines all poetry, its characteristic manner of verbal expression in creating "speaking pictures". However, the technical resources available to diction of this kind – figures of thought such as the metaphor and simile, as well as acoustic figures, like metre and rhyme – were developed to fulfil a single, distinctive purpose: to make information memorable; to pass on knowledge from one generation to the next; by using standardized musical forms in language to create the only existing mnemonic system (perhaps the respected members of the jury would oblige by attempting to speak the text of a song without humming the tune …); by using set phrases and portmanteau expressions (Homer's "cunning Odysseus," for example, or our "dear God"); by lending trenchant characterisation to things by means of visually suggestive comparisons ("rosy-fingered Eos"); by then synchronising sound-track and visuals to produce a cinema of the mind, comprising newsreel as well as entertainment, sweeping historical romance and educational documentary, propaganda and moral edification; through which facts, circumstances and values could be passed down, making culture possible in the first place.

It was for this purpose alone that poetry had been invented. To this end too had it generated the stock formulae that constituted a language transcending time. The traditions on which it was able to draw in so doing were far older than the few millennia in which it had assumed a literary form. But this was precisely the crux of our problem. For it was with the invention of the alphabet that poetry had suddenly lost its function and raison d'être. The advent of script meant the formulaic language of poetry was no longer essential to the transmission of information, and that ideas and facts could be recorded in writing without prior transformation in the matrix of poetry. The advantage was that entire fields of knowledge, including the natural sciences, philosophy and the Law, became emancipated from the constraints of poetry, and established themselves as autonomous disciplines – for their material could now be directly set down in writing. New poetic genres were born of this development too, like drama, whose actors could now record everyday speech.

The disadvantage was that the inventory of poetry suddenly seemed superfluous.

Poetry has never wholly overcome the loss of its central function, which, incidentally, was also the beginning of all its trials, of all the proceedings brought against us. It was tantamount to our expulsion from Paradise. Plato had already indicated as much by giving to poets their new name. By nature inclined to nostalgic retrospection he had lamented the demise of the ancient *Aoides* – the singers, seers and prophets invested by the gods and history – whose tasks had given them a monopoly on the transmission of culture. Following the revolutionary introduction of writing, however, a reversal no less radical than that of the later computer age, the *Aoides* were transmogrified as "poets," godless "makers," puffed up artisans of the language, barking phrasemongers and two-bit verbicides. Who had forfeited all authority, all auctorial significance, and had mutated as mere "authors". Thereby losing their last vestige of authenticity.

Having ascertained the state of the facts – revered members of the jury – we shall now proceed to our defence. In which we shall table evidence to the effect that the conduct of the defendant, notwithstanding circumstantial evidence to the contrary, has been without blemish – but that his profession, given the magnitude of the upheavals already referred to, must henceforth be judged in a different light. For what has remained intact of the original character of oral poetry, an art form that was probably many thousands of years old? Very little. What *has* survived is mainly the enjoyment we experience in listening to a poem, whether in the discretion of one's own language, the distinctness of a foreign language, or in sound poetry. It is something that inhabits the quality metrical language owes to music: a communal experience that seems to unite reciter and audience, their breathing and heart frequency synchronized by the regular pitch of the verses. An experience in which bookish words reclaim their archaic corporeality. Giving rise to a form of communication that once was peculiar to oral poetry, whose origins, we remember, lay in the service it once performed to religion. An experience, in other words, in which communication becomes communion. If the truth of this development largely escapes the scrutiny of reason, the same cannot be said for its methods. For therein survives its persuasive force, harnessed to this day by political demagogue and advertiser's copywriter alike, or by all who seek, through the insinuations of verbal euphony, to sell a message which they intend to remain sacrosanct.

However, this does not explain why the propensity of such brainwashing to engender conflict should be a matter of concern in respect of religion, the economy or populist politics, but not of poetry. The reason is that poetic devices are plundered by the former to a clearly defined and commonly intelligible end, while poetry, on the other hand, seems to have become an end in itself. It is therefore essential, esteemed members of the jury, that we elucidate the matter of its authorization. Authority was once conferred upon oral poetry by the ruler who praised it, the gods it celebrated, the audience it sought to entertain, and the knowledge it transmitted – on the condition that it remained no less subordinate than Adam and Eve in the Garden of Paradise. With the advent of writing, however, which he soon adopted for his profession, my client bit into the bitter apple (as the Germans say) and ate (if I may be permitted to use this motif one last time) from the Tree of Knowledge, that is: self-knowledge. Henceforth he became his own legislator. The Muses no longer gave authority to his poems, as they always had done in the past, nor sanctioned his enthusiasm as "possessed by a god". Instead, he was henceforth forced to find his own justification for what he produced.

With newly acquired literacy, however, poetry also forfeited its unequivocal status. Not only because, as Plato complained, writing was open to interpretation, consisting merely of words and lacking entirely in the facility to register intonation, facial expression, or gesture, which were what actually showed what people meant. No, for besides growing in ambiguity in this way poetry had also declined in universal comprehensibility and accessibility. Whereas the epic extemporizing of oral poetry, with its concise items of information, its generalized formulae and continuous repetition had taken the short attention spans of its listeners into consideration, poetry was now confronted with readers. For whom the poem was a visual as well as a limited entity. To be read as often as one wanted. This was the beginning of the "text" – whose ever denser weft and warp became transparent only on repeated reading. But it was here too that poetry took leave of its wider audience. For the members of the latter were generally more interested in the "cinema of the mind" – that is, in the film itself – than in the constitution of the screen.

As you can see, we are apt to deal with the defendant a good deal more severely than any prosecuting counsel preceding us. And this, in order finally to foreground what makes poetry unique and inimitable. Thereby to prove the truth of its case at last.

The more poetry was made for paper, pen and the discerning reader, the less important became all those redundant factors that were dependent on memory, recitation and listeners: instead verse became more concise, and more complex. But this had yet another effect: for having lost its function as the significant medium, poetry had no alternative but to make a subject of itself. It now began to focus its gaze on its own rules and resources. The most important of these is probably the metaphor. In the words of that most ancient of our colleagues, Aristotle, who defended poetry against Plato: "the greatest thing by far is to have a command of metaphor. This alone cannot be imparted by another; it is the mark of genius, for to make good metaphors implies an eye for resemblances."

The value of poetry has come to lie in its ability to turn analogy into its central concern. While metaphor had previously been little more than a device to outline things in more trenchant terms, it now became a faculty of the understanding. With its own use value: for every invention or discovery can be traced to the *aha*-experience of Archimedes in his bathtub, to the insight that one thing is like another. It is this principle of resemblances that drives the think-tanks and creative studios, the leading edges of science and technology, even providing the basis of wine criticism (or have you ever read a gourmet columnist writing of wine that tastes of grapes?). But it goes further than that: in fact, this x=y mechanism is the only way we have of giving meaning to things. With its help we have named our world and rendered it comprehensible. Beginning with ourselves, from our awareness of our own bodies, we have used metaphor to appropriate the things that surround us – from the leg of the table to the foot of the mountain – because we are incapable of imagining anything that does not exist. For every new invention is evolved out of what went before, and every new discovery is only brought to light by comparison with phenomena we already know. And the discipline that considers such matters its foremost concern is poetry. With which we conclude our first argument.

Second argument: whereas oral poetry was a feat of memory during which rhapsodist, poem and listeners merged to a moment of pure presence, the impact on poetry of writing has been to elicit its timelessness. The consciousness of pure presence is probably confined in our own day to the moment of poetic inspiration, which continues – as our client is fond of repeating – until the man of Porlock knocks at the door. What ensues is the elaboration of the idea, the construction of the poem according to the pretensions of its form – which in fact amounts to a re-construction of that special moment. At the same time, the subject of this work is self-referential: memory itself.

Our memory is no video-recorder, taping and rewinding films to requirement. On the contrary: whenever we remember, we reconstruct the past anew, rearranging fragments differently each time to create a novel entity. If oral poetry was comparable to a film, lyric poetry has more in common with a photograph; where the former saw its remit in presenting a broad canvas whose validity was universal, the latter can claim to lay before us snapshots of reality – however local and subjective they may be – whose definition and exposure is expertly handled. And whereas poetry in its epic capacity passed on the world of the past for the benefit of the future – oral poetry being a trade that was dependent on time – today's poetry is more likely to see its own activity as detached from time, its lines suggesting moments that are suspended outwith that dimension.

The reasons for this lie in the musical constraints of metrical language, in rhyme, and in the strophic form. These three have one characteristic in common whose significance, though practically negligible with regard to oral poetry, has come to the fore as poetry has become more self-referential: the retrospect occasioned by their essentially repetitive structure. Rhyme is but an echo of a pre-determinant word-sound; the refrain takes us back to the beginning; the euphony of the lines implies the monotony of the eternally recurrent. It is this that enables a poem to restrain time, or indeed to bring it to a standstill, making it the only form to give lasting quality to a subjective factor that neither celluloid nor digital plastic can render.

However, its ability to transcend what is merely private or purely individual is due to a second factor which, like music, has managed to survive the revolutionary impact of writing intact: the figurative language of poetry (literature since has added nothing to its panoply of rhetorical skills). It is thanks to the objectifying consistency of its diction that the highly subjective bearing of most modern poetry attains supra-individual significance. It does so by rendering the personal as the exemplary, representative and universal; and this in poems that are "total" works of art, comprising image and sound, language and music, the intellect and the emotions. The totality of a moment reduced to its most human dimension. Only a poem can do this – for it is something which prose narrative cannot comprehend, and which drama cannot act out.

But what of truth? A good poem is distinguished from a bad poem by the extent to which it meets its own formal requirements – whether these be semantic and logical, allegorical and metaphorical, visual (like the Alexandrian calligrammes in which writing was shaped as Eros' wings) or mathematical (like the formal rules of combination used by magical charms, the hypograms, whose existence Saussure proved in Martial's poems, songs by Guihelm and Villon based on the medieval practice of gematry, or the constraints developed by the Oulipians). In the case of sonnets that imitate the logical closure of a syllogism, or of an allegorical poem intent on exploring every aspect of its semantic frame, the criterion of truth is relatively unproblematic. But what kind of truth inhabits poems such as those by Inger Christensen, in which the world is arranged in Fibonacci-sequences? Or – viewed simply – in stanzas structured by the consonance of terminal sounds?

It may seem too absurdly logical to be true, but even the ancient Sumerians were drawn to the conclusion that similarly sounding words were related in kind at a fundamental level. Startlingly, their belief has been confirmed by research in neurology: a person conditioned in a language laboratory with electric shocks whenever he or she hears the word "rhyme" will also flinch on hearing that someone has had a good "time," or committed a "crime". It is apparent that rhyme has a basis in biology, a reality with a claim to its own criteria of truthfulness. But what of poems that incorporate textual graphics, what of object poems? Here too we need a poetics that is up-to-date – and which has yet to be written. One thing that can be said, however, is that visual figures of this kind are also ultimately preoccupied with the figurative imitation of structures which occur in Nature, thereby giving substance to the ancient Greek notion of mimesis: understood as the interpretation and portrayal of the real. There is probably no other art form which can execute these in more concentrated a form than the poem. That would normally suffice to conclude our plea, but there is more that needs to be said.

We submit once again that poetry foregrounds the rules of its own genre: the different systematic arrangements of language. Since language and thought influence each other, both automatically include reality; poetry of whatever make is *true* if only because it is rooted in words. In this sense the poem – to hazard a modern frame of analogy – can be seen as a kind of module, the stanzas as circuit boards, and the lines as circuits. Taking this IT-jargon a step further we can see that while the carefully encoded language of poetry acts as a conductor between reality and consciousness, the poem *in toto* defines the various modalities by which reality can be mapped, as well as the experimental set-up that permits access to it in the first place. The decisive factor here is the conductivity of the poetic chip. If we now go on to question the truthfulness of poetry in this context, we are in fact addressing the problem in relative terms, for here it is more appropriate to speak of "good" or "bad" than "true" or "false". The more stringent the formal principle ordering the language, and the more rigorous its execution, the more efficient the poem will be as a vehicle for investigation and discovery – for only the poem's intrinsic precision can minimize the babble of data in the module. No matter what programme it is intent on carrying out, it will always be able to tell us something about reality, and be all the more truthful in doing so, the more comprehensive, efficient and integrated the performance of its inner circuits.

What these relay to the screen are diagrams – diagrams like world maps: some recording rainfall, sea currents or wind direction; some recording geological patterns, altitudes or temperatures, others still demographic concentration or other statistics. Ladies and gentlemen, the thrust of my argument will be apparent: for each of the many maps generated by this programme a specific aspect of reality is revealed. Permit me to submit this as my third argument.

This covers only one characteristic of poetry, however. The poem defined as a module with its ins and outputs of subjectivity and the world constitutes anything but run-of-the-mill IT. Esteemed ladies and gentlemen, members of the jury, when my client – looking too blasé by half after all these technical metaphors – views his verses in more pragmatic terms, as a speech act, then he is fully aware that they deviate from the truth quite deliberately, in as far as truth represents some kind of secret convention between human beings. This is because, a) he is usually more interested in originality than truth, which he often finds banal; b) because language as a medium lacks precision; and c) because of all the different styles of poetic diction. But also d) because of the complexity of its literariness, and e) because several principles of organisation are quite likely to concur within a single poem, and are therefore also equally likely to compete with one another: grammar with the elliptic line, both with the demands of metre and the patterns of sound, all these together with the logic of their various tropes and picture planes. It would be like a crossword puzzle attempting to incorporate several languages into its chequered pattern at once – and still make sense. Which is one of the reasons why there are so few good poems.

To persevere in one's attempt to encounter the *one* truth that would be valid at every level, that, in the classical Greek sense, is the Eros of poetry: the desire to reach out and touch what cannot be grasped or held. More important than the gesture itself, however, are the ambiguities generated by the method it stands for. The way polysemy is produced at the intersection of the different linguistic planes. And contradiction. The way one part of a metaphor can thoroughly convince us and, at the same time, point to a second dimension that is unfathomable and cannot be thought through, a dimension that is metaphysical. This is the true achievement of poetry: in trying to portray the world as it is, it reveals the seeds of paradox wherever two words clash. Its truth is to show where and in what manner the dimension of contradiction begins. With the Wittgensteinian clarity appropriate to its hermeneutics, a poem supplies the criteria by which it must be judged as well as foundations upon which such criteria are based. So that we can retrace the way one word joins another in making something that transcends every dictionary and every language.

The true freedom from contradiction which belongs to poetic truth can be summarized thus: a poem reaches out to the utmost bounds of philosophical knowledge by asserting, via its contradictions, that all poems, like all Cretans, lie – in as far as they are also telling the truth. Submitted as argument No. 4, this might seem excessively philosophical to any jury that were really hostile to our plea. But the ambiguities set up by poetry also have a thoroughly practical effect: they lay claim on behalf of the imagination to a space that cannot be confined or controlled, to areas where thought is free to roam and play. That is the reason why my client has felt gratified, indeed honoured, by accusations of subversion, demagogy and pornography. Because these have only served to expose the totalitarian systems whose show trials were intended to force him to his knees. Which they had good reason to do. Because under such dictatorships poetry – the oldest trade in the world – once more remembers its ancient Mediterranean traditions and reverts to what it once was: a universal organ of speech, albeit in this case underground, in *samizdat* form, as the secret cant of prisoners. It is for this reason too that my client is not especially perturbed to learn that my honourable colleague, the public prosecutor, has tacitly decided to drop all charges brought against him, for that is a sign that times for poetry must at least be good enough. For better or for worse, poetry is taken so much for granted now that nobody notices just how ubiquitous it has become. Indeed possibly too omnipresent – on every TV-screen after all, and every hoarding, every radio programme and every printed page. Which has set my client wondering ...

Jochberg, 5 May 2003

INVENTORY I

At the edge of the track between Amguid and Tamanghasset in the Algerian desert a plaque marks the Tropique du Cancer. To reach it you have to skirt the foothills of Garet el Djenoun, passing through a region where, in the fifties, the French tested hydrogen bombs in underground shafts. In Libya the 23.5° north latitude marks the beginning of the Aozou strip, which extends as far as the Tibesti Mountains, site of the ancient Garamantian emerald mines. Today the most striking thing about the place is its clutter of burnt-out machines left over from the war against Chad. Where the same latitude meets the intermittently mined Egyptian-Libyan border a rocky massif rears up on the plain, its precipitous face decorated with Stone Age engravings and rock paintings recalling a time when this was a place of rivers and lakes. Further east lies Aswan, the ancient city of Syene. It was here that Eratosthenes computed the Earth's circumference by measuring the angle of the sun's inclination in a well. But the further south you travel from this parallel towards the Tropic of Capricorn the more the sun in its career appears to tilt away behind your head, until eventually its position at noon is north.

Between the tropics lie regions whose aridity is broken only in the equatorial zone, where a shallow layer of parasitic vegetation continues to cling to the eroding continental crust. Beneath its canopy are rotting tree trunks and the high-pitched whine of the insects. Impressions of the kind Darwin recorded in the *Voyage of the Beagle* of a sublime, majestic jungle, its hostility and impenetrability placing it on a par with the desert, show Nature wholly engrossed in itself, seemingly intent on exposing how naked the Earth is, and how vulnerable the life that inhabits it. Here is evidence of yet another meridian, linking the poles of the organic and inorganic, its extremes culminating in the equator and the tropics framing it.

To refer to a landscape as hostile or inaccessible is to think of it in human terms. Nature, however, is nothing if not indifferent. To express that indifference in language one would need somehow to get outside the categories of human thought. But since they are all we have, we can think of it only as difference – a paradox we try to grasp through the concept of sublimity. It is a conundrum that lies precisely in our inability to put it into words.

What we *can* say is that the various definitions of the sublime – which have characteristically overlapped in the course of the centuries with notions of terror, beauty, the picturesque and the Romantic – suggest a constant: affective experience in the face of nature, and the position we adopt as subjects relative to that experience. Ultimately, the sublime is nothing but the expression of an existential attitude, which, defeated persistently by the intangibility of nature, nonetheless takes its bearings with regard to that insuperable breach. That is as succinct a definition as the terms will allow. It is in these terms too that we may approach a poem that sets out to map the topography of the sublime on the grid of its tropes.

In respect of height or depth, distance or proximity, the north sought by a dipping needle is always the foreign, the Other. But when a compass takes its orientation from the sublime its cardinal points change their names, displaced to a transcendental plane: the majestic and the unfathomable, the immeasurable and the oppressive.

Extending the metaphor we could say that the sublime is based on a projection, one whose contour lines give shape to its relief. To find the right scale and align the sublime with the coordinates of a certain place and a certain time one looks for natural landmarks, aware that whatever one sees will inevitably depend on one's own point of view. Representations of the sublime in language thus are subject to distortion, but it is this, too, that alerts us to its strangeness, its resemblance to allegory in the original sense: sublimity as an Otherness permitting different readings. The void that is manifest here also gapes elsewhere: in the face of the mountains or the sea. It is a gap to which the gaze repeatedly returns, as if to a vanishing point.

But this only demonstrates the extent to which all such meridians and parallels rest on illusion, on bearings no less deceptive than the notion that the sun rises in a certain place and circles the earth, or culminates at some time in the day at a point where it casts no shadow. They are nothing but human perspectives, constructed to relate the history of light and its spaces, an optics invented to bring us closer to things, and to the elementary truths that hold them together.

The sea in Homer is purple, white, or the colour of wine, and the sky bronze or iron – but never blue. A Babylonian clay tablet describes Sirius with a coppery gleam, but for Ptolemy it was a yellowish colour, while Seneca saw it shining red, and Manilius blue – to us it appears white. Views of the sublime are similarly heterogeneous: as a product of the imagination, argued Kant, it is nothing but pure form, without substance. To describe the indescribable one must therefore fictionalise it – to the effect that the interfaces between subject and world, chaos and order, assume an emblematic reality of their own. In this sense the paradox of sublimity is reflected in the nature of light: we see because of it, we see through it, but we don't *see* it.

Optike in Greek meant to "see clearly," but the true nature of light was no clearer then than it is today. The Pythagoreans thought the eye emitted a ray, the atomists Leucippus and Democritus that fine films, simulacra, continually emanated from the surfaces of things, while the Platonist Academy attempted a synthesis of both approaches. The Arab philosopher Ibn al-Haytham (known to the West as "Alhazen") came up with the idea that the eye was simply a receptacle for rays of light which it resolved to a point in the cornea – a theory considered of minor importance in his own day, but which later led indirectly to the invention of perspective and its visual pyramids. It was this theory too which removed the beholder to a position outside the picture; from now on he stood back and viewed the interior of the picture as through a window. This emphasis on the subjectivity of the observer would find a later echo in the Cartesian rift between mind and matter, a gap sublimity was subsequently required to re-fill.

In describing light phenomena geometric optics from Euclid to Newton had assumed that rays of light travelled in a straight line. The experiments of Thomas Young challenged this assumption, however, launching the idea that light was dispersed in waves – until Einstein declared both ideas to be complementary. Under the influence of quantum theory the science was renamed "physical optics". It was through quantum physics too that the (microscopic) world became ultimately imponderable, existing solely in the eye of the beholder, presenting wholly different aspects of itself from one instant to another – for depending on the nature of an experiment light can be measured in terms of particles, waves, or energy. Moreover, every observation is itself deemed an intervention, changing the properties of the object. As Niels Bohr put it: "It is wrong to think that the task of physics is to find out how nature *is*. Physics concerns what we can *say* about nature."

It is this act of speech that by virtue of reaching out into the world keeps one at one's desk: therein lies the first draft of every poem. Rational thought has its own ways of establishing the rudiments of things. Here and there it retraces the lines, occasionally suggesting its own line of investigation, annotating the margins of the verses, reviewing the genealogy of an idea.

"To maintain 'the sublime' in the old sense" would be "wrong from the start"; it would be no less wrong to see it as a monolith, a block of poems, a single voice. Instead it resides in cadences and subtle inflections, in fragments and folds, in the unexpected proximity of different strata. These may interlock, but we cannot finally unlock them – poetic memory conforms to words only to give them a second, tropical meaning: the gaze into the zones of geography, rendered in figures of speech.

INVENTORY II

Thought yields in the figurative language of the tropes to concepts and phrases that depart from their literal sense. Figures of speech can reverse cause and effect, substitute a part for the whole, refer to one thing in terms of another, or compare different things. Sometimes they are given to circumlocution, to insinuating the opposite, or negation, of what is actually said. Used in this way words switch their focus from the things they usually mean to vanishing points far beyond their horizon. The rhetorical trajectory of the tropes, like the curve of the sun between the tropics, turns through figures of speech to seek an equator of language and nature.

In the critical treatise by Pseudo-Longinus – *Peri hypsous* – the "exalted" exists because nature "has implanted in our minds an eternal desire *(Eros)* for anything which is great or, equally, for what we consider demonic." What this sentence invokes is a two-fold discrepancy. On the one hand sublimity is conceived of as a surrogate for a notion of divinity that goes beyond the purely canonical to comprehend whatever is overwhelming or all-powerful from every sphere of existence – including the "profound". On the other hand the sentence also addresses the rupture between mortal and immortal – all the examples cited in the text itself refer to different forms of the struggle with death: war, mortal danger, torture and agony. Sublimity implies an approach to something that transcends the quotidian in human affairs in order to experience life's finitude. The insight gained would be inspired by the voices of greater and lesser divinities – however overwhelmed by terror, mankind still enjoyed the protection of the gods, and it was from these gods too that humans received an inkling of their own greatness and bestiality.

But such voices have grown quiet. What remains is the terrifying, eternal silence of empty space, described by Pascal in his *Pensées*: "For, finally, what is man in nature? He is nothing in comparison with the infinite, and everything in comparison with nothingness, a middle term between all and nothing. He is infinitely severed from comprehending the extremes; … he is equally incapable of seeing the nothingness from which he arises and the infinity into which he is engulfed."

Attempting nonetheless to find words for the sublime one ends up with concepts whose meaning, through the necessary addition of "un-," "in-," "im-" or "over-," is erased in the same breath. One can no more limit the scope of the sublime than reduce it to a single formula. Certainly, it announces its presence by way of style: sublimity is an aesthetic category because it is through aesthetics that we defamiliarize the world, and because only the unfamiliar is capable of expressing the sublime. In the Longinian text the tropical figures are therefore examined at some length. The unaccustomed light thrown on the world by the tropes reveals analogies whose paradoxical quality is capable of adumbrating aspects of nature that could not otherwise be grasped. The most radical figure of thought in this respect is the hyperbole: "Man is a speck of dust next to the size and duration of the universe".

The Augustan period in which *Peri hypsous* was written had a different term for the elevated, one whose context has since slipped into the background: the august. This was derived from *augere*, which originally meant "to grow, or multiply," but also "to honour, or exalt". The two were linked in the archaic role of the poet as the master of ceremonies at fertility rites and performer of paeans, themes treated in the surviving work of Hesiod, in *Theogony and Works and Days*.

The verb *augere* relates to "augur," the official whose duty it was to divine portents and find words for their sublime truths. With the help of his crooked divining staff the augur marked out the boundaries of his *templum*, a rectangular observatory where he would carry out hepatoscopy and the auspices, interpreting bird flight and branches of lightening. The augur's gaze is implicit in the first syllable of the word, *aug*: Indo-European **oc*, which, via *oculus* (Latin, eye), becomes the German *Auge*.

The history of the traditional Latin word for the sublime – *sublimitas* – adds further layers of meaning. Limes was the marked border or march of a piece of land, limus the fertile mire of the field, sublimare the act of raising demons from this underworld to the upper world. Sublimiter meant hovering to avoid enervation by earthly contact, while subliminis pointed to the lofty realms of the sky and the flight of birds. The latter connotation returns us to the eye, limis aspicere meaning to "glance sidelong at the sky". We have come full circle to the tropical gaze: a gaze through a verbal lens to the figurative focal point. The sublime exists solely in the picture we are capable of making of it.

In terms of this picture *sublimitas*, like the Necker cube, is a kind of reversible image. The sublimity it denotes lies literally "under a threshold," suggesting an alternating perspective: a looming eminence that is nonetheless below something else, a gaze whose sense of scale is indwelling, but which nonetheless looks down from a point that is far beyond its apparent boundaries. Is this meant to be Janus, the god of thresholds? Does the image relate to the sill below or the lintel above the doorway? Is its sense linked to the notion of transitions, of border-crossings, or does it refer to the architraves of the temple, whose dimensions were gauged an appropriate size for the gods? The paradoxical nature of the sublime encompasses changing proportions no less than alternating viewpoints that only a metaphor can bring into alignment.

The sublime stands as a substitute for the gods and Man – and for consciousness of the rift between them. Its subject is nature in the raw, as well as its various geographical determinants. Aristotle's model of the cosmic order dominated thinking until well into the Middle Ages. Above the earth began the celestial sphere within which the planets moved; this was surrounded by the hollow ball of the fixed stars, whose initial motion was caused by a divine demiurge and trickled downwards, ending with the circling moon: the inner limit of the universe. The drama of the sublunary sphere, its perennial discovery of sublimity in the mountains, was its longing to overcome that limit: to pile mountain on top of mountain, Ossa on top of Olympus, and Pelion on top of them, in an attempt to catch sight of heaven.

The German word for beauty *(das Schöne)* was derived from looking *(German, schauen)* and appearance *(German, Schein)*. This engendered a corollary in the mid-eighteenth century when two works appeared almost simultaneously: Burke's *Philosophical Enquiry*, which popularised the sublime, and a theoretical work by Baumgarten introducing the concept of "aesthetics". The term in its original Greek had meant nothing more than perception in the optical sense. Baumgarten made it the subject of a science, which – untrammelled by logic – he applied to the "lower cognitive abilities" which culminated in poetry via the "sensory memory". Burke's treatise on the sublime covered similar ground: both thinkers invented schemes for emotional response and sensory impressions, thereby giving shape to ideas of the beautiful and sublime.

The criteria for so doing had changed fundamentally since Pseudo-Longinus, however. The Renaissance had come and gone, and its experience of beauty now seemed rigidly symmetrical, its notion of the divine frozen by convention. The new ideal championed intimations of the chaotic forces concealed beneath the mask of form, the delicious thrill aroused by the sensation of fear, responses to silence and empty space. As if such stillness could be described with audible force, or as if it were the attempt to hear absolutely nothing – absolute nothingness.

What had brought nature back to the centre of attention was the discovery in it of structures that could be read as signs. A modern definition of sublimity would be aware of the anthropomorphism implicit in our temptation to see in apparent laws of nature the expressions of an intellect. Even the waves of the ocean never seem purely arbitrary: their dynamism suggests a moving body. As if nature had a script whose alphabet we could partly decipher, without being able to reconstruct the entire language.

The influence of speculative ideas generated by the natural sciences of the day was as contagious as it was conspicuous. Metaphysics transformed itself into empiricism. The idea of the sacred gave way to a deism that still saw the world in the hands of Providence but had long been sceptical of revelation. A new ethics saw the rage of the Homeric hero displaced by the pathos of the petit-bourgeois *Kleinbürger* and his voyeuristic awe of majesty. In Newton's mechanistic universe, soon to find its correlative in the mechanisms of industrialisation, sublimity was synonymous with violent emotion that conveyed on the subject a sense of his own superiority, its symbols attending the construction of sentiment appropriate to the dawning age of technology. A rudimentary form of perceptual psychology, no less influenced by the science of the day, provided a theoretical framework for explaining such processes. According to Hartley complex ideas depended on the action of the senses, for "when external objects are impressed on the Sensory Nerves, they excite Vibrations in the Aether residing in the Pores of these Nerves." And Burke wrote: "Whatever is fitted in any sort to excite the ideas of pain, and danger … is a source of the sublime; that is, it is productive of the strongest emotion which the mind is capable of feeling." A precipitous mountain, for example, gigantic enough to send forth individual rays of light from a vast number of points at once, all of which make an impression on the retina, causes a painful tension of the eye (while a hill gives rise only to a gentle fluctuation of light impulses). The pleasurable sensation of the sublime derives from the knowledge that the apparent threat it poses is unreal, that it exists only in a virtual sense, so to speak – and that nervous tension will soon abate. "It is a natural inclination that leads us to admire not the little streams … but the Nile, the Danube, the Rhine, and above all the Ocean," as the Longinian text claims. "Nor do we feel so much awe before the little flame we kindle … as before … the craters of Etna, whose eruptions bring up rocks and whole hills out of the depths." The sublime amounts to an aesthetics of first occasions: familiarity breeds contempt, which is why the sources of sublimity can never be momentous or impressive enough, before they too lose their edge.

The reaction against the cult of the great heights and of magnitude, whose initial setting, Haller's Alps, shifted during the age of Darwin to the Amazonian and African tropics, before ceding to the polar icecaps, was a return to the archaic notions of profundity: the mire, the demons of the underworld, the inward gaze. On the entrails of the earth geology had now gained its hold, and chemistry had discovered the sublimate as a transitional aggregate between two different states. Applied to the "hepatoscopy" of the soul, however, the true figures of the sublime were those made manifest by – sublimation. This was a kind of twilight phenomenon that entered the language via the tropes of irony, litotes or periphrasis.

"Bold, overhanging, and, as it were, threatening rocks, thunderclouds piled up the vault of heaven, borne along with flashes and peals, volcanoes in all their violence of destruction, hurricanes leaving desolation in their track, the boundless ocean rising with rebellious force, the high waterfall of some mighty river, and the like." According to Kant, these were the paramount symbols of the sublime. But the heights of Mont Blanc are unlikely to inspire much awe today, and even the ascent of Parnassus can be undertaken by cable-car. However, the sublime can still be revisited in connection with vast or empty spaces, or in the fundamentals of our modern conception of the universe. The incommensurable has become that which cannot be measured, while unsoundable depths have simply become unsound. In its attempt to explain them the scientific imagination runs up against the conceptual boundaries of nature, embodied in the sublime. The word itself is the substantivization ("that which is sublime") of a certain adjectival quality that cannot stand by itself. Its subject is not nature, nor is it the human being, but their relationship to each other – in as far as they are able to shape each other.

In attempting to define the sublime as an event in nature one turns again and again to the (lost) notions of the divine, the transcendental and the metaphysical that informed the pattern of its early interpretation. Behind every storm towered the spectre of a god hurling thunderbolts; receding from the picture plane the orthogonal lines of the sublime could be confident of a vanishing point in an almost tangible beyond. It is a view of the phenomenon which has no place in the modern definition. Linear perspective has gone; the projected lines run on in parallel and converge only because the eye and calculus see it that way. The blank spaces beyond have been shaded in by the sciences, which have engineered the collision of light beams to produce matter, predicted an endlessly expanding universe, and computed the probability of elementary particles generating in a void.

The tropes we employ to make sense of these things have not changed, but they have assumed a different sort of reality. In Benjamin's words, writing of the historical turning point of the First World War, what they now project is something like "the open air, amid a landscape in which nothing [is] the same except the clouds and, at its centre, in a force field of destructive torrents and explosions, the tiny, fragile human body."

Castletownshend, 30 June 1998

THE PALE MOUNTAINS

geysers and seething mud · sulphur that stifles
all breath still · boiling lava idly slapping
at the cavity's inner walls like surf mounting
the face of a cliff · the amphitheatre of typhoeus
from the lip of the crater only smouldering gashes
and in the dark a fiery rain of quartz and porphyry
then arid earth · the rigging-loft of the night
lowering the next landscape · patches of scrub
on the inkling of a desert a dried-out riverbed the sky
like molten lead in the jaws of the mountains
and in the foreground a layer of petrified snails:
the nameless is always greek — bellerophon crippled
and miserable roaming the plain till the overture
ends · the ocean parts like a curtain corals
and sea urchins set in scarlet the waves warm
as blood · reefs in the lagoon and mussel shells
deposited as the white of jagged peaks: the pale
mountains · enter pangaea with the continents
as painted symbols on her cloak · each pirouette
reveals a little more naked flesh under the folds
and again a change of scenes · basins overthrust
stood on end then fractured and lifted to their present
height · a gravity turning the whole to marble
the schlern a block of ice from which the sun breaks
off its chunks · then the tenor bound for verona
dieudonné sylvain guy tancrède de gratet de dolomieu
who along the route taken by the post chaise finds
a paving stone that will later be given his name
the year was that of the french revolution the theory
of the earth an opera of fire and water · cavities ruptured
under the crust a flood poured forth to the
equator and the world rested again on its own
rubble · its origin had already been calculated as
falling on a sunday 23rd october 4004 b.c. · man came
after god · and with him the unity of action and time

völs am schlern, 7.4.97

ON THE SUBLIME VI

    quota 33 · sometimes the seagulls batter
their heads on the leaded panes behind the altar
    for the smeary light in the flurry of stars appears
to them as spray · but seen from the sacrarium

    during the memorial service the sea
stands flat as if against the windows of an aquarium
    the sluggish mass of march · water viscous
as tar before the octagonal tower of a lighthouse

    that has never sent a signal · in the thick
walls the urns are invisible and the stone resounds
    with the murmurs of the guard of honour like

an echo from somewhere below · in this gallery
    of the dead the first regiment of the young *fascisti*

and the aryans and italian workers lie devoutly
    united in spirit · even the missing fell to uphold
immortal values and cherished an idea eternally
    young as inscriptions barely ten years old

attest · but most of the marble slabs are empty
    reflection · the silvery relics of an army

 grids on a map of the cold · *raff. liturri, castellamare,*
    serg. · on the wall here and there are lists
of names to bury lives not up for state or crown
    or glory tricolours solemnly wagging now

to fame the wind · here downwind no one resists
                      tell el eyssa, el alamein, 2.3.96

ISAAC NEWTON – *PRINCIPIA*

it was a tuesday · out on the grass
the chairs and white-washed table where i ate
with my stepsisters · it was warm

and the faculty shut for the plague · a glass
of water and the gutted fish upon the plate
were nauseous to me: that black coagulum

and thin intestine · our talk was idle
i saw them mouthing soundless words
and behind their backs something like a wing

but with its edges clipped · as if a passing angel
had tried to weigh their thoughts with its caress
then an apple fell and everything

that was the world was held · the gateway
the house the hill · no beginning now could
meet its end at the appointed place · it withstood

that natural urge for order · a burden lay
on things and from their mass there came a gravity
forcing them apart · to indefinity

woolsthorpe, 1666

ISAAC NEWTON – *OPTICKS*

i took the sun to my chamber
in my window-shut i cut a half-inch hole
and placed the prism at its entrance

at first i saw but a glimmer
then a kind of shelf dividing the further wall
into the parts of a day's alchemic substance:

paper potash red lead grass and orpiment
quicksilver copper sulphide indian dye
blue flowers violets and bubbles of every colour

barbels of a weever a trace of golden pigment
the blue tincture of spanish wood mulberry
juice and peacock plumes · i had no measure

for all this it was intangible and outward
the vibrations of corpuscles that strike
the retina and like the sounds emitted by a body

resemble the notes of a scale: red
orange yellow green blue indigo violet · light
of their intervals is composed bowing to the eye

cambridge, 1662

PHYSICAL OPTICS VIII

the first day after ramadan · rain over
　damascus · the barrier of light and the split pin
　　of a minaret that sticks from the cogs and chains
　　　of its crossbar · water towers oil tanks and factories

50s cars parked on the cracked sidewalks
　opel chevrolet and dodge · beyond the crossing
　　lies the scrapped rump of a *syrian air* machine
　　　like a send-up of the fear of flying and the valkyries

emerge from the nearby ferris wheel
　with the tripping gait their black chadors
　　only just permit and get on the bus · in the silence
　　　of this half-dazed day that could hardly be holier to the dead

a girl with a plastic flower and a bow
　in her short hair chews at the armrest
　　and the boy at my side takes no notice · god knows
　　　what he is dreaming with his green eyes · perhaps

some day he will see that the wet glare
　of the refinery towers behind the fence embodies
　　exactly the same perfection as the doves that cower
　　　brown in the dust because the trees no longer bestow

any shade · life is nothing but an exhausting
　of extremes at the barbed-wire mesh · hunger gnaws
　　through all things in the end · at the barricades and road
　　　blocks in the suburbs the soldiers guard this no-man's land

of light that now drips hissing on the warm tar
   rain over damascus · and the sky like a perfect
      pour · the trough of a crucible in which things alloy
         on the road to jerash tadmor mosul bagdad (800 km)

the glowing white flow from its taphole
   slackens at the dam of the mountains · streaks
      of iron billows of steam over a canal straight as a ruler
         through the steppes · the windscreen wipers drag and jolt

across the smooth surface of the milestones
   like the wings of a bird · military bases bedouin tents
      and fires · in the ditch a tanker with the hand-painted
         logo of a *syrian livestock car company* · then only sand
                                tadmor, 21. 2. 96

LA ZISA

and returned to the enclosed garden · eden
the peaks around the bay far in the hues of narcissi
and amid this court of summer the *sebihl*
a marble fountain · ribs rippling one by one
as if water welled on water
to flow into the rivers four · it is still
trees full of oranges and mirrored in the faience
of calm blue pools your silhouette · an image
inhering in itself: the lucidity of this absence
agleam · high above on the capitals peacocks spread
their feathers · with imperishable flesh
fans kept the sun in their eyes · i tried
to steal it back for you: that is what words
can do · open windows for the wind blind arcades
and a clear view over cupolas · in that niche perhaps
one proffering the cup chess-players in mosaic acrobats
amphorae in the sand over arches in the shade
threads of saffron in the palm · something bowing
to you and gone · all perfection only ever becoming
                grande albergo & delle palme 4.1.01

CEFALÙ

when the town was in the hands of saracens
women plunged clothes into freshwater basins
by the sea · streaming up canals the waves flushed
the soapsuds out and ebbed away · above the crush
of houses a massive rock of shelly chalk rose
shaped like a head: and its face was
of the purest white · otherwise one held lead
to the blaze for a lustre close to marcasite
green rust came as verdigris from greece
a salt gotten from things copper · turquoise
for the mosques was from nishapur its green
a mirror of the sea and from beyond it ultramarine
powdered lapis-lazuli from the hindukush
that died on the flame and left white glass
indigo was rasped from indian woad with a file
but the women washing linen called it *al-nil*
for its powder was as blue as the river
they had never seen and smyrna tincture *al-azarah*
juice of the dyer's madder root · but little
was dearer than a rock whelk's secretion: purple
that petrified to the red seashores · *rehj al-ghar*
by contrast found in caves was a powder of ore
that vaporized · on the waves though and their light
its ruby orpiment disintegrated night for night
to the gold-grained pigment of the sun
and the serifs with which all suras here begin
the sea a vast folio whose battered margins
the cliffs have bleached · a cold burning
up the lime to reclaim the white of morning

when the town was in the hands of saracens
women wrung their clothes on slabs of stone
to hang out the washing they went up to the gardens
a picture of summer · half-shadows that quivered
in the heat words in an afternoon lull that carried
far and no one ever to render them in script
a language whose flowing letters i only adapt —

sinuous descenders i set like coasts harbours too
marked in as dots above – to write you:
like others who may never have written a letter
but returned from afar with little bags of colour
because they had no other way of saying it
than pouring dark dye powder on an empty sheet
their gaze turned towards the one they loved

atelier sul mare 31.12.00

M'ONNA LISA

what it looked like when he painted it is anyone's
guess · the dark gauze of the varnish the lines
of the *craquelure* she wears as centuries of tiny
wounds that do not heal but only cut more deeply
into her indeterminate face · the sketch
of all love's derelictions · nothing to expect
nothing to hope for all memory made to wait
and yet how composed · whether mother too young
wife mistress or much-wooed courtesan
she raises her brows · the veil however signifies
grief's retreat inward · the days
falling about her are all she retains · her smile grown
vapid sometimes affectedly ambiguous wearies
of surrender and is full of night: what is left
of names whispered to her nape · but a haven
rare · both arms pressed to her belly until
she wakes fitfully reluctant and yet drawn to all
whose undoing she has been · but clinging still
knowing she has been loved less for herself alone
than because she has betrayed herself to no one

paris 18.02.01

CASTÈL DI TUSA II

if in this catalogue of the eternally adulterous
goddesses names i chose for you then more in defiance
of them than to find you famous friends: no matter

what antiquity a venus reborn to her morning
bubbles may look back on – with eye-lining curled lashes
and eybrows plucked the features feign a countenance

whose daily victory over age would prefer
a second home in samothrake to the tackiness of haling
from a mud village in babylon

whatever she was called before her many marriages
to dodge sore feet standing in the shadow of a temple wall
meant having to develop a talent for playing on

the little grandeur she still had without overdoing its mysteries:
the superficial in the unattainable
is what suitors have always gone for – the philtre

of a studied lust that only just allows one to make the grade
and so i watch you creaming
your legs shaving your bikini line dabbing lipstick

smudges off white teeth and sure: it's a taster
though for something more apt to sap than sate
but what gives you away – as you set to clearing

this hotel out of freebee bottles of scent and talc –
is your appetite: never have i seen your eyes
so wide your gaze so impatient for something else

atelier sul mare   1.1.01

TROPIC OF CAPRICORN

relict mountains · blocks of black and shining
slabs · i'd seen them through binoculars the day before
dash upward flank to flank pause nose to the air
and off again a traverse through the glare

heavy beasts whose flaming manes alone
betrayed them against the rock · wind

on my cheek i climbed in the impassable in ravines
boulders broken by frost polished by sand

and come to rest in that transient suspense
whose scale of time supposed a measure
outwith breaths and throbbing blood
its dimension was this scree · i crouched motionless

in the morning light waiting under an overhang
tension of the kind only perseverance can exhaust
thought i heard stones crashing a snorting and believed
them long scared off by me because i had lost

my eye for it and everything around me hardened
and saw it some arms' lengths away
scraping its horn on the ridge · the yellow ring of the eye
its coat like dark oats no: sand bending back

its neck and turning its head away · and kept still
as before as if one could have this moment interlock
with all things past · then the echo of hooves
in the debris filling in a silhouette with what is real

tin haberti 11.1.02

Translated, from the German, by Iain Galbraith.

One of the most prominent younger German-language poets, Raoul Schrott was born in 1964 and grew up in Tunis and Tyrol. His most recent volumes of poetry are Hotel *(1995),* Tropics *(1998),* Gilgamesh *(2001) and* White Book *(2004). A prolific translator and essayist, he has also published the novels* Finis Terrae *(1995) and* Tristan da Cunha *(2003). His novella* The Desert of Lop, *translated by Karen Leeder, was published by Picador in 2004.*

Iain Galbraith is a poet, essayist and translator, born in Glasgow. He now lives in Weisbaden, Germany. His translations of Michael Donhauser appear in the third issue of IRISH PAGES *(Vol 2, No 1).*

BEACHCOMBINGS

Francis Harvey

ALTER EGO

The day you told me I had two faces
was the day I was walking on wet sand
towards Moyne Hill and, with each step I took,
watched another step ghosting and unghosting
on the strand around the prints of my feet.

THE SKYLARK

was a singing speck in the sky
far above their heads
as the lambs in the dunes below
were showing it how even the earth-bound
are able to go skylarking on the ground.

SNOW IN THE SUMMER

That August day when I found
a gannet
the tide had washed up
on the shore dead
I thought of the first time
I'd pissed in snow
as I looked
at its neck and head.

DUNLIN

Far out over the sea
in a sunlit sky
feathered with white cloudlets
constellations of stars
twinkle in broad daylight.

BLUBELLS

June and, as I was caught out
telling a lie to you,
a shimmer of blue and green
on a grassy islet
in Loughros Beg Bay
was striving unsuccessfully
to counterfeit aquamarine.

WALKIES AND TALKIES

The ringed plover, dashing about the beach
in spurts of manic energy,
seems intent on showing me
and the dog how frantically
it's been rehearsing for its role
in the next early Chaplin movie
until the dog decides to become
a barker for the talkies
and the plover goes walkies
in a way that would not be possible
for Chaplin or the dog or me.

THE TIRELESS SEAMSTRESS

The incoming tide that unstitches
the seams and irons out
the tucks and pleats
in this beach's cloth-of-gold
will shortly recede and leave
new seams, tucks and pleats, holes
in the cloth-of-gold
for the next incoming tide
to unstitch, iron out, darn,
on and on *ad infinitum*

CHINOISERIE

The eyes of the girl with the pigtail
in the coolie hat on an Irish beach
among the tiny pagodas on sea sandwort
go suddenly Chinese in the sun's glare
as she places the willow-patterned dish
of picnic sandwiches
on the reed mat made in Hong Kong.

THE CRYTOGRAPHERS

When it's not drawing circles and half-circles,
what the marram grass inscribes on the sand
with the fine point of its rusting nib is
as enigmatic as the cryptograms
these flocks of waders have printed with their feet.

SANDHOPPERS

A cloudless blue sky and the patter
of raindrops that, no matter
how long they fall, will never wet a single one
of these windrows of seaweed drying in the sun.

BARNACLES

I've found a vast mountain landscape
of extinct volcanoes,
each one the shape of a cone,
on this tiny seashore stone.

FRUITS OF THE SEA

Look how today on a distant sandbank
in the estuary where clouds are shoaling
the seals are curled up like black bananas.

THE MATHEMATICIANS

God, you said, with a sweep of your hand
taking in the big picture
of sky and sea, had to be
a mathematician but I
was looking at the small picture
as the marram grass bent to its task
of drawing circles and half circles
on the sand as perfect as the ones
I used to draw at school with compasses.

LUGWORM

If I could join together these pieces
of string heaped on the beach I'd have a line
long enough to fly a kite to heaven
or plumb the ocean's deepest abysses.

MIRROR MIRROR ON THE STRAND

Here I am again space-walking
through the sky and the clouds looking
at myself looking for words
to describe what the tide
has provided for the vanity
of me and a flock of preening birds.

HAREBELLS

On a sunny day of late summer
a flight of estuary waders
preparing for touchdown
warily circles the machair
confused by a quivering array
of blue windsocks indicating
a steady force six blowing
from every conceivable point of the compass.

Francis Harvey, a poet and novelist, lives in Co Donegal. His most recent collection is The Boa Island Janus *(The Dedalus Press, 1996). An extract of his unpublished novel* The Diarists *appeared in the second issue of* IRISH PAGES *(Vol 1, No 2).*

A FIELD OF LIGHT

Michael Longley

On the life of adverbs.

It is thirty-four years since I first visited the Yeats International Summer School. I was invited here to give a lecture in 1969 by A.N. (Derry) Jeffares. My name had probably been suggested to Derry by his Deputy Director, Brendan Kennelly. I felt terribly nervous. Who was I? I had just published my first slim volume of poems and I reviewed poetry occasionally for *The Irish Times*. I was hardly a critic at all and in no way a scholar. The title of my lecture reflected my sense of my limitations. I spoke on "Yeats's Effect on Young Contemporary Poets."

The lecture went down well enough for me to be invited back the following year. I think it was then that I sat in on a committee meeting and suggested that lectures on poetry other than Yeats's might be given at the School. The redoubtable Frank Wynne considered this a good idea; the door opened wider, and the achievements of such as Austin Clarke, Patrick Kavanagh, John Hewitt and W.R. Rodgers were chewed over.

For several years my wife Edna and I came to the Summer School whether or not she or I was giving a lecture. We were joined gradually by other writers from the North – Paul Muldoon, Frank Ormsby and, once, Derek Mahon. We returned again and again in order to meet up with the new friends we had been making at the School, many of them regular performers at the lectern – friends from the South like the UCD historians Francis Byrne and Kevin Nowlan, friends from Oxford like John and Christine Kelly, friends from Canada and America like Lester Conor, Maurice Elliott and Desmond Maxwell, friends from Sligo like Mary Lappin, John Keohane and his daughter Catherine.

Those were frightening and tumultuous times in Ireland, and especially in the North. The Yeats Summer School in Sligo was for us Northerners an oasis of conviviality and graciousness. We found here the extended hand of friendship rather than the clenched fist of hatred. I love those lines of Yeats's about introducing the new friend to the old. He would approve of this community of minds, this network of relationships that stretches around the world and brings individual lives together. The illumination we receive here is more than intellectual and aesthetic. Though it features academics and writers, the School was conceived by (and continues to be overseen and sustained by) a committee of local people, each one a civic hero. It is first and last a municipal achievement. With its wide horizons and deep roots, the School epitomises what we might call "civilisation". If I may quote a couple of lines from a poem in my last collection: "Who was it who suggested that the opposite of war / Is not so much peace as civilisation?"

I would like to share with you a few memories and images from decades ago, beginning with the two historians from UCD:

– Francis Byrne, white with exhaustion, always the last to go to bed;

– Kevin Nowlan rationing out the fizzy-orange vitamin C tablets;

– Gerry, the Imperial Hotel's slow-moving but heroic night porter, on the verge of implosion;

– The Imperial Hotel itself on the verge of nervous breakdown, a major player in all of those labyrinthine shenanigans;

– In the Imperial dining room overcooked sirloin steaks and mixed grills around a huge circular table;

– Having one's literary knowledge probed between mouthfuls;

– A Japanese professor spooning sugar into his oxtail soup: "Very strong tea";

– "Yeats & Wilfred Owen," Jon Stallworthy's shapely lecture about the great man's silly exclusion of Owen from *The Oxford Book of Modern Verse*;

– Francis Stuart who had married Iseult Gonne talking more positively about "the Yeats he had known" than Yeats ever did about him;

– Jimmy Simmons hugging his guitar and singing "Claudy," his great ballad of lamentation for the bombed town;

– Sean Lucy's repertoire of Irish songs lasting all night (or all eternity, it seemed!);

– Seamus Heaney beckoning me into his room and trying out some nervous sentences on Yeats, then a day or so later taking everyone's breath away with a scintillating lecture;

– The English poet Geoffrey Hill shyly singing "She Moved Through the Fair": then his majestic Saturday morning poetry reading, possibly the best I've ever heard;

– After gritty readings by a quartet of chain-smoking Northern Irish poets, Kathleen Raine's delicate fastidious tones;

– Being introduced at the New Bridge to Robert Lowell who immediately started to talk about some of my poems as though he had read them;

– At a seminar Basil Bunting interpreting a complex Persian meter as the mimesis of the footsteps of native women counterpointed by the slap of their breasts against their ribcages;

– In the Imperial Bar apologising to Basil Bunting because my son Dan, now a molecular biologist but then a raucous toddler, just wouldn't leave him alone. "What's wrong with this Summer School," he complained, "is that there aren't enough children around!" To amuse Dan the great man waggled his ears. The poet of *Briggflats* could have won a gold medal for ear-waggling.

My love affair with Sligo and the Summer School came – temporarily – to an end in 1979 when, on the grounds that I – along with some other Northern delinquents – had taken too much drink, the then Director Gus Martin barred the bards from the evening session in the Yeats Room, the inner sanctum. No doubt Gus had a point, but wasn't there a hint here of the pot calling a row of kettles black? It certainly wasn't a case of "Lord, what would they say / Did their Catullus walk that way?" I felt mortified, and didn't return to Sligo for some years. Mind you, I wasn't invited! Anyway, here I am. I read in this year's programme that I am a "distinguished poet" and that today is my birthday. So let me be – for a few hours – "a sixty-four year old smiling public man."

As I said earlier the first lecture I delivered here was called "Yeats's Effect on Young Contemporary Poets." On the morning of 12 August 1969 I began by stating: "As a reviewer of new verse for *The Irish Times* I am often depressed by the decline of the subordinate clause. A deftly worked adverbial clause of concession or consequence is hard to come by nowadays." It was a fateful day. As I spoke the Bogside erupted. The Battle of the Bogside broke out in Derry. And West Belfast was soon to go up in flames.

The following Saturday in the "Sayings of the Week" column of *The Irish Times* extracts were printed from the urgent speeches of such figures as Ian Paisley, Major James Chichester Clarke and Jack Lynch (his now famous statement about "not standing idly by"). A sentence from my lecture was included – ironically no doubt – as my comment on the crisis: "I am often depressed by the decline of the subordinate clause." Meanwhile, Professors Francis Byrne and Kevin Nowlan had absented themselves from the School and driven for the afternoon across the Border to inhale the atmosphere of revolution in Enniskillen. They returned to Sligo as though from a dangerous reconnaissance. But the nightmare was happening on my home ground. My "Saying of the Week" did indeed sound comically inadequate. Had I been found wanting? In my Yeats lecture the following year I tried to answer that question. I argued that "my political and grammatical anxieties intersect at that point where the tensions of Ulster might be considerably alleviated by a few deftly chosen subordinate adverbial clauses of concession."

Although dumbfounded by the ferocity of the violence, poets of my generation did face into history and in time were able to respond to our community's pain. Yeats showed us the way forward – into and out of the darkness. We had in fact been considering his example for some time. Way back in March 1966 (when she was still an undergraduate at Trinity) Eavan Boland wrote to me about a new poem of hers and about her excited discovery of Yeats's note to "The Stare's Nest by my Window", part VI of "Meditations in Time of Civil War". Here are Eavan's words:

> [It] struck me like lightning. You can wander around for years carrying a helpless feeling like a child on your back, then one phrase wakes it, gives it life and sense and crowns it prince of all your impressions. In this note Yeats describes how, during the Civil War in Galway, he became desperate not to lose his understanding of beauty and not to become embittered: "Presently a strange thing happened. I began to smell honey in places where honey could not be." Out of this hallucination he wrote that exquisite poem "O honey-bees / Come build in the empty house of the stare." That sentence of his is the most perfect expression I've found for the way in which a poet rescues his imagination from violence and sorrow – in fact I can't put it in words, but its meanings seem infinite.

The engagement with Yeats goes back even further. The previous year – 1965 – I wrote for BBC Northern Ireland a film biography of the poet to mark the centenary of his birth. In my commentary I describe Yeats's reaction to the Easter Rising: "Yeats is doing a lot more than commenting on a single political event. In the ensuing creative period the eruption of violence in Ireland joins in his mind with the anarchy of the First World War and a philosophical conviction that a new destructive era of human history was beginning ... he was now facing as a poet universal disorder." Sustained by Yeats my younger self asserts: "Poetry is for me man's biggest and bravest endeavour to make sense out of all that is chaotic in his life." I praise "Meditations in Time of Civil War" as Yeats's most prodigious attempt to "exalt a lonely mind" with "befitting emblems of adversity," and declare that "to clear a devastated site and build on it, as Yeats did, is the most responsible, the indispensable, achievement of a great poet."

In those long-ago Sligo lectures my concern for the health of the subordinate clause was no more than a humorously tentative approach to Yeats's syntactical virtuosity and "the vastness and the humanity of his formal achievement". The great stanzaic and metrical tradition of poetry in English was, and is, galvanized by his practice. Like Wilfred Owen in the trenches of the Great War, Yeats demonstrates again and again that the complex, intense lyric poem is capable of encompassing extreme experience. For the thirty years of the Troubles he helped poets to clarify their own responses to almost daily violence. In the Shakespearean altitude of his great tragic lyrics he instructed us to remain true to our imaginations. We did not write in his shadow. Rather, in dark times we worked in the lighthouse beam of his genius. Today, it is my privilege and pleasure to invite you all to follow me into that field of light.

This address was delivered at the Opening of the Yeats International Summer School, Sligo, 27 July 2003.

THE HOLLY BUSH
in memory of Dorothy Molloy

Frosty Carrigskeewaun. I am breaking ice
Along the salt marsh's soggy margins
And scaring fieldfares out of the holly bush
And redwings, their consorts, chestnut-brown
Flashing one way, chestnut-red another,
Fragments of the January dawn-light
That Killary focuses on the islands
Before it clears the shoulder of Mweelrea.
Caher Island and Inishturk are frosty too.
In the shortlived spotlight they look like cut-
Outs and radiate apricot from within.
I learn of your death in this weather and
Of your book arriving the day after,
Your first and last slim volume. Dorothy,
You read your poems just once and I was there.
The poets you loved are your consorts now.
A hundred or more golden plovers turn
And give back dawn-light from their undersides.
The edge of the dunes wears a shiny fringe.

Michael Longley was born in 1939 in Belfast and attended Trinity College, Dublin. His tenth volume of poetry is Snow Water *(Cape, 2004).*

AN OFFICE OF READINGS

Enda McDonagh

Beyond the rule of men.

In the search for alternative spiritualities many Irish people disillusioned today with conventional religion have recourse to the arts in various forms. This is not a new or a peculiarly Irish phenomenon. Serious art works have always been recognised as nourishment for the human spirit just as they are products of it. Art critics and commentators, even theologians, have encouraged this approach, while at their best they sought to maintain the integrity and autonomy of the art object. Despite this, much contemporary "art-spirituality" remains at a superficial level or is too general in reference to provide real nourishment. This essay concentrates on a single work by a single writer, John F. Deane's *Manhandling the Deity*, in the hope that the close interaction of poet and theologian may yield some genuine spiritual fruit.

Between theology and the arts there has been at best an ambiguous relationship over the millennia. Religion, of which theology is the intellectual servant/master, would appear to have an easier and more intimate relationship with the arts as its imaginative sister, but with recurrent and serious disputes over issues of truth and morality. This applies in particular to Christianity which in its various traditions both rejoiced in and rejected imaginative creations of artists, verbal, visual and musical, from the catacombs to the basilicas, through the medieval Cathedrals and Renaissance churches and palaces, to the less ambitious, less explicit and less frequent interactions between Christianity and the arts in our own time. A more rigorous and rational presentation of Christian belief and practice in creed and moral system has often militated against imaginative freedom; yet the great mysteries of creation, fall, redemption and resurrection in their biblical and doctrinal forms have proved of enormous inspiration to poets, painters, sculptors and musicians.

In a western culture where these mysteries are largely alien, their creedal formulation as in the Apostles' Creed, or the doctrine of the Incarnation, may have little purchase on the creative imagination. Biblical and other religious narratives with their own creative and imaginative base engage reader and writer more concretely. They also provide more immediate inspiration for prayer in meditation and other practices. Even then the biblical language and imagery may prove too strange and remote a faith and prayer-base for many contemporaries. The Word of God in its biblical form may need the mediation of the creative human word, a gift more available to the poet than to the preacher. In a whole series of volumes, John F. Deane has grappled with the mysteries of humanity and nature in the context of biblical narrative and even Christian creed. This volume provides a still more intense example of his struggle.

According to the blurb on the back-cover, "John F. Deane shapes his new collection, *Manhandling the Deity*, in a framework that calls to mind the Roman Catholic mass, celebrated for the living and the dead." Despite the deeply religious nature of its celebration of the living and the dead, I am not sure that the overall framework of the collection is easily related to the shape of the Catholic mass; certainly not in the way a Mozart mass is or a more relevant example, *Mass for Hard Times*, by fellow-poet, R.S. Thomas. However, Deane's volume has a discernible liturgical feel and structure to it, most obviously in the *Officium* poems introducing each main section and in the closing poems, "Recessional" and "Canticle". For this reader and perhaps others, the variety of poetry, nature, love and explicitly religious poetry may be enjoyed in another related interpretative key.

A Liturgy of Reading

In the recent rush to spirituality in a rather shallow secularist world, one of the better responses of Christians has been that known as the *lectio divina*. A form of meditation based on reading (or better, listening) to the Hebrew and Christian scriptures, ancient in origin, *lectio divina* has developed new techniques of engagement which many people find increasingly attractive. For too many these scriptures are still a closed book and alternatives, serious and shoddy, from high art to New Age frivolity, are readily available and eagerly availed of.

A rather solemn introduction to the delightful and truly poetic *Manhandling the Deity*. Yet even the book's title, formidable as it is, at once reveals and obscures my point. For many committed and searching Christians, for whom the scriptural *lectio divina* is not immediately or permanently fulfilling, poetry among the arts can offer a significant spiritual alternative, whether or not it leads to reading the scriptures or to any explicit Christian commitment. In this work, as in so many others, John Deane has multiple explicit and implicit Christian references manifesting a deep religious sensibility. His manhandling of the deity is in the tradition of stable birth and criminal execution. The beauty and music of language and image already herald the resurrection appropriate to his and indeed God's need to promote justice for our manhandling of the God and our mishandling of God's human family and world. Reading these poems aloud, as I prefer, or in silence, one is moved reflectively from the world of the *lectio naturalis et humana* of a true poet to at least the possibility of the *lectio divina* of the true God.

All of this needs much further exploring. Here a threefold division will also be followed, but a rather different one from that of Deane in the collection itself. The first stage of the exploration and reading will concentrate on some of the nature poems and on what may be called a *lectio naturalis*. In the second stage, the focus will be on poems dealing with specific human beings. This may be described as a *lectio humana*. In the final section the more explicitly religious poems will be considered. Of course, none of these are what you might call pure forms. Nature, human beings and the deity intermingle in most of his work. However, it is helpful to look at poems where one or other of these themes predominate. And these distinctions are particularly important in a poet of such religious sensibilities and concerns as Deane.

In the current secular culture, it is often difficult for someone characterized as a religious poet to be properly appreciated as a poet. The devoutly religious as well as the non- or anti-religious may crush the poetry beneath the religion and both sides fail to see the poetry as poetry. This may be a parable with wider application as people suborn true humanity to some ideology, religious or non-religious. A religion like Deane's, true to the doctrines of creation and incarnation, should be able to resist that temptation.

Lectio Naturalis *in* Manhandling the Deity

The natural world in its beauties and cruelties is read brilliantly and expressed musically in many of Deane's poems, nowhere more concisely and effectively in this volume than in the short poem, "Runt Bird". Only the full text can do justice to the beauty and cruelty.

RUNT BIRD

Today the adult birds
were inveigling the young from their nest;
come on in, they were calling, the sky is lovely.
The last, the smallest, came

fluttering downwards like an autumn leaf.
I hold it now forever, small as the human heart,
certainly as scared, and its claws
cling to my manflesh. If I fling it into air

it may soar like brother Icarus for one
glorious moment, or fall
on the hard earth where cat and magpie
will be busy in the rutted slaughtering places

and I must tell myself again that this
is runt bird, incapable,
and that the universe that claims us
thrusts on, beautiful and without compassion.

This moving nature poem occurs in the third main section of the collection and after the equally moving but more hopeful and (in the double sense) graceful "House Martins". While "the adults waltzed and tangoed down the air," the young, "cowled and fledgling monks," will soon "have fled the nest, a little/ groggily, but proud as prelates, and you know again/ in the secret place within that houses grace, that everything beyond the rule and filthying of men/ is whole, and holy, and unsoiled."

The ecclesiastical images for the young as "cowled fledgling monks" in the nest and "proud as prelates" on fleeing, reflect Deane's religious mindset and prepare the reader for the secret place of grace and everything that is "whole, and holy, and unsoiled". Deane's nature poetry here and elsewhere retains its own natural integrity and beauty while reflecting religious sensitivities, whether implicitly as in "Runt Bird" ("I hold it now forever") or explicitly in "House Martins" and in the neighbouring poem, "The Wild Meadow" ("the wild meadow of our universe marvellously wrought"). These and other nature poems such as the final "Canticle" reflect what might be called the *lectio naturalis* of the poet, his reading of nature which in all its ambiguity retains for the attentive poet as reader and listener intimations of nature's divine origin and destiny: "(A) night wind mistles through the poplar leaves/ and all the noise of the universe stills/ to an oboe hum, the given note of a perfect/ music." As the music of the universe inhabits the poet and finds fresh expression in the poem, reader and listener are offered the twofold gift of the poem in itself and as new entrance to the natural world it captures. The adult house martins "who waltzed and tangoed down the air,/ each one/ a muscle perfected into flight" can never look the same again because the reader/observer can never be the same again. The *lectio naturalis* of the poet, become the *lectio humana* of the reader, involves a conversion process which parallels the poet's own and does not necessarily stop at the human and natural phenomena if poet and reader are sufficiently alert to "the wild meadow of our universe marvellously wrought," that miracle of creation.

Lectio Humana

In his "human" poems, if one may describe them as such, Deane reveals the extraordinary beauty in the ordinary round of the "egg-woman" in "Elliptic," "generous/ with the flesh-browns, the buttermilk-whites/ her movements always/ close to repose, like the imperceptible/ elliptical motion/ of the spheres." But that ordinary and extraordinary were never far from the harshness of "her space/ poverty, and her time/ labour." And the sons she "birthed" – "Sons, to boys, to men; she cried/ each time they left to build/ Birmingham and Liverpool." "Between times she tended/ the graves of the parish, seasoning/ loss with flowers, sheening – /with her dank sleeve, her chicken-wing/ dusters – the incised names of those/ who had migrated/ to eternity."

The emigration patterns of his native Achill have given Deane a keen sense of the generations lost particularly to the West of Ireland. "The Emigrants" recalls his boyhood memories as in the early morning "the creaking ... cart" brought emigrants and families to the bus of departure as he heard "the urgent, hushed, voices,/ nervous shiftings against the dark;/ ... then those awkward gestures and voices,/ embarrassed kisses and knobbled words/ like sand ramparts against a rising tide,/ how the hurt was held back, the way/ you hold your palm to your side/ to contain the suffering."

Not all of human life even in Achill was so sad. The joy in fishing and living, the very frenzied joy of all living comes through as father and son drifted in "a small row-boat on Keel Lake ... till suddenly mayfly were everywhere,/ small water-coloured shapes like tissue,/sweet as the host to trout and – *by Jove!*/ he whispered, old man astounded again/ at the frenzy that is in all living."

And not all human sadness is in the countryside. "In a Shop Window" is such a compressed account of Deane's capacity to be invaded by the suffering other and to recognize his own failure and that of the comfortable class to respond adequately that it is like "Runt Bird" worth quoting in full. Indeed, as with "Runt Bird" in the *lectio naturalis* section, it may provide the best illustration of Deane's *lectio humana*.

IN A SHOP WINDOW

He curls into a city doorway,
his night-home refrigerator packing cases,
his mattress last month's newspapers;

the clattering of footsteps past him has grown less,
chocolate wrappers whip in the wind and a can
dances passionately in the gutter;

shaven-headed and unshaven, he is a gathering
of man-stench and garbage smells;
his eyes are dried-out seeds and you look

quickly away. Sometime in the night one hand
will fall heavily out along the pavement, palm
upward to the stars, fingers bent so you can see

the perfect quarter-moons of his fingernails,
the lifeline like a contour map of the sky.
This is the very image of God's abdication,

foolish, unlovable, the sheen on glass
throwing back our appalled faces where we stand,
immersed in self as in lambswool coats, certain

of our place in the world, our destination.

An obvious temptation with a poem like this is to concentrate on the content and then perhaps paraphrase moralistically in commentary. It happens frequently in homilies on the Sunday scripture readings in Church. With a poem, it is particularly easy to ignore the music and the imagery in search of meaning or moral. Both meaning and moral might be said to be clear here. However, for the reader/ listener to take the poem into herself, she needs to read and listen again and again, to let the poem not only sing to her but to sing in her so that her capacity to see, listen and share in the condition of the doorway refugee matches that of the poet. That should make commentary superfluous and conversion to action possible. Otherwise, we remain immersed in self and our worldly certainties.

There are many other rich examples of Deane's *lectio humana* in this collection. "Alice's Harbour Bar" tells the moving story of one man's search for solace and courage in "the sickening/ frisson of excitement: to be caulked/ in companionable darkness, drink/ comforting, the world/ shaping itself to manageable forms: or face/ reproach and silence, the harshest judgment/ in her sorrow, in the children's eyes/ watching him with barely hidden terror." And for all that, a deeply sympathetic poem about a good if broken man. But the "image of God's abdication" in shop window beckons towards the more explicitly religious poetry and the poet's version of the *lectio divina*.

Lectio Divina

The *Officium* prayer-poems, variations on a theme and psalm-like in form and content, which preface the major sections of this "Mass" collection, might seem the best introduction to the Deane *lectio divina*. They require little commentary and read beautifully if mournfully. In their "psalmist misery," with their emphasis on the sin and suffering of humanity, they may mislead the reader into thinking that the poet has little time for praise, hope and charity. That this is a mistaken reading of him was already apparent in the nature poems. His is a complex relationship with a broken world spelled out with power and majesty in the long and to some shocking religious poem, combining real "shock and awe", entitled "Between Clay and Cloud".

It proclaims an Ascension Day affirmation of faith in a "self-broken" God, whose "love ... spun the universe and its derivatives; that he created man in his own image/ self-broken and incomplete". The Deane credo continues:

And [I believe] in his only Son,
enigma, the Jesus-
word uttered
when he spoke
his impulsive foolishness;
creating power
become love become
man. A man, like men
broken.
After the measured
ballet of reason we step
on the ice of mystery.

The foolishness of God which for St Paul confounds human wisdom finds expression not in "the measured ballet of reason" but in human brokenness, the brokenness of the Cross. Deane, like Kavanagh, does "not ask for reason's payment, / Nor analyse God's breath in common statement." Human sinfulness looms large but:

> sometimes the sun shines silently in
>
> and the beauty of our confined spaces
> shatters us into praise; sometimes,
> when faith, like a firefly, comes glimmering.

For Deane, "God's breath" completes his Christian and Trinitarian credo in a sweep that can leave the theologian only breathless:

> And in the Ghost, the aspiration,
> breath of his utterance,
> bolero of winds on the wild meadow,
> frisson of wisdom along the spine ...

He concludes: "O broken God be with us always, / now, and at the end of time."

His conclusion to another major poem, "The Wild Meadow," referred to earlier as nature poem but like so many with religious undertones and overtones, takes up again the theme of our brokenness but in a more hopeful mood:

> There was one child, East Timor, our time, who fled
> terror through the night, who fell and died,
> her body splayed where even her doll lay spread
>
> in cruciform shape. Our lives are fragile as the thyme
> and celandine, all of us lacking wholeness in our days:
> cormorants, militias, God. Attempt the ordering of rhyme.
>
> Attend, be guardian. Love, and offer praise.

The very image of God's abdication in suffering humanity and in a universe without compassion expresses how far the poet is inhabited by breaking humanity and a broken world. Few Irish poets capture the pain so vividly or so beautifully. None recasts it in the cruciform shape that is prelude to resurrection, in the human song that is prelude to praise and prayer. Deane relocates our agony and that of Christ in "the wild meadow of our universe marvellously wrought." Mary Pieta and Mary Magdalen are companions on the *via dolorosa* that began with "His coming so still/ To his mother's bower" and concluded with the drifting woman, her skirt hiked up, only to be surprised that "she'd be the one to knock first on the tomb's door."

As in the beautiful cover with its reproduction of Tony O' Malley's "Good Friday" (1964), rumours and glimpses of Resurrection abound. And all this is summarized in the final poem, "Canticle," as "all the noise of the universe stills/ to an oboe hum, the given note of a perfect/ music." And above "there is a vast sky wholly dedicated/ to the stars and you know, with certainty,/ that all the dead are out, up there, in one/ holiday flotilla, and that they celebrate/ the fact of a red gate and a yellow moon/ that tunes their instruments with you to the symphony."

In the Deane office of readings, it would be right and proper to add the categories of *musica naturalis et humana* to that of *lectio naturalis et humana* in preparation for *musica et lectio divina* accessible to us even now in this "wild meadow of the universe."

Father Enda McDonagh is one of Ireland's foremost theologians. He recently edited, with James Mackey, Religon and Politics in Ireland *(Columba Press, 2002), a collection of essays by 19 theologians. He teaches at the National University of Ireland, Maynooth.*

CLIMBING ERRISBEG

Tim Robinson

A draught of space.

Because I have climbed Errisbeg Hill in Connemara some fifty times, I rarely head for the top nowadays, but prefer to wander to and fro on the lower slopes, just above the "mountain wall" that divides enclosed and cultivated land from open commonage, looking at oddly shaped rocks and the twisty paths sheep have made between the roundish clumps of western gorse, as if I could never sate myself with detail. Along the south flank of the hill the boundary between enclosure and commonage coincides with that between the pale granite of the coastal strip and the dark gabbro above it, and the latter must be much the harder as the slope steepens markedly at this level. But geology calls for overviews and is better left for hilltop consideration; in fact any hill suggests a progression from close-up observations of what is immediately under the climber's hands and feet, through rests for breath-catching and retrospection and glances ahead at intermediate delusive skylines that hide the ultimate goal, to the triumphal horizon-sweeping outlook from the summit and the crushing realisation of the depths of time that weigh on a mountain top and even on the mere 987 feet of Errisbeg.

I usually come onto the hillside through the mountain gate at the top of the lane from Roundstone, and turn south-west from it along the mountain wall; here I am following what used to be the main road of the district, before Alexander Nimmo came in the 1820s to found the village and its harbour and to build the present road, which keeps lower down and nearer the coast. The original road, which would never have been more than a rough track, came southwards from Ballynahinch and climbed across the eastern flank of Roundstone Hill and round Errisbeg to Murvey, from which it followed the same line as today's road to Ballyconneely and, more importantly in those days, to the castle of Bunowen. Here and there along this route are traces of habitation, now deserted in favour of houses nearer the shore and today's coast road. Half a mile south of the mountain gate is the old settlement of Coogla (a name that trails more history than I can cram into a digression here), now consisting of five or six small farmhouses along a quiet sideroad; the old Ordnance Survey map shows dozens of open rectangles representing roofless buildings scattered among the filigree of field-walls around them. Here my contact is Tommy O'Donnell, a neatly-built and neatly-dressed countryman, full of years and memories of the hillside, on which he has pointed out from his cottage a dozen or so places with interesting names, most of which I have had difficulty in relocating in subsequent explorations by myself. The Malthouse, for instance, where poitín, the illicit spirits of barley, used to be distilled; the Fairy Woman's House, of which no story survives that I can come to hear of; Meall Daing, the first word meaning a knoll, and the second being unknown to me. One of the difficulties of locating these places from Tommy's descriptions is the sheer complexity of the hillside above Coogla, of which I am only beginning to assemble a mental map, after many years of rambling it. There are six or seven narrow gullies running down south-eastwards towards the village, deeply incised and edged with low cliffs further up but all quite shallow and tending to the boggily indeterminate near the foot of the hill. Some of these have minute streams in them, trickles only a few inches across that disappear into oozy patches or widen into shallow puddles here and there, by which I sometimes stop to watch the whirligig beetles – shiny-black, apple-pip-sized, each one paired by its shadow on the streambed – dashing about the surface as if madly scribbling their names on water. On one of these occasions I was distracted from my exploration by another tiny shadow on the stony bottom of a pond, which had a completely different pattern of behaviour from the frantic cursive of the beetles; it moved in short darts, resting immobile for a second or two, shifting almost instantaneously a couple of inches, resting again for an instant, and flicking away in another direction. This shadow was much more noticeable than the tiny grey-brown water-skater on the surface of the streamlet that was casting it. Small enough to have been drawn on the nail of my little finger, the shadow was shaped like a four-leaved clover, and each lobe of it had a delicate golden rim. Looking at the water-skater itself I could see that its front and hind pairs of legs were flexed as if to support its weight, so that each of four feet would have been slightly depressing the surface film; these depressions were evidently acting like concave lenses, dispersing the sunrays falling through them and concentrating them into a narrow band around the dark circles they projected onto the streambed. Peering more closely again at the clover-shape I could see two more even smaller dots of shadow on either side of it: the impressions of the creature's middle pair of legs, which were longer or straighter and did no more than touch the water surface, and with which presumably it propelled itself like a rower in a skiff. It seemed at most only marginally comprehensible that such a display of minute clockwork jewellery should be staged by sunlight and insect and the laws of refraction to the delight of my eye, but quite incomprehensible that it should be sparkling unobserved in a million sun-drenched pools all over the bogs at that moment.

Tracking these little streams up and down the hillside, I eventually managed to associate one of them with the Malthouse. From his cottage Tommy had pointed out to me a notably smooth slanting rock outcrop, some forty feet square, as marking this place, and when I made my way up to it I found that the outcrop formed the north side of one of the gullies, the south side being a massive glacially moulded outcrop like a recumbent dinosaur, with the stream flowing in a slot a few feet deep in the peat against its flank. Some stones had been placed in the stream to dam it, so that it widens into a pool at this point – one of the few pools on this hillside big enough for its purpose, which would have been to supply plenty of water to cool the "worm," the coil of copper piping in which the distilled whiskey was condensed. In fact the whole place was well suited to its function; the vertical rockface by the stream providing shelter for the men tending the turf fire under the pot and topping up the barrel containing the worm, and the slanting outcrop commanding a wide outlook down to the village and the main road for the man on the watch for the police. Having found this splendid rock sheet I lay on it for a time, feeling myself as closely applied to it as lichen, and let my eyes rove over the fields and houses below, the deserted island of Inis Leacan just offshore, as flat on the water as I was on the rock, and the mysterious low domes of St. Macdara's Island and Deer Island farther out, all these places being replete with memories and stories for me, and I planned how, place by place and page by page, I would someday write them into this book.

Conscious of work to be done, and driven by my obsession with place, I then got up, followed the stream three hundred yards downhill until it disappeared under the mountain fence and became a ditch in Coogla, and having pinpointed that end of it, followed it uphill again past the Malthouse, rather breathlessly, to where the steepening gully narrows between rock walls and is almost blocked with a mass of scree. It is the prominent knolls of rock between the upper ends of these gullies that give the hill its characteristic gap-toothed skyline. Three of these projections are especially salient; Tommy names them, from left to right, as An Goibín Géar (meaning the small sharp beak), Clochaí Whitewash (a slight garbling of Cloch an Whitewash, the stone of the whitewash), and Aill na gCuinneog, the cliff of the churns. These are one's intermediate goals in climbing the hill from the direction of Cúgla, and each is worth scrambling around in detail. An Goibín Géar sticks out like a canted pyramid, the south face of it being an almost vertical drop of twenty or thirty feet into the gully passing below it, and its north face an easy scramble. I stood on the point of it once with a compass, trying to take bearings of some landmarks in order to fix its position for my map of Connemara (it is too insignificant a feature to figure on the official maps), but I found that the compass needle was completely disoriented and eventually settled down pointing south rather than north, probably because the point had been struck by lightning at some time, magnetising the rock. Clochaí Whitewash is a smaller pyramid overhanging a gully, with a patchy crust of whitish quartz on its southern face; for some reason the Coogla men used to scratch their names on it with a stone, as I am told by the grandson of one of those obliterated signatories. Aill na gCuinneog is a substantial cliff forming the north side of the deepest of the gullies, and sheltered a booley or summer milking pasture. There is a ruinous little building, hardly more than a heap of stones now, under this cliff, called Púirín Chúgla, a *púirín* being a hut or hutch. The "cliff of the churns" always reminds me of a little anecdote of his childhood told by a Connemara man in the 1930s; I translate it from Seán Mac Giollarnáth's *Peadar Chois Fhairrge*:

> I saw my mother churning milk at the booley. One day she couldn't get the butter to set with the churn-dash. She put the churn on her back (there would be a rope round the churn and a breast-sling) to take the churning home. When she was coming down Leitir Chaisil [near Carna], she let the churn down off her back and took the lid off it. When she looked into the churn the butter was made. I was with her. "Come here," she said, "and see what I've got." There was nothing to be seen in the churn but butter.

The womenfolk and children booleying by Aill na gCuinneog would have had only a short trot down the gully to reach home, clearly visible half a mile below, and probably would not have overnighted there as was the custom in more distant booleys. They would have been able to watch their menfolk at work in the little fields or even on the shore beyond, where wavering towers of smoke would have been rising from the kelp kilns. They would have been able to identify each of the scores of currachs and hookers fishing around the islands sacred to the boatman's saint Macdara and to his rival Coelan, and the turf-boats sailing out to the Aran Islands, which appear from this height as a grey-blue plume laid along the horizon. It was a homespun, hard-worked, world, as closely woven, rough-textured and worn ragged as their everyday garments, but above and around it the sea and sky flaunted silks of a splendour beyond the reach of envy. Today there are no potato-diggers in the fields or kelp-burners on the shore; in summer streams of cars head along the road to and from the beaches. On the hillside one very occasionally meets a man checking where his sheep have wandered to; a woman or a child, never. The sound of churning is not to be heard at Aill na gCuinneog.

But these brief evocations of other times and places, to which I shall return, are interim views, hastily drawn like the breaths one takes when resting for a moment in a climb, turning away from close-up engagement with the next step of the slope to look back into the distances already traversed, as if a draught of space were as necessary to the body as air. Then one goes on, as in this particular walk I go on, picking my way over the scree to where the glen opens out into a boggy arena surrounded by the many peaks of Errisbeg Hill. The very highest is straight ahead; Tommy and the few others who still know the hill call it the Windmill because in about 1950 the Electricity Supply Board planned to install a wind turbine here, and mounted an apparatus for measuring wind speeds, like a windmill about 10 feet high, says Tommy, who was paid to go up to take readings from it every day. Whether there was too little or (more likely) too much wind, Tommy does not know, but the plan came to nothing. To the east of the highest point, just above Aill na gCuinneog, is a roughly domed knoll that looks as if it is the real summit as one toils up towards it from Roundstone; it is called Tower an Phúca, but what story connects it with the *púca*, the goatish hobgoblin, I have not learned. Looking back east from this eminence one sees Roundstone, just over a mile away, as a clustering of white and grey and ochre flecks, then the narrow waters of Roundstone Bay between it and the long, arthritic finger of Inis Ní, and more distant branchings of the sea surrounding and penetrating further lowlands to which Cnoc Mordáin forms a lazy recumbent skyline. The coast to the south and west of Errisbeg Hill is best surveyed from the Two Towers, a peak with two little cairns on it, south-west of the highest point of the hill. Directly below are the two famous back-to-back beaches of Goirtín and Dog's Bay, one on either side of a sandy spit joining a low island of grey granite and green pasturage to the mainland. This unusual mushroom-shaped landform is the *iorras beag* or small peninsula from which the hill and the townlands that share it, Errisbeg East and Errisbeg West, get their name. To the west lies the district called Iorras Mór or Errismore, the big peninsula, a wide low wedge of land driven into the Atlantic; the lighthouse of Slyne Head at its farthest tip is hardly visible against the glitter of the ocean.

Finally, it is from the topmost peak that Roundstone Bog becomes visible as a whole for the first time, stretching away to its indeterminate limits, which are often blurred with haze: the coast road with its scattered holiday homes to the west, the outskirts of Clifden six miles to the northwest, the main road to Galway skirting the foothills of the Twelve Pins to the north. Alexander Nimmo, who carried out a survey of the bogs of west Galway in 1813, was the first to give an overall description of what then was a nameless wilderness:

> From Mannin Bay to the river of Ballynahinch is an extensive flat moor of a singular appearance: from one of its principle districts I have named it the Moor of Orrismore. This tract is about seven miles by four, and, generally speaking, is a plain, not much elevated above the sea; it is however intersected by many low ridges of mica slate, and in the hollows between them are a multitude of lakes. I have an exact survey of the moor, and find the number of the lakes to be about 143, of different sizes, many of them having numerous and intricate arms. When viewed from an elevation, this appears to be a complete labyrinth, in which it is difficult to perceive the direction of the drainage.

Nimmo was reporting to a Commission set up by the House of Commons "for enquiring into the Nature and Extent of the Bogs in Ireland, and the Practicality of Cultivating them," and his recommendations might have presaged the end of this particular bog:

> The ridges aforesaid prevent any navigation from being easily led into these lakes from the limestone tract [of central Connemara], but in the event of an extended cultivation, something of that kind might be effected; for example, a dam upon the stream near Ballinaboy would throw it into one narrow sheet of water to the upper end of Lough Fadda, with various arms penetrating the moor, so that limestone or calcareous sand loaded at Ballinaboy, might be transported over most of a tract of about two miles long. A similar instance occurs on the north of Orrisbeg hill, where a great congeries of lakes are all nearly on one level, and from which a navigable cut might be brought very near to the Roundstone bay where lime coral and sea weed may be easily procured …

However, in those torpid post-Union years when most of Ireland lay "unimproved," he could not recommend throwing money into this morass:

> With the exception of a few of the smaller lakes, which are mere bog

pools, and may be easily bled, the most of them are high in the bank, and have rocky mouths, so that they cannot be drained at moderate expense; and where so much land is still to be reclaimed, such an application of labour would at present be unadvisable. The best purpose to which they can be applied, is by the judicious position of farm steadings, to derive all the benefit possible from them in the way of water-carriage through the arable grounds. And in the mean time it is obvious that they greatly facilitate the business of drainage and enclosure.

The ending of the Napoleonic Wars soon after the date of this report, and the consequent collapse of agricultural prices, initiating a sequence of crises culminating in the Great Famine of 1845–9 and continuing into the last century, meant that such "farm steadings" never were established; so, it is to human suffering and failure that we owe the preservation of the unique and beautiful terrain visible from Errisbeg.

I have tried several times to describe this landscape. Not long ago I went up to look at it again from the top of Errisbeg, trying to find an adjective for it, and the one that came spontaneously to mind was "frightened". The outline of each lake bristles with projections, every one of which is itself spiny; they stab at one another blindly. There is a fractal torment energising the scene, which is even more marked in aerial photographs, in which the lakes seem to fly apart like shrapnel. Of course all this is purely subjective and projective: I was the only frightened element of the situation. For a moment I felt I had identified the force that drives the expansion, the self-scattering, of the universe: fear. But when I collect myself to analyse the view from Errisbeg and to relate what forms I discern in it to what I read in geological texts on Connemara, the results are deeply perturbing to my sense of the human scale. Studying the apparently random distribution of land and water, of rocky hillocks and sodden levels, one regularity at least is soon identified: a chain of long narrow lakes and reedbeds, with lengths of stream linking them, running north-north-westwards from the western foot of Errisbeg and including the largest of all the lakes, Loch Fada, which simply means "long lake," near Ballinaboy. On a map this alignment of linear features is very striking. A geologist would immediately know that the explanation of it is a fault, or a bundle of parallel faults, cutting through the underlying rock and making it more vulnerable to erosion along a narrow zone. In fact the "Murvey Fault," as it is called, runs from Dog's Bay to Clifden and beyond to Cleggan Bay in north-west Connemara, and has been traced on the seabed as far as the straits between Inishbofin and Inishark. And it is not just a crack in the rock; the land on the west of it has been shifted southwards along it relative to the land on the east, by nearly half a mile. This is hardly noticeable at first glance since erosion and bog growth have long ago obliterated differences between the terrains on either side of the fault, but on a geological map of the area it is clear that various boundaries between rock types make sudden jumps southwards where they cross the fault line. One evidence of this relative displacement is however visible from the top of Errisbeg. A stream flowing westwards marks a lesser fault that intersects the Murvey Fault at right-angles just below the hill, and the continuation of this lesser fault can be seen as a long hollow following the same westwards direction but offset to the south. The work of giants, one might think, but in fact this is a relatively minor effect of the earth-shaking forces that have shaped this landscape. A much greater, if less visible, one is the Mannin Thrust, a roughly horizontal fault plane across which a huge block of land – most of what is now western Connemara – has been slid southwards and now rests on rocks that used to lie many miles offshore from it. In one area of seven or eight square miles to the north-west of Errisbeg, all the rock above the fault plane has been eroded away in the millennia of millennia since this movement took place, so that the rock that was overridden now forms the surface. This area is called the Delany Dome from the geologist, Frances Delany, who first identified it. Seen from Errisbeg it is all flat bog like the rest, but on walking across it and examining the rock wherever it shows above the peat one can see that it is very fine-grained, all the crystals in its structure having been milled to dust and reconsolidated by the enormous pressures and stresses to which they have been subjected. To understand something of the nature of these rocks and of the forces that shuffled mountain ranges one across another, one has to look into the births and deaths of lands and seas, the history of geography, in which, as it happens, the terrains constituting what is now Ireland have repeatedly been in the thick of the collisions of continents.

Because of the heat of radioactivity in its interior most of the Earth's substance is plastic enough to flow in convection currents that ascend, spread and descend in a perpetual rolling motion, the brittle crust forming the continents and the ocean floors being spat out, carried to and fro, torn apart, piled up, and swallowed again by these currents like flakes of scum on a boiling pot. All this happens so slowly that the distances between continents have only changed by a hundred paces or less during the whole of human history. The Earth is something like four and a half billion years old, and the oldest rocks of Connemara were formed around 700 million years ago. Rocks of the same types and origins occur in Mayo, Donegal, Antrim and Scotland, and are called

Dalradian (from the medieval Scottish and Ulster territory of the Dál Riada); they are mainly sedimentary rocks that have been much metamorphosed – altered and re-crystallized – by all the folding, crushing, stretching and heating they have undergone since they were first deposited. At that period nearly all the continental masses of the globe were gathered together as one supercontinent, which was just beginning to be ripped in two by the ascending and diverging currents of hot material beneath it. As the crust thinned and sagged below sea level an incipient ocean formed along the zone of tension, and rock eroded off the surrounding lands was washed into it grain by grain, piling up into great thicknesses of sands and muds slowly consolidating into stone. As rifting of the supercontinent began volcanoes pierced through the crust, and layers of molten gabbro – a coarsely crystalline rock rich in iron and magnesium – were forced between the strata of sedimentary rocks. By 500 million years ago the new ocean, which geologists have named Iapetus, was perhaps as wide as the present Atlantic and was beginning to narrow again; to the south of it lay Baltica (the present-day Scandinavia) and the vast continent of Gondwana, while the landmass to the north of it, called Laurentia, comprised what are now North America and Greenland. Two smaller fragments of continental crust on opposite sides of the ocean were pushed together as the ocean ceased to exist; this new conjunction hardly formed an entity as yet, being only a small part of a continent put together out of the old Laurentia, Baltica and other pieces of the jigsaw, but another few hundred million years would make it Ireland. What is now Connemara was part of the northern fragment of this future Ireland; initially it was adjacent to what is now Donegal, but as the continental margins drove together it was chipped off and squeezed southwards, to dock against what is now Mayo. In the last stages of the collision of continents, not only were the Dalradian sedimentary rocks metamorphosed by heat and stress, folded and buckled in ridges hundreds of miles long and several miles high, but in Connemara a huge block of these metamorphic rocks and the sheets of gabbro intruded into them were rammed outwards over an arc of volcanic islands that had lain off the southern coast of Laurentia. So it comes about that the rock now exposed in the Delany Dome is in origin a rhyolite, an igneous rock like a fine-grained granite, representing the roots of those long-annihilated volcanoes, while the rock surrounding it and underlying most of Roundstone Bog is amphibolite, which is gabbro that has been highly metamorphosed in the course of its movement across the Mannin Thrust; in fact the amphibolite strata have been completely inverted like a rucked-up carpet, so that older layers lie above the younger. Errisbeg Hill itself is of metagabbro, i.e. a gabbro that has been metamorphosed but not so extremely as the amphibolite; both sorts of rock originated as molten intrusions emplaced deep in the Dalradian rocks below a volcanic arc, perhaps the same one that gave rise to the Delany Dome rocks, and have been exhumed by subsequent ages of erosion.

The compaction of these marginal terrains during the fusion of the two continents not only piled up mountains but forced rock far down into the hot depths, where it melted and rose again as a light magma that cooled some way below the surface to form huge domes and bulbs of granite, a coarsely crystalline rock chiefly composed of quartz and silicates of alkali metals. At this stage, one has to remember, the Atlantic had not yet come into existence, and the new "Caledonian" mountain chain, perhaps as huge as the Himalayas, ran from the present Appalachians through the northern parts of Ireland and Scotland to Norway. Soon after the creation of this vast range, exposure to all weather regimes from the tropical to the glacial wore the Irish mountains down to a plain. (The Twelve Pins, a tenth or less of the height of their bygone ancestors, are the glacially carved remains of a plateau raised in a much more recent period of mountain-building.) Similarly, erosion has bared several of the granite rock-domes and levelled them off to form most of the present southern coastal region of Connemara, including the lower slopes of Errisbeg.

That, in rudimentary summary, is the geologists' understanding, or my limited understanding of their understanding, of how the main elements of this apparently eternal and peaceful scene, the view from Errisbeg, have come into their present and temporary conjunctions. Re-reading what I have written I note the use of a rhetoric of violence: collision, stress, tearing, crushing. The timescale of the world's building and unbuilding of itself can only be related to the scale of lived experience by the chilly abstractions of arithmetic, of powers of ten, or by metaphor. The same processes could be presented as constructive: the continents dance together and conjoin, or in parting scatter the seeds of new countries; the chemistry of the depths concocts the subtle colours of minerals and the perfection of crystals; soil is provided out of stone. If metaphors of destruction predominate it is because the geological timescale threatens our sense of our own significance. Our awarenesses as individuals last between, say, a tenth of a second and our allotted three score years and ten; we can just about catch the dart of a water-skater at the one extreme, and the dubious symptoms of global warming at the other. Outside that range scientific instrumentation and the collective resource of historical record mediate a secondary and ever more interpretative access to the milliseconds and the millennia. But as single biological entities we sail on a tiny raft of timescales between the atomic and the cosmic; we know that in the blink of an eyelid a world of things happen, and in a lifetime, next to nothing. To Pascal's two spatial abysses of the infinitely great and the infinitely small, between which the human being is suspended, we have added two abysses of time. As to the outer abyss, I can deduce something of it through a survey of its works in the landscape seen from the top of Errisbeg, but its presence weighs upon me more intimately as the absent stack of rock overhead, thousands of feet thick, that has been worn away, layer by layer, grain by grain, to free the stone I stand on.

Roundstone, Co Galway 2004

This essay is from a book on Connemara to be published by Penguin Ireland in 2006. The author wishes to express his gratitude to Professor Paul Mohr of the National University of Ireland, Galway, for geological guidance.

Tim Robinson, cartographer, naturalist and writer, lives in Roundstone, Co Galway. His two-volume Stones of Aran *(The Lilliput Press) appeared in 1986 and 1995. His most recent book is a collection of fictions,* Tales and Imaginings *(The Lilliput Press, 2002).*

From PIERS PLOWMAN

Bernard O'Donoghue

THE PEOPLE THROUGH THE MEADOW STRAYING

In the season of summer   with the sun at its highest

I dressed in my work-clothes   like any poor shepherd,

In the garb of a hermit   but for worldly work

And set off through the country   to find what I'd find.

I met many wonders   and uncommon sights,

Till one morning in May   on the hills behind Malvern

I fell sound asleep,   worn out by the walking.

As I lay on the ground,   resting and slumbering,

I'd this marvellous dream   I'll describe to you now.

I saw all the good   that live in the world

And the bad just as busy,   you can be certain of that:

Loyalty, betrayal,   let-down and cunning –

I saw them all in my sleep: that's what I'm saying.

I looked to the East,   in the track of the sun

And saw a great tower –   Truth's home, I imagined.

Then to the westward   I looked shortly after

And saw a deep valley.   Death lived down there,

I'd no doubt in my mind,   with all evil spirits.

I saw in the middle   between these two points

A beautiful meadow,   thronging with people

Of every station,   the poor and the needful

Who slaved at their labours   as this hard world requires them.

Some trudged behind ploughs   with no chance of a respite,

Sowing and seeding.   They worked without ceasing

To win for the people   what the greedy would waste.

Some got all proud   and dressed up accordingly,

Their faces and get-up   a sight for sore eyes.

But many more,   it has to be said,

Lived in penance and prayer   for the love of Our Lord,

In the confident hope   of ascending to Heaven.

As monks and nuns   they remained in their cells,

Never wishing to   dash round the country

On the lookout for luxuries   o pamper their whims.

Some took to business and did very well –

At least as we see it – "getting on in the world."

More had a fine time,   acting the clown

With dancing and singing   and swearing their heads off,

Inventing daft stories,   making fools of themselves.

Such people imagine   that work's a poor option.

(Prologue: C-Text)

The long poem Piers Plowman, *by William Langland, in three versions, dates from the late fourteenth century and is one of the most important Middle English literary texts. It is written in alliterative metre and is an allegorical dream-poem mixing religious belief, mystical vision, satire and moral exhortation.*

Bernard O'Donoghue, a poet and scholar, teaches Medieval English at Wadham College, Oxford. His most recent collection of poetry is Outliving *(Chatto, 2003).*

FOUR POEMS

Gary Allen

CANAAN

I have found my name
cut into the threshing-floor

cold slabs indented by the flail
till wrists, arms, shoulders
were numb with repercussion

the *thud*, *thud*, *thud*, steady and surreal
down through the years

and the fine dust,
the grain separated from husks and straw,
in which a child saw the God his fathers feared.

The high windows of barns and spireless churches,
dry as a father's love,
tell a child that nothing good is obtainable

obedience the only truth.

It matters not how blood is spilt
or what it's given for –
see how your ploughshares

have been turned back into swords:

this bridge choked
with tractor, slurry-spreader, harvester –
I have carried a knife in my lunch-box,

ready to kill.

Hazlett reached this age
pulled from his hiding-place
among the dank pools of flax

spreadeagled on the threshing floor,
fifty lashes tore the skin from his back.

Oh father, what is it that sets us free
if not the same mistakes that bind us:

farm machinery pushed aside
down the slopes to a dried-up riverbed,

and a baker's honed knife
flung to the long grass.

THE REVIVAL

All these girls clothed in white
without a word,
blow down the street
to meet their brothers.

The clouds are high in the sky –
it is summer.

The trains from Belfast
stand at the station
carriage doors flung open.

This way –
my great-grandmother's hand in mine
though I am forty years older –

come down to the river's edge

where Moses waits
a long beard of bullrushes —

a man from Monaghan come upcountry
having set Dublin in flames.

See how she shines in the water
a child become gold
voices singing free of poverty
bare feet slapping stone.

NORTH OF NOWHERE

These are cows that move dumbly
across the gorse and thistles,

but they could be human

alive in their own stream of piss
their inattention to what surrounds them:

in that shed over there I stretched gut
ten hours in salted water

hands ballooning — the bloated maggoty carcass
of one who got too close to the river,

the child who left us to swim the floods.

These beasts are giant
munching the car-lights on the motorway
striding the black slated roofs of the housing estate.

Where do cows go to sleep at night mister?
my ma says standing in fields

have you ever seen a bull's balls,

or a pit-bull snapping a herd
into the barbed-wire entanglements round the substation,
or the great staring eye
before the bolt is shot?

I stand outside, covered in shit and blood
and like a fool I pray.

What are cows used for?
Handbags, belts, shoes –

and sometimes, like humans, they look at the moon.

A BRIEF HISTORY OF THE DEAD

You talk of death,
but we have pulled skeletons by the cart-load:

so many bones,
the century groans under them.

Take this man here,
digging a shallow grave in the forest

no less precise in his terror,
or is he resigned,

numb from blows,
submersions in a bathroom of winter water-light

and what priest is it
that can come here to give the last rites?

as if God can find any grace here.

It is only another birth gone wrong,
carried away sublimely

like smoke rising above bogland
or terraced streets

or furnaces and factories across Europe.

It is a strange reaping:
ask the men digging in the fields,

holed skulls among turnips and beet

or the suck-suck of flattened faces
cut from peat-banks.

So let's not talk of death
as though it in some way could console us

with some kind of passive release.

Instead, we shall remain silent
turn our ears to stone, our eyes to our feet,

and make martyrs of the living.

Gary Allen was born in 1959 in Ballymena, Co Antrim and lived for many years on the Continent. His first book of poems, Languages *(Flambard/Black Mountain), appeared in 2000.*

POEM

—

Seamus Heaney

BEACONS AT BEALTAINE

Phoenix Park, May Day, 2004

Uisce, water. And *fionn*, the water's clear.
But dip and find this Gaelic water Greek:
A phoenix flames upon *fionn uisce* here.

Strangers were *barbaroi* to the Greek ear.
Now let the heirs of all who could not speak
The language, whose ba-babbling was unclear,

Come with their gift of tongues past each frontier
And find the answering voices that they seek –
As *fionn* and *uisce* answer phoenix here.

The May Day hills were burning, far and near,
When our land's first footers beached boats in the creek
In *uisce*, *fionn*, strange words that soon grew clear.

So on a day when newcomers appear
Let it be a homecoming and let us speak
The unstrange word, as behoves us here,

Move lips, move minds and make new meanings flare
Like beacons signalling from peak to peak,
From middle sea to north sea, shining clear
As phoenix flame upon *fionn uisce* here.

This poem was read by the author as part of the ceremony marking the formal accession of 10 new members of the European Union. The event took place in Dublin owing to Ireland's six-month Presidency of the Union.

AUTHOR'S NOTE

In the Celtic calendar that once regulated the seasons in many parts of Europe, May Day, known in Irish as *Bealtaine*, was the feast of bright fire, one of the four great quarter days of the year. The early Irish *Leabhar Gabhala (The Book of Invasions)* tells us that the first magical inhabitants of the country, the *Tuatha de Danaan*, arrived on the feast of Bealtaine, and a ninth-century text indicates that on the same day the druids drove flocks out to pasture between two bonfires. So there is something auspicious about the fact that a new flocking together of the old European nations happens on this day of mythic arrival in Ireland; and it is even more auspicious that we celebrate it in a park named after the mythic bird that represents the possibility of ongoing renewal. But there are those who say that the name Phoenix Park is derived from the Irish words, *fionn uisce*, meaning "clear water" and that particular coincidence of language gave me the idea for this poem. It's what the poet Horace might have called a *carmen saeculare*, a poem to salute and celebrate an historic turn in the *saeculum*, the age.

Seamus Heaney was awarded the Nobel Prize for Literature in 1995. His most recent volume is Finders Keepers: Selected Prose 1971-2001 *(Faber, 2002).*

A VETERAN AWARENESS

Seamus Heaney & Luzius Wildhaber

I

Remarks by Seamus Heaney on the occasion of the formal opening of the Bar Library, Belfast on 21 November 2003.

The first lawbook written in the West, the only lawbook with which I am in any way familiar, is the third part of Aeschylus's trilogy, *The Orestia*. The final play in that great group was performed in Athens in the fifth century BC and is generally known as *The Eumenides*.

But the play could equally well be known as *The Court of Athens* or *The Athens Truth and Reconciliation Commission*, because the story it tells is of the end of a world where the Furies were the dominant force and of the beginning of a new world where authority would henceforth be vested in a system of law. The Furies embodied the spirit of retribution, the need to have crime avenged, and in particular crimes of blood – avenged, if necessary, by the spilling of more blood. But the play shows how this ancient blood-for-blood ethic gives way to the word of the goddess Athena, goddess of wisdom, goddess of Athens, patron of the first court of twelve citizens, patron of a system of civil and administrative justice which she institutes and authorizes. The Furies become the Kindly Ones, the Eumenides of the title. They submit to what Athena calls Holy Persuasion and are welcomed into ground beneath the city, acknowledged as fundamental realities, their dark provenance the other side of the bright Athenian coin.

I bring all this up because at the opening of this magnificent new law library, it seems appropriate to remember how fundamental to civilized life is our agreed respect for the workings of the law and the courts, and how fragile. And indeed the people of Northern Ireland have a veteran awareness of these matters, a deeper than average experience of both the impulse towards furious retribution and the need for a reconciliation that is both tough-minded and civilized. But I also bring up the memory of Athens and the matter of the law because the mighty doors to this building are now adorned with an image of the heroine of another great Greek tragedy – the image, that is, of Antigone; and Antigone, let us not forget, experienced what many on both sides of this society have also experienced: a deep conflict between the things decreed by government and the things decreed by their own deepest pieties and principles.

It so happened that when Carolyn Mulholland was starting on her commission to furnish these beautiful, burnished, biblio-epic doors, in consultation with the chairman of your Arts Committee, Donnell Deeny, I was starting on a commission to translate Antigone for the Abbey Theatre's centenary in 2004. We both recognized that these were parallel projects with the result that I ended up almost as excited about Carolyn's work as she was. I know, ladies and gentlemen, that we are here to celebrate several other artists whose work adorns this place and many of them are friends of mine, but I hope they will forgive me for making special mention of the doors, because Carolyn has been a close friend of ours now for almost forty years. We kept on at any rate, free-associating about various law legends and law locations, about *brehons* in Ireland and Vikings at the Althing, about the tables of the law and the temples of the gods, about Portia, about the *polis*, and about images associated with all these things – those images, as Yeats calls them, "that yet/Fresh images beget." Carolyn moreover, is doubly gifted as an artist since she believes in words as well as images, and it is one of the glories of these doors that she has been able to incorporate oracular words from so many different places and periods. Words like the original Irish copyright law, "To every cow its calf, to every book its copy"; or the gnomic Icelandic maxim, "With law our land be built or with lawlessness laid waste"; or the tragic recognition of the Chorus in *Antigone*, "Wise conduct is the key to happiness. Always rule by the gods and reverence them."

The words *law* and *library* are hallowed words. So is the word *art*. They belong in that cluster of the humanist vocabulary that has to be made credible and operative over and over again by jurists and artists and architects and all men and women of good will, all those who would do what Yeats, in another noble phrase, once called "the spiritual intellect's great work". The pictures on these walls remind us that the artists who have lived through dangerous times are not necessarily changed utterly, that they don't necessarily bring forth terrible beauty but rather counter the times with true and vivid forms, true temperaments as different as those of John Kindness, Felim Egan, Graham Gingles, Clement McAleer, Simon McWilliams, Jack Packenham, Martin Wedge and Paddy McCann. The images on the doors are memorable, bold and archetypal. The grand design that Carolyn has executed will stand for what it is, bronze cast in commanding forms to engross the eye and the mind. But it will stand also as a reminder of the absolute value and necessity of that ongoing work of spirit and intellect, of its power and indeed its glory.

II

Speech by Luzius Wildhaber, President of the European Court of Human Rights, on the occasion of the formal opening of the Bar Library, Belfast on 21 November 2003.

Judges, members of the Bar, ladies and gentlemen:

It is a great honour and privilege for me to be asked to take part in the opening ceremony of this wonderful new Bar Council Library Building. I am sure that all those who will spend their professional lives working here will find themselves inspired – as I have been – by the sense of light and openness to the community which graces this building. As we have discovered with our own relatively new building in Strasbourg, architecture can be a source of inspiration for busy professionals, though not always a source that is recognised with a unanimous voice. Building for lawyers is – I would venture to say – necessarily a contentious exercise.

However, the opening of a building is always a fitting moment to reflect on the wider picture. Allow me to do so with reference to our common pursuit; the protection of human rights through the legal process.

One insight comes to mind on this occasion. James Madison – one of the Founding Fathers of the Constitution of the United States – has spoken eloquently of liberty and learning each "leaning on the other for their mutual and surest support". Working as a President of a chronically busy international tribunal which examines human rights complaints from forty-four jurisdictions, I am struck by the aptness of this observation. There is an obvious interdependence between learning and the protection of human rights and maintenance of the rule of law. We rely on the knowledge and skills of advocates to assert and plead human rights issues before the national courts as an essential part of the process that leads to judicial recognition and enforcement of rights by the national courts. Learning equally informs the reasoned decision of the judges. We also rely on these skills when a case is pleaded before the Court in Strasbourg and I can assure you that the adjudicatory task is made easier – indeed greatly assisted – when the matter is artfully pleaded in a manner which encompasses the essence of the argument with the sharpness and clarity that we have come to expect from lawyers trained in the common law system.

But there is also a wider sense in which the observation is true, that relates directly to the work of the European Court of Human Rights.

The Convention system is essentially a system of last resort which should only come into play when redress for the complaint has been first been sought before the local courts. In this sense it is often described as a system which is subsidiary to that of the national system – a system of outer protection, if you prefer. The underlying philosophy of the Convention system is that human rights should first be protected at home and that the national courts should be afforded the opportunity to apply the provisions of the Convention to the issues at hand, preferably (but not as a matter of obligation) against the background of Strasbourg case law. It is only if this is not possible or if there is discord between the rules applied locally and Strasbourg jurisprudence, that the Court would step in. I would add, in parenthesis, that given the large number of cases brought every year to Strasbourg, the future of the system now depends on the effective protection of human rights at national level.

Of course, the Convention system works best in States where incorporation has taken place. I am well aware that there was a time when judges in Northern Ireland or in other parts of the United Kingdom were not receptive to Convention points being raised before them. There existed what could politely be called a "constitutional resistance" to national courts applying Convention standards, or indeed even interpreting administrative law principles against the background of the Convention. But that belongs to the past. Convention law is now an integral part of your legal system and lawyers can now plead Strasbourg jurisprudence directly before the domestic courts. This in turn makes it easier for the Court in Strasbourg to adjudicate when it is confronted with a fully reasoned national judgment where the courts have sought to establish the relevant Strasbourg law and to apply it to the case under consideration. It also means that the national courts are in a position to contribute to the development of human rights law throughout Europe to the extent to which their judgments inform and influence the development of Strasbourg law by the European Court. The judgments of the United Kingdom courts in *Pretty*, *Goodwin*, *Stafford* and *Amin* are excellent examples of this. The poet's observation that "the law makes long spokes out of the short stakes of man" has never been truer.

This respectful exchange and dialogue with national courts on a continuous basis through the medium of decided cases not only aids the adjudicatory process but enlivens and enriches the quality of the Strasbourg Court's case law. It is based on a notion of partnership in the common task of ensuring the protection of the Convention's guarantees, a partnership which has become a practical necessity in a Convention community involving 44 Contracting States with a combined population of some 800 million Europeans.

Of course, it depends heavily for its success on an active and informed legal profession as well as on the judges. It falls to lawyers to identify appropriate cases in which to raise a Convention issue and also to keep abreast of jurisprudential developments. As those of you who have been involved in human rights cases will know, this may be no easy task for it calls on a breadth of vision which goes beyond the provincial or indeed the national. It is not uncommon for the Court to be confronted, in important cases, with citations from the superior courts in the USA, Canada, South Africa, and now the House of Lords. Modern means of technology have promoted this development which, in my view, can only be beneficial since it taps into the wisdom of other experiences and other jurisdictions. Exposure to alternative ways of analysing constitutional issues can only be seen as a healthy challenge to traditional habits of thought. The recent decision of the United States Supreme Court in *Lawrence v Texas* offers a recent example. The willingness of the Strasbourg Court to refer to decisions of both the US Supreme Court and the Inter-American Court of Human Rights is a further example. In this sense also, liberty and learning rely on each other for mutual sustenance.

Let me just add one final note on incorporation which places the emphasis more on practical experience than on either liberty or learning. As lawyers from a jurisdiction which has given rise to some of the Court's leading cases, you will all be too well aware of how incorporation actually works in practice. I can only hope that you do not recognise yourselves too closely in the following advice given by a senior British counsel to his pupil. The counsel said: if you have the law on your side, you should argue the law. If you have the facts on your side, you should argue the facts. But, said the pupil, who obviously had a bright future, what if you have neither the law nor the facts on your side? Well then, came the reply, just tell the judge it's a human rights issue.

It is clear to me on the joyous occasion of the opening of this building – and judging from your response – that incorporation of the Convention into Northern Irish law has a great future ahead of it.

Seamus Heaney was awarded the Nobel Prize for Literature in 1995. Luzius Wildhaber, a native of Switzerland, is President of the European Court of Human Rights in Strasbourg.

THE LAW LIBRARY DOOR

Carolyn Mulholland

One of Ireland's most versatile sculptors, renowned for her work in bronze, Carolyn Mulholland grew up in Lurgan, Co Armagh and now lives in Dublin. Her panelled bronze door for the new Bar Council Library in Belfast (above and facing) was unveiled at the building's formal opening on 21 November, 2003.

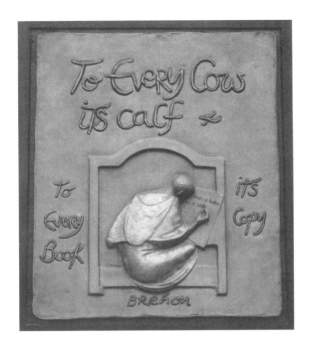

Photographs by John Minihan

POEM

—

Adrian Fox

SUNDAY MORNING

Belfast 1970 – a grey sky hung
Mucus of tar, the scent of hatred
And spent shells' residue.

A woman loved for a moment
By the enemy, cried like a gull
Embedded in an oilslick, somewhere
Off the coastline of my heart.

The etched guilt of a one-night stand
Tied to the lamppost. Some men
Passed wrenching *traitor*, *slut*, *cunt*
And *greenhorn* from their throats,

That slithered on the black tar
Of her breasts, seeping into
The feathers of her heart.

Adrian Fox was born in 1961 and grew up in Ardoyne, Belfast, where his father was a member of the IRA. A selection of his poems appears in Poetry Introductions 1 *(Lagan Press, 2004). He now lives in Craigavon, Co Armagh.*

AT THE BAR OF JUSTICE

Biljana Plavšić

A war criminal repents.

Mr. President, Your Honours, Madam Prosecutor, Counsel: I'm thankful to have this opportunity to speak today. Nearly two years ago, I came before this Tribunal, having been charged with participating in crimes against other human beings, and even against humanity itself. I came for two reasons: to confront these charges and to spare my people, for it was clear that they would pay the price of any refusal to come.

I have now had time to examine these charges and, together with my lawyers, conduct our own investigation and evaluation. I have come to the belief and accept the fact that many thousands of innocent people were the victims of an organized, systematic effort to remove Muslims and Croats from the territory claimed by Serbs. At the time, I easily convinced myself that this was a matter of survival and self-defence. In fact, it was more. Our leadership, of which I was a necessary part, led an effort which victimized countless innocent people.

Explanations of self-defence and survival offer no justification. By the end, it was said, even among our own people, that in this war we had lost our nobility of character. The obvious questions become, if this truth is now self-evident, why did I not see it earlier? And how could our leaders and those who followed have committed such acts?

The answer to both questions is, I believe, fear, a blinding fear that led to an obsession, especially for those of us for whom the Second World War was a living memory, that Serbs would never again allow themselves to become victims. *[During the Second World War, the Nazi-backed Ustashe regime in Croatia launched a genocidal persecution against the Serb Orthodox, Jews and Roma — the Editor.]* In this, we in the leadership violated the most basic duty of every human being, the duty to restrain oneself and to respect the human dignity of others. We were committed to do whatever was necessary to prevail.

Although I was repeatedly informed of allegations of cruel and inhuman conduct against non-Serbs, I refused to accept them or even to investigate. In fact, I immersed myself in addressing the suffering of the war's innocent Serb victims. This daily work confirmed in my mind that we were in a struggle, the international community was our enemy, and so I simply denied these charges, making no effort to investigate. I remained secure in my belief that Serbs were not capable of such acts. In this obsession of ours to never again become victims, we had allowed ourselves to become victimizers.

You have heard, both yesterday and today, the litany of suffering that this produced. I have accepted responsibility for my part in this. This responsibility is mine and mine alone. It does not extend to other leaders who have a right to defend themselves. It certainly should not extend to our Serbian people, who have already paid a terrible price for our leadership. The knowledge that I am responsible for such human suffering and for soiling the character of my people will always be with me.

There is a justice which demands a life for each innocent life, a death for each wrongful death. It is, of course, not possible for me to meet the demands of such justice. I can only do what is in my power and hope that it will be of some benefit, that having come to the truth, to speak it, and to accept responsibility. This will, I hope, help the Muslim, Croat and even Serb innocent victims not to be overtaken with bitterness, which often becomes hatred and is in the end self-destructive.

As for my own people, I have referred today to their character. I think it, therefore, important to explain what I'm speaking of. There now stands in the centre of Belgrade a great domed church, still under construction, the construction begun in 1935. Our people have persevered in building this church as a monument to a man who more than any other formed the character of the Serbian people. That man was the great St Sava. The path he followed was marked by self-restraint and respect for all others. A great diplomat who gained the respect of his people and the world around him, a man whose character has become deeply ingrained in the Serbian people. It is the path and example of St Sava that the great Serbian leaders have followed, even in our own times, demonstrating a noble endurance and dignity, even in the most difficult circumstances. One need only point to Bishop Artemije Radosavljevic, who to this very day is a voice crying out for justice in what has become for Serbs the wilderness of Kosovo.

Tragically, our leaders including myself, abandoned this path in the last war. I think it is clear that I have separated myself from those leaders, but too late. Yet, this leadership, without shame, continues to seek the loyalty and support of our people. It is done by provoking fear and speaking half-truths in order to convince our people that the world is against us. But by now the fruits of this leadership are clear. They are graves, refugees, isolation, and bitterness against the whole world, which spurns us because of these very leaders.

I have been urged that this is not the time nor the place to speak this truth. We must wait, they say, until others also accept responsibility for their deeds. But I believe that there is no place and that there is no time where it is not appropriate to speak the truth. I believe that we must put our own house in order. Others will have to examine themselves and their own conduct. We must live in the world and not in a cave. The world is always imperfect and often unjust, but as long as we persevere and preserve our identity and our character, we have nothing to fear.

As for me, it is the members of this Trial Chamber that have been given the responsibility to judge. You must strive in your judgment to find whatever justice this world can offer, not only for me but also for the innocent victims of this war.

I will, however, make one appeal, and that is to the Tribunal itself, the Judges, Prosecutors, Investigators; that you do all within your power to bring justice to all sides. In doing this, you may be able to accomplish the mission for which this Tribunal has been created.

Translated from the Serbian and delivered before the Judges of the International Criminal Tribunal for the Former Yugoslavia, The Hague, The Netherlands, 17 December 2002.

Prior to the outbreak of the Bosnian war in 1992, Biljana Plavšić – a well-known nationalist intellectual and writer – taught in the Department of Biology at Sarajevo University. With Radovan Karadic, Ratko Mladic and others, she held a wartime leadership position in "Republika Srpska," the secessionist Serb-Orthodox para-state (now an autonomous region within a reconstituted Bosnia) that engaged in massive ethnic cleansing of Muslims and Catholics, culminating in the murder of over 7,000 men and boys at Srebrenica in July 1995.

FOUR POEMS

Hugh Dunkerley

CHILD

You were sleeping when they found you,
curled in a ditch, long summer grasses
bending down to touch your senseless face.
You never heard the clatter of the circling helicopter,
never noticed the men and women
in dazzling overalls combing the fields,
the batter of bristling cameras
waiting for you at the end of the lane.
You were silent when they asked
about the men who'd taken you,
what they'd done to you
with hands, threats, caresses
how for weeks the grasses had gradually
closed out the light until you were finally
cocooned in a green darkness.
You never woke when they lifted you,
naked, from your hiding place
and carried you away,
some skin cells, a few stray hairs,
floating down onto the broken ground
already finding their way
in the long slow sift of matter.

FAST

For days you must have lived on air,
the exaltation of hunger,
your stomach shrinking to a knot,

until you couldn't feel anything,
not even the cold that had wracked you
through your thin sleeping bag, night and day.

In the tent crumpled biscuits, chocolate,
a half opened-tin of condensed milk
were scattered out of reach, the remnants

of a rite you'd long forgotten.
In the granite light the mountains wavered
while at night the stars rustled, tugging

at you with their tiny gravities.
You must have thought you were close then,
the chrysalis perhaps of something unimaginable.

When the last agonies came, the muscles,
the organs, consuming themselves in a final blaze,
what a purification it must have seemed.

Verity Linn, a Breatherian, was found dead near a remote Scottish loch in 1999.

AFTERWARDS

I catch myself in the mirror,
the familiar topography of my face

altered somehow; the eyes she scrutinised,
the lips that pressed against hers

almost someone else's.
Does it change us a little each time,

this melding of our bodies,
the subtle interchange of DNA?

I remember the first time,
the strangeness of knowing

I'd been inside a woman,
looking down at myself,

the raw part of me
still sluiced in her wetness.

I had given something away;
a wholeness that had finally been broached.

LAZARUS

As white as a tuber,
still filthy from the grave,
I stagger back into my life.

The house is shuttered in mourning
and I hide in its dark,
unable to bear the sun's bright lances,
the baying crowds that grow
like a pestilence with each new day.

Their words crash through doors.
"What is heaven like?
Will we burn for our sins?"
I can tell them nothing:
death was dreamless sleep,
his voice an agony calling me back.

My sisters bring me food,
indecipherable tastes, everything
tainted with the odour of putrefaction.

At night I slip out,
walk the familiar dusty streets.
People I have known since childhood
cross the road to avoid me,
their heads averted.

I see it in my sisters' eyes;
the memory of the opened grave,
something pallid and awful
stirring in the graveclothes.

Hugh Dunkerley teaches English and Creative Writing at University College Chichester, in the South of England. His first collection of poems, Walking to the Fire Tower *(Redbeck Press), was published in 1997.*

FIVE POEMS

―

Sarah Maguire

THE GRASS CHURCH AT DILSTON GROVE

Papered with clay
then seeded with fescue and rye,

the church walls fur
with a soft green pelt,

filaments trying the air
before climbing the light.

The church is damp;
it smells of a tool-shed:

mineral,
soil coating tines and boots,

vegetable, with the sap
of lifted plants.

At sunset
small boxes of yellowing sunlight

plot the grass as it fades
through cross-hatched windows,

loose panes stove in,
the lead curled back.

Memories of redemption
wane in the rafters,

communion forgotten
in the emptied nave,

a mission beached
without a flock,

the lost souls lost
to the docks.

Pebble-dashed agglomerate:
these are the rough-cast walls

of the first concrete church in London.
And now the grass comes home

as a box of green metaphors
opens

while I watch.
How old I have become.

Everything the grass has asked of me,
I have done:

I have taken the grass for my path,
for my playground, and for my bed;

I have named grass seeds,
I have borne volumes of turf;

I know the stuff of clay,
the weight of sods,

the bloom of *Agrostis*
on mended soil.

Everything the grass has asked of me
on this earth, I have done

except give my self
up

except lie
under its sky of moving roots.

PASSAGES

Decree: clear skies
over the heart
of London: cirrus

nothing less
flaming
the far edge of blueness,

nothing less
marking
the absolute boundaries

of air, of resolution.
A cast of slowing jumbos,
emptied of fuel, begins

the descent:
trawling
the long southern flight path

down into Heathrow.
When the huge wheels
hatch

from that cold,
aluminium belly,
will a petrified figure

plummet down
(this time)
into a carpark,

breath frozen midair,
the wrapt human form
seared

on the landing gear
tossed three miles clear
from touchdown,

from migration?
The big silvered craft
run the gamut of light,

taking in evening
buoyant, journeyed:
pushed to the edge

of the city: now exposed,
with its parcel of lights,
its human freight

inching homewards
through dusk, mid-September,
as fear

slips its cold roots
through the known.
The dull muddied Thames

is full of the equinox,
dragged by the moon
the dun waters

flush to the Barrier:
a ruined city checked,
a whole rumoured ocean

balanced in abeyance.
Tides dissolve memory:
history

loosens its cargoes
into the tides
promiscuously mingling,

forgetting,
heading out to the open.
But the silt sifts on,

turning and sorting:
as the docklands fall
out of sight,

cargoless,
trafficless, winches abandoned,
ceilings stove in

to the skies.
And the skies are rivers
freighting

the burdens
of rivers: transhumance
precious and raw

now landing on tarmac.
The jets tick
as they cool,

boxes contracting
on earth,
as rivets ease back:

the hulk
emptied of passengers
now filling

with migrants:
labouring in the site
of exile and arrival.

The swallows
left weeks ago,
with no notice:

one afternoon
the skies
were abandoned:

lack
takes them southwards.
And in the formal garden,

the last hybrid roses
flare rose-pink and
salmon and mauve,

but the sap's on the turn.
And the earth is balanced,
day equaling night:

and is equally
unbalanced
as rumours are pieced

into news.
After this: winter.
The youngest vixen repeats

her sharp scent,
doubles back, excited
back again,

crouching,
back now to the rough path:
slips

under the light paling fence
and is
gone:

EUROPE

Merely an idea bruising
the far horizon, as a cold mist tightens into rain –

but at dusk we still wait
by the Bay of Tangier, on the old city walls, gazing northwards

till the night comes on,
and a necklace of lights gathers the throat of the sea.

The young men burn –
lonely, intent on resolving that elusive littoral

into a continent of promises
kept, clean water, work. If they stare hard enough, perhaps

it will come to them.
Each night, they climb these crumbling ramparts

and face north
like true believers, while the lighthouse of Tarifa blinks

and beckons,
unrolling its brilliant pavement across the pitiless Straits.

LANDSCAPE, WITH DEAD SEA

Flat out on brine
    at the bottom of the world –
        not one wisp of cirrus

can mar this cobalt blue dome
   nailed to a dry bowl of hills,
       pastel hills folded in stillness.

Buoyant on bitterness –
   the tonnage of fluids transfigures
       into haze above my very eyes,

to a mist heavy with minerals,
   molecules of sweet water
       shipped up slowly to infinite blue.

These deep, barren waters
   are riddled with toxins and salts.
       At the shoreline I harvest

the dark, sybaritic mud –
   worked into my flesh, its granular
       astringency erodes my dead skin.

Down south, Potash City –
   acres of evaporation pans
       and chimneyed factories,

ringfenced depots stacked up with salts,
   with phosphates in boxes
       and sulphurous drums.

At sunset, the western, mineral sky
   ebbs through carmine into mauve.
       The lights come on in Jericho.

I imagine what I cannot see –
   barbed wire threaded with jasmine,
       sharp enough to smell.

This riven land: here
   the great tectonic plates glide asunder
       as fast as my fingernails grow,

riding the molten core of magma –
    the invisible, radiant heart of the earth,
        burdened by geography, charged with life.

COTTON BOLL

From here, the cotton fields stretch further than an ocean,
undulant green, pocked with foam.

Little bush, burning in the catastrophic heat,
how far did you come

to set root in this thick black earth, humidity rising,
staggering belief?

Sheets, winding-sheets, underthings, handkerchiefs —
a polity of garments

spun from that one fine thread, yanked
straight out of your heart.

Dyed, dark-stained with sweat, how invisible is the yarn
that ties the weaver to the woven

when all we grasp is stuff —
the loosening fabric of desire, or of utility,

that we labour to possess, unlace, discard,
then burn.

Sarah Maguire was born in 1957 in West London, where she has lived all her life. Her third book of poems is The Florist's at Midnight *(Cape, 2001). She is the Founder and Director of the Poetry Translation Centre at the School of Oriental and African Studies, University of London.*

PARSLEY OF ALEXANDRIA

—

Michael Viney

Directions and misdirections.

The plant peering in my workroom window has not so much grown up there as entered stage left, such is the power of its stately, shimmering presence. It is a weed or wild herb, according to one's sensibilities, but at nearly two metres tall and half that in girth, it is clearly not to be plucked out in passing or picked and stuck in a vase. An upside-down chandelier, it radiates dozens of flower-heads, each a fractal hemisphere of hemispheres and all the same pale greeny-yellow, a colour shared with little else on my tangled acre. This luminous hue provides much of the distinctive instress, in Hopkins' word, of *Smyrnium olusatrum*, the herb commonly called alexanders.

The growth of the plant this spring has astonished me: the only one I've seen in Mayo and certainly a solitary specimen on our hillside. Here it is in full glossy sail under my nose. Where did it come from? I have no clue as to its origins; the marvelling has to come first.

John Fowles once deplored the habit of approaching nature in quasi-scientific mode, reaching for names of species, their habits, degrees of rarity, rather than the feelings of the moment: "We have quite enough facts now". My guilt was relieved by his later, post-Zen decision, almost a *volte face*, that "living without names is impossible, if not downright idiocy . . . [The] two modes of seeing or knowing could in fact marry and take place almost simultaneously, and enrich each other." What was really alienating us from nature, he thought now, was our obsession with utility: "We shall never fully understand nature (or ourselves), and certainly never respect it, until we dissociate the wild from the notion of usability – however innocent and harmless the use."

The alexanders (now trembling under the restless clasp of a blue tit, searching its umbels for tiny flies) offers itself in the proper exercise of knowing. Not for nothing is it made like a diagram drawn at brainstorming sessions, all slashing lines and circles. And those ancient – now garbled – names, progressing and changing through history's herbals (*herba Alexandrina*, *petroselinum Alexandrinum*, the parsley of Alexandria (some parsley!) – what should they bring to mind but the lost library of Egypt, now reinvented as the Internet. Tap in *Smyrnium olusatrum*, and the facts come scrolling up, recycling and supplementing the many elegant books that, in turn, recycle the old herbals and their seemingly imperishable woodcuts.

All celebrate the plant's long use by humanity, as medicine and food. In a further splendid resonance, the great medical school of Alexandria founded the tradition in which Dioscorides, father of pharmacognosy, wrote *De Materia Medica*, a standard text for 1,500 years. Herein, the seeds of *hipposelinon* (the Greek name for alexanders), drunk in wine, made it one of the myriad emmenagogues that haunt herbal history, in apparent obsession with the need to promote menstruation (or abortion?). Later, in Medieval Europe, it was to prove carminative, aperient, depurative, diuretic, antiscorbutic. Its more plebeian virtue, however, was as a vegetable. The long, wrist-thick winter tap-root lent itself to pickling, and the spring shoots were chewable as a rather tough celery: the secret, as Geoffrey Grigson discovered too late, is to blanch them, thus avoiding a "decidedly bitter and forbidding" aftertaste.

A food plant in Egypt long before the pharaohs, it was carried by the Romans as far west as Britain, where it has turned up in appropriate excavations, along with figs, lentils and asparagus. Medieval monks grew it as a pot herb, and the Augustinians, taking its seeds to the Somerset island of Steep Holm, were to change its natural history thereby. Nourished by a limestone soil and copious gullshit, alexanders now forests the island in summer and by autumn an estimated 75,000 plants have produced 450 million black seeds weighing 22 tonnes. Duly impressed, I have attempted to count the flowers in each cluster on the bush outside the window, the clusters in each umbel, the number of umbels on the stems, but averaging the variables proved too much.

With such an output of seed, and widespread cultivation both in Britain and Ireland, alexanders escaped freely into the wild, finding warm and cosseting corners on frost-free coasts. In Kerry, for example, its records cluster around the ruins of castles and monasteries, but the plant also claims an occasional niche among the other burly umbellifers – hogweed, cow-parsley, etc – of roadsides and hedgerows, where an Irish name, *lus na ngrán dubh*, plant of the black grain, endorses its antiquity. Indeed, the centuries up to the seventeenth heaped the Irish plate with vegetables in a variety later quite eclipsed by the fatally obliging potato. Peas and broad beans, so easily dried for winter, were among the earliest, and cabbage a special favourite of the monks. Onions, with garlic and leeks, were by far the most valued vegetable of medieval Gaelic Ireland and part of the food-rent levied by a lord upon his clients. There was alexanders, yes, but also the umbellifer called *cerrbacán*, "the bent, crooked one", Ireland's most widely eaten medieval root. This is now identified, if with some hesitation, as *Sium sisarum*, a water parsnip from China, widely grown in Europe, with a cluster of sweet and knobbly tubers. Today called skirret, it would have thrived in Ireland's general bogginess, yet has now quite disappeared from the island's flora, leaving only its even more marshy relative, the great water parsnip, *Sium latifolium*, as a rarity of the Shannon and the Erne.

In Europe, the taste for alexanders was steadily overtaken from the seventeenth century onwards, when the Italians improved, by selection, the sweeter wild celery, and by the nineteenth century it was almost completely forgotten. After Rio, however, with biodiversity in global crisis, the Food and Agricultural Organisation of the United Nations decided to look again at neglected species that have fed humanity throughout history. There were thousands of plants that, but for economic or cultural accident, might still be nourishing the hungry poor, but today a mere dozen provide three-quarters of our food. This "involution," as an FAO report termed it (as in the withering of aged limbs) has "increased the vulnerability of agriculture and impoverished the human diet." Sifting through neglected Old World crops, candidates for improvement or donation of useful genes, there, indeed, was alexanders, wedged between blue-starred borage and scorzonera, the "viper's grass" of the Mediterranean, with a succulent, black-skinned root. I have grown and savoured scorzonera and also its white-skinned cousin, salsify, with amethyst flowers that open only in the morning.

The FAO report's Spanish authors were not encouraging: tastes have changed in the Western world. "The trend has been away from dishes rich in spices and hot ingredients towards milder dishes which respect the flavour of the food itself or enhance it. This is perhaps the case with celery vis-a-vis alexanders [which is] more bitter and pungent and not as tender as sweet celery …While cultivation of alexanders is waning, cultivation of celery is by contrast on the increase, as is its importance in cool, subtropical and tropical areas of Latin America and the Far East."

I thank them for resonant images of celery crunched under Mexican moustaches and Peruvian bowler hats, by tribal canines in New Guinea and gold molars in Hong Kong. Nonetheless, I shall save a few seeds of my alexanders, some to be sown for a pungent chutney and some to be crushed to see if they do, as promised, release the scent of myrrh, a Christmas mystery since childhood.

My father would approve. Harry Viney, son of a Hampshire village carpenter, came from the older order of rural England, not many removes from peasantry, with apple trees behind the house and rhubarb round the privy. His knowledge of plants as food was to profit his family in World War II, when he claimed the derelict land around the bankrupt builder's shed across the road and banked up beds of soil behind redundant girders. Here, crouched in his shadow, I scored furrows with a stick for the sowing of seed. Sometimes, sowing carrots or cabbages on my own acre now, I notice the way my finger and thumb work slowly together to let the seeds fall, one by one; how I save those left over by trapping them in a crease of my palm and trickling them back into the packet. It is Henry William Viney who seals the packet, scoring each tiny fold, a whole concertina of folds, with a chipped and grimy thumbnail.

His packets were the cheapest brown-paper envelopes, stored in a dark, dry drawer. Their rustling contents, sifted out by an aproned seedsman in generous quarter-ounces or even, as with peas and beans, half-pints, were of vegetable varieties unchanged in that part of the country for decades, perhaps generations. The plants did well in the hot, breezy summers of the south-east coast and in a soil well limed by chalk. Most seed was "open pollinated" – that is, ripening from flowers naturally pollinated by bees or hoverflies, rather than in the purposeful hand-pollination, under glass, of the modern F.1 hybrid. It could be saved from the plant from one year to the next and still grow true, whereas the re-sown seed of a hybrid loses the exuberance of the "first cross" (F.1) and reverts erratically to poor copies of its parents.

Open-pollinated varieties are themselves the product of centuries of constant selection, refining the favoured qualities of the wild plant (biggest, juiciest, tallest, tastiest, hardiest), seizing eagerly on any promising natural mutation, and weeding out any throwbacks to earlier states. The very earliest selections are almost parables of paradox: how wild peas, with pods timed to explode to throw the seed as far as possible, had mutations which held the peas in the pod, thus providing the strain that was picked, taken home to eat, and re-sown; or how wild wheat, which needed to collapse its stems to bring its seeds to earth, sported odd plants that held the grain aloft, to be picked, taken home to eat, and sown again.

Such stories can suggest that human intervention rarely served the wild plant's own survival: a subtle seed to plant in the mind at this juncture of science. By selection and consolidation, genes of a comparative handful of plants have been led into forms almost as different from the original as mastiffs and dachshunds are from the wolf. Cabbages, cauliflowers, brussels sprouts, savoys, kohl rabi and most kales, for example, all juggle the same eighteen chromosomes of *Brassica oleracea*, the wild cabbage of cliffs and islands, and, if allowed to flower and set seed, will still cross with each other with a promiscuity that would have quite defeated Abbé Mendel.

(The text continiues after Portfolio)

PORTFOLIO

—

Rachel Giese Brown

Field Work

Trees Marked for Cutting
Les Landes, France

Rachel Giese Brown was born in 1936 and divides her time between France and the United States. She studied with the American photographer Melissa Shook in the mid-seventies. Her books of photographs include The Donegal Pictures *(Faber, 1988),* Sweeney's Flight *(Faber, 1992, with poems by Seamus Heaney), and* Solstice *(Privately Published, 2002).*

i

Haystacks, November
Pays Basque, France

Botanical Garden, Winter
Aveyron, France

Black Shed
Northern Ireland

Silage under Snow
Northern Ireland

Pont de Tanus
Aveyron, France

Turf Stack
Donegal

Cotton
Texas

Field of Sunflowers
Near Goujounac, France

German Blockhouse on an Eroding Coast
Cap-Ferret, France

Hayloft
Catalunya, Spain

Water Level Gauge
Néouvielle, Pyrénées, France

Road in Ariége
France

Boats Wrapped in Plastic, Winter
Cape Cod, Massachusetts

Abandoned Cars
Donegal

Stepping Stones Across a Bog
Donegal

Years ago, friends sent a pinch of seed of the so-called "asparagus" or "hungry gap" kale. Both names are well-deserved. A vigorous, lanky brassica, spending many months in the ground, it puts out a multitude of shoots in spring at just the time when the vegetable garden offers very little greenstuff. Hurried into the steamer before they can wilt, the shoots are tender, epicurean and full of Vitamin C. Every few years, I let the best plant shoot up into flower: a spire of yellow blossom, safely solitary on the hillside, that buzzes with bumble bees for weeks. By summer's end a multitude of pods begin to brown and curl open. Their seeds, in glossy thousands, would fill most of a jam-jar and would sow the whole acre several times over; half an egg-cup is enough. I watched my father sort the biggest, strongest carrot from the root-store established in the foundations of our terraced house (the trap-door was under a rug). Planted out in spring it grew a stem four feet high and made enough free seed for the following year's crop, or even two: but this, again, was a carrot that left pollination to the bees.

The breeding of F.1 hybrids has been described by Colin Tudge as "a wonderful, essentially teutonic exercise in observation and logic," to which one's image of hand-pollination with a fluffy paintbrush, dusting pollen from one greenhouse flower to another, is clearly inadequate. It demands close study and selection from millions of offspring of thousands of crosses, attempting to map (abstractly, not under the microscope) the locations and pathways of desirable strings of genes among the 30,000 on offer. A single gene may be snatched and isolated by repeated back-crossing with a wild or foreign plant with particular resistance to disease, thus adding several more seasons to the process. This is plantsmanship at its most patient and cooperative with nature. Even with computers to keep track, plant breeding is time-consuming, and therefore costly.

The rise of the F.1 hybrid was a product and instrument of the social change that continued to separate people from growing their own food. Expanding cities, fuller employment, consumerist convenience all conspired to concentrate the seeds of food plants, and their produce, in the horticulture industry. As acreages expanded into windy prairies of tillage, commercial competition and plant breeding were entwined in ever more elaborate genetic control. F.1 hybrids were now tailored not merely to improve yields and resist diseases and pests, but to organise the nature of plants for industrial farming. Cereals must bow to the wind on shorter stems, apples must grow bigger on smaller trees with steeper branches. Vegetables must mature all at once, on a closely predictable date, this to be advanced or retarded through the year in optimal defiance of the seasons. Crops must be uniform in shape, size and colour, and so arranged on the plant that machines can do the picking (as in long-stemmed tomatoes and peas without leaves). Tough skins, long shelf-life, turgid stems, intense and durable colour were bred for supermarkets and cling-film packaging.

Many of the older, open-pollinated varieties of vegetable had been sold by most seedsmen: "everybody" sold Autumn King as a reliable main-crop carrot, as they should. But as breeders, notably in Holland, developed the costly refinements of hybridisation, the value of the seeds as products became markedly greater. Thus, in a current catalogue for gardeners, a packet of Trafalgar F.1 hybrid brussels sprouts ("sweeter . . . the children come back for seconds") holds 40 seeds for £2.69, while the "well known and reliable" open-pollinated sprout, Bedford Fillbasket, promises 100 seeds for only £1.29. (A website lists 230 brussels sprout varieties in North America, most of them hybrids from Dutch breeders: an obsession with breeding novelty surely not equalled since "tulip mania").

Such reordering of value, and the constant introduction of real or promised improvement, have swept thousands of older seed strains out of existence. The trend can be blamed first on the engulfment of seed companies by a handful of multinationals, but it was aided and abetted in the later twentieth century through the impulse of the EEC (now the EU) to tidy up, harmonise and regulate. It was bothered by the large number of seed varieties, old and new, that seemed so nearly synonymous. By the 1970s, it became a punishable offence to sell varieties that were not on a national list or in Europe's new Common Catalogue of Varieties. In order to be registered, a variety had to demonstrate Distinctiveness, Uniformity and Stability, a mantra that seemed to seal the separation from wild nature. By 1980, more than 1,500 plant seeds were deleted, many of them non-hybrid varieties, owned by nobody, but adapted to local soils, climates and diseases. The loss of such valuable landraces was an obvious sin against biodiversity and part of the genetic erosion that has come with globalisation of patented seeds.

In the microcosm of the garden, the saving of old and threatened (and therefore, inevitably, "tastier") vegetable varieties was co-opted to the wider mission of the organic movement, whose members have kept forbidden seeds in cultivation and circulation. In America, where commerce alone had winnowed out the seed-lists, the private exchange and cultivation of "heirloom" seeds began with token sharings of beans and maize and blossomed along with the alternative subculture, now supporting dozens of small, independent seed companies (one of which, in Washington state, is a rare and pleasing repository of asparagus kale).

An Ireland too moist and cool to ripen its own seed commercially has remained in thrall to Dutch, British and American suppliers. Shorn of the green-fingered middle-class sensibilities which might, in a different history, have borrowed some husbandry from the Big House kitchen gardens, it waited upon blow-ins to show interest in a heritage of food-plants adapted to an over-humid isle. An American, Anita Hayes, founded the Irish Seed Savers' Association which has tracked down "native" brassicas, onions and potatoes. It has searched out and rescued more than 140 different types of old Irish apple trees living in retirement in mossy, pre-fungicidal orchards, their boughs arthritic but canker-free, their fruits resistant to scab and mildew and often with intense, revelatory flavour. A German, Michael Miklis, has gathered in 40 varieties of grain – 25 kinds of oats alone – developed by Irish farmers over the generations or discovered in seed-banks as distant as Norway and Russia. His fields in County Kilkenny recycle these "landrace" seeds into production, thus conserving their potential for animal and human food, bedding and thatch.

In the scale of global concern for biodiversity, such local efforts may not, perhaps, amount to a hill of beans. But in microcosm, it seems to me, they connect significantly with Edward O. Wilson's concept of "biophilia," which he defines as "the urge to affiliate with other forms of life." Asked why they save seeds, ISSA members range widely through human satisfactions, from "that magical feeling of sharing the secret of creation" to "thumbing my nose at big corporations," but convictions of a solidarity with nature and an almost physical solicitude for its plants are common to all. Luther Burbank (1849-1926), the greatest plant breeder in American history (stoneless plums, white blackberries, etc) believed, with the geneticists in Monsanto, that "there is not a single, desirable attribute which, lacking in a plant, may not be bred into it" and he would sacrifice whole fields of plants to find one worth propagating. But then "you must love it . . . be gentle with it" – which does not sound much like a motto for the wall of Monsanto's laboratories.

This spring saw the FAO accepting the potential of GM crops "as a new tool in the war on hunger," subject to environmental risk assessment, case by case, and the wresting of biotechnology from the clutches of corporate profit. "Neither the public nor the private sector," it declared, "has invested significantly in new genetic technologies for the so-called 'orphan crops' such as cowpea, millet, sorghum and teff that are critical for the food supply and livelihoods of the world's poorest people." (Teff is a primitive, tussocky grain that eases two-thirds of the hunger of the people of Ethiopia). The high-yield grain varieties of the Green Revolution of the 1960s and 1970s were produced as free public goods, the result of altruistic public sector research. They certainly increased production, but at the cost of great damage to traditional farming ecologies, yet the FAO still sees small-scale farmers as being "trapped in subsistence agriculture." The Gene Revolution, driven primarily by private corporations, will have even less interest in their security on the land and may put an end to their seed-saving. Human, genetic, even soil erosion seem doomed to proceed hand-in-hand.

The patient passing of genes between plants whose shared ancestors and evolutionary kinship lets them interbreed – what Professor Steve Jones has called "botanical diplomacy" – has nothing in common with the implant into strawberries of anti-freeze genes obtained from an Antarctic fish, or, rather more persuasively, implanting rice with beta-carotene to create a golden grain with Vitamin A. "Genetic engineers," says Jones, "deny the central facts of evolution: that the action of a gene can depend on the species in which it finds itself and that all species were once varieties (which means that the boundaries between many can still be breached)." The discovery of an alien gene from GM oilseed rape in bacteria in the stomach of a bee has seemed to hint at unconsidered transitions.

At the height of Ireland's home-grown resistance to GM crops, notably to trial fields of modified sugar beet in the Republic, there were academic spokesmen for the view that genetic engineering was "no different" from traditional plant breeding: a misdirection especially troubling just as the Irish Government announced its endowment of biotechnology on a heroic scale. At such paranoid moments, one could see that the geographical isolation of the island supplies a secure and quarantined laboratory.

My alexanders, meanwhile, has briefly attracted a passing red admiral. In the *Journal of Ecology* last year, one R.E. Randall spent almost 7,000 words on fitting *Smyrnium olusatrum* into the natural scheme of things, among them the 137 species of insect – flies, bees, wasps, ants – seen to visit its flowers. Micro-moths stick eggs beneath its leaves, and caterpillars spin webs about its umbels. Biochemists, probing the oils and resins that run through its veins, from roots to fruits, found enough to fill half a page with rolling polysyllables. Just one plant, all by itself, provides a great deal to know.

Michael Viney, naturalist and writer, lives in Carrigskeewaun, Co Mayo. His acclaimed column, "Another Life," appears weekly in The Irish Times. *His book on life in the West of Ireland,* A Year's Turning, *was published in 1996 (Blackstaff Press). A new volume,* Ireland: A Smithsonian Natural History *(Blackstaff Press), appeared in 2003.*

TECHNOLOGIZING LIFE

—

Casey Walker

Meet the opposition.

INTRODUCTION TO BIOTECHNOLOGY

This century's battle royale.

I

Biotechnology creates living things out living materials. It applies knowledge from the life sciences to the design and creation of life. Its consequences are directly tied to each individual and the whole of the living world. These consequences are of an order entirely different from existing technologies. Biotechnology is not like any other artefact – an automobile, nuclear energy, computer, or satellite communication – which is an inanimate thing created out of inanimate materials.

II

Transgenic biotechnology creates living things that would not be alive otherwise – salmon with human and chicken genes, tobacco with firefly genes, potatoes with pesticides – launching a new order of artifice that is distinctly different from the bits of paper, plastic, or aluminium cans we pick up as trash on the sides of roads and recycle. These new life forms will interact as living things do within the living world – giving off pollen and roots, swimming, flying, running, mating, multiplying, eating, being eaten, dying and decomposing. These inventions will be subject to the same system of values and rights as all living things.

III

Biotechnology is the technology of an industry which – as is true of all industries – has the sole purpose of making money. Its power to make money rests on two conditions: that it be well-capitalized and that it correctly predict robust markets. Biotechnology's current and/or projected markets include: (1) genetic engineering for crops, livestock, fisheries, and forest; (2) genetic engineering for humans who are unborn, sick, maimed, physically or mentally nonconforming; (3) genetic information useful to numerous databanks, including those of national and domestic security forces, criminal forensics, institutions of education and employment, and medical, life, and disability insurance companies; (4) some predict human clones as perpetual organ/limb/skin factories, and imagine genetically engineered chimeras (part human, part primate) as a new labour class; and (5) bio-warfare, with products targeting genetic populations of crops, livestock and people.

IV

Biotechnology creates living inventions that affect ecosystems in ways that cannot be recalled like faulty brakes, cannot be cleaned up like an oil spill, and cannot be stored like radioactive waste. Genetically-engineered live viruses meant for influenza immunisations or for cancer treatments can mutate beyond targeted host cells and create new, epidemic viruses. The escape of genetically engineered crops, livestock, fish, or trees into wild populations can irrevocably mix with wild species, homogenizing the genetic materials of artificial, domestic and wild species' genes (a new form of extinction), as well as render that species vulnerable to single pathogens. Collateral effects to biodiversity losses from genetic "weediness" within any ecosystem are incalculable – with impacts extending from those on microbes, soils, insects, birds, and plants, to oxygen levels, dew points, and weather patterns. Conversely, if current and future attempts to resurrect extinct species (such as the Tasmanian tiger in Australia and the Huia bird in New Zealand) are successful – Jurassic Park-style – and each animal is subsequently introduced into zoos, parks and wild ecosystems then equally new and different ecosystemic impacts will occur. In all cases, the natural evolution of species and ecosystems will be corrupted and suffused with artifice.

V

Biotechnology as an industry is not self-correcting or self-regulating and has little precautionary regulation or oversight in place. Moratoriums and bans on genetically engineered organisms have been difficult to impose and harder to maintain. International trade law to date has refused to recognise genetically engineered foods as different from non-engineered foods, and has mandated patent systems in every country to accommodate and enforce ownership of genetically engineered organisms. The United States is the world leader in genetically engineered organisms. The US Department of Agriculture is a co-owner, with Delta Land & Pine/Monsanto, of the terminator technology (which disables seeds from germination and obliges farmers to buy new seed each year). Industry officials expect US agricultural exports to be 90 per cent genetically engineered within a decade. In April 1999, President Clinton awarded four Monsanto scientists the National Medal of Technology for the birth of agro-technology and for placing the US at the forefront of a new science. Thus far, food labelling and safety testing have not been required for the highest-yielding, engineered crop and livestock byproducts commonly consumed in milk, cheese, ice-cream, eggs, meats, potatoes, tomatoes, corn, soya, fast-food burgers and french fries, corn and potato chips, and baby formulas and baby foods. Further genetically engineered organisms are legally regarded as the intellectual property of their inventors through US patent law. Throughout the 17-20 year span of an awarded patent, inventors are ensured exclusive legal ownership for the commercial application of genetically engineered life forms.

VI

Until recently, public criticism of biotechnology has been virtually nonexistent in the United States. Public acceptance or support for biotechnologies is convergent with cultural beliefs that technological innovations are progressive, inevitable, and the best means to economically compete and succeed in global markets. Additionally, the mediated world of a predominantly consumer/entertainment culture is convergent with the spectacular, limits-defying feats promised by biotech. Public ignorance of ecological, moral, and human social issues presented by biotechnology can be attributed to: (1) *de facto* censorship through corporate intimidation and law suits; (2) self-censorship of career journalists and corporate-owned media; (3) aggressive public media campaigns by biotech industries; (4) contractual ties between biotech industries and universities, which tend to foreclose contrary research and contrary voices; (5) a failure in education to emphasize values, human beings, consciousness, questions, and conscience, as well as a lack of ecological literacy (preschool through university); (6) weak engagement of spiritual consciousness or practice; and (7) a politically disengaged public.

VII

Advocates tend to characterize biogenetic engineering as problem-solving. Critics tend to re-describe both the problem and the solution. One compelling problem has been identified as world hunger, with biotech advocates arguing for a "Second Green Revolution" to meet the needs of an estimated human population 10-12 billion in the twenty-first century. Critics argue that feeding hungry people is a distribution not a supply problem, a problem best solved in any case by small-scale agriculture with ecologically sustainable strategies that are independent of genetically engineered seeds, monocultures and factory-style livestock. A second problem area covers health and medical issues ranging from conditions as simple as diarrhoea in Third World countries to complex medical conditions such as diabetes and cancer. Critics argue that the root causes of many medical conditions are industry-related environmental toxins and contaminated air, water, and food supplies, for which bioengineering solutions are merely palliative. Beyond strict medical applications, there exists a strong cultural bias for the techo-eugenic elimination of human imperfections, inferiorities, aging, and even death through genetic engineering. One group, called Extropians, hopes to solve the problems of biological barriers and become post-biological post-humans: "persons of unprecedented physical, intellectual, and psychological ability, self-programming and self-defining, potentially immortal, unlimited individuals." An Extropian conference at UCB, August 1999, featured such well-known scientists as Gregory Stock (University of California, Los Angeles), Cynthia Kenyon (University of California, San Franciso), Calvin Harley (Chief Scientist at Geron), Eric Drexler, and Roy Wolford. Critics argue against ideas of biological imperfection and perfectibility as diminished and diminishing views of humanity and life processes.

VIII

Biotech scientists, writers, and industry advocates frequently disregard criticism as ignorant, hysterical or sentimental. Yet, a growing number of cellular and molecular biologists (such as Stuart Newman and Richard Strohman) persuasively argue that the science behind genetic engineering is incomplete, that most human diseases and complex traits are not genetically determined but shaped by epigenetic and dynamic processes. According to Richard Strohman, "Most human diseases, and complex traits in all organisms, depend on non-genetic processes. They are shaped by environmentally sensitive regulatory networks of molecular agents that obey dynamic rules. These 'epigenetic' networks are generally unappreciated, and their rules are little understood by modern biotechnology. To prematurely initiate large-scale genetic engineering – whether of vast areas of cropland or of human beings – based on genetic knowledge but epigenetic ignorance is to practice incomplete science and to invite disasters of unknown proportion."

IX

Biotechnology industries are also extensions of information industries. As Bill Gates said, "This is the information age, and biological information is probably the most interesting information we are deciphering and trying to decide to change. It is all a question of how, not if." In Silicon Valley, the leading edge is not in building computers, but in telling computers what to do – the who's who of new money are software designers. Entrepreneurs are currently working to create digital clones with "reality merge," functions that will enable people to translate their bodies into digital data to go shopping and have clothes fitted on-line, seek medical advice, or play interactive games. Such a view of information and of the body's information as linked to providing newer, more efficient and powerful "options" for the modern person feeds into the globalizing economy and electronic herd described by Thomas Friedman in *The Lexus and the Olive Tree*. Ideologically, biotechnology as an information technology ignores a natural world in which animate life is part of the larger-than-self, non-arbitrary, non-socially constructed, non-virtual processes.

X

Biotechnology is, as USDA Secretary Dan Glickman said, "The Battle Royale" for the 21st century. Beyond its battle for markets and control, such a battle fundamentally exposes rapidly diverging worldviews between those often referred to as "globalists" (a.k.a. *homo economicus*) and those often referred to as "localists" (a.k.a. *homo eroticus*). Globalists tend to view the living world in economic terms while localists tend to view economics in terms of the living world. As biotechnology is powerfully convergent with a globalist worldview and stands to create entirely new terms and conditions for the living world, the burden of articulation and argument falls on localists. Such a debate is a world-historical debate that forces to the surface heretofore taken-for-granted or dimly intuited meanings and understandings of the living world. Its kind and quality will depend on all the arts of civilization – from science, literature, philosophy, theology, history – and it will depend on a public demand for it.

THE END OF HUMAN NATURE?

The lived truth of creation.

Biotechnologies can be assessed on a number of levels – the scale of genetically engineered and transgenic crops, livestock, and fishery foods currently grown and consumed; the scale of projected engineering for human beings; corporate incentives and industry strength; patent and trade law on intellectual property rights; regulatory vacuums; incomplete and flawed biological science; real and projected impacts on the living world and on human beings; and issues of ethics, morality, activism, and worldview. All of these issues, as we can see from the daily news, are rapidly gaining attention. Yet the question of what can and should be done with biotechnologies rests within a still wider and more urgent problem. Coupled with rising new technologies such as molecular electronics, nano and terraformation technologies, we are suddenly contending with the capacity to structurally design and create biotic and abiotic matter from scratch.

How do we best respond to these newfound and exceedingly powerful capacities? What can we do now that will enable us to look back years hence and say that we responded wisely, contributing our best efforts to discovering rather than ending possibilities for existence on earth?

These questions turn us, I think, away from arguments for or against the use of such technologies in terms of safety, efficacy, or rights. While these concerns should be pursued in order to identify harm, check abuse of power, and slow the consequences of premature deployment, they are not radical enough. For *even if* each new engineering technique were proven safe to all donors, recipients, and succeeding generations; *even if* each were guaranteed to do its job precisely and accurately; and *even if* all concerns for democratic process and equal rights were met and approved by a unanimous, global culture, still such standards would not in themselves prevent the creation of a world devoid of human or wild nature – the creation of a technohive in a technosphere.

And even if a technohive in a technosphere sounds promising in its defiance of material and biologic limits (as it does to a number of people), its promise is merely for an existence of a kind – which is neither progressive nor inevitable. More significantly, such a world permanently forecloses on a human and wild nature akin to those any of us have ever known throughout our entire human history. Thus, the radical argument – the challenge to be taken up – is that of the "possibility of existence". Is human or wild nature possible by design, and if not, are we willing to engineer ourselves into our own peculiar extinction?

As philosopher Keekok Lee argues in her book *The Natural and the Artefactual*, there is a key distinction to be made between something that looks natural and something that is, in fact, natural in its *being*. We cannot say that any single thing – whether it be a plant, animal, acre of soil, freshwater lake, or child – that has been designed at its structural level to fulfil the intents and purposes of its designers is in fact "natural". It is a cultural artefact. It lacks its own being for its own sake and will always be an artefact imposed upon a world that is already, and cannot be otherwise, living out deeply embedded and emergent relationships.

Further, regardless of whether any artefactual entity fulfils the plans of its designers and meets the expectations of its consumers, it cannot be thought of as a product that is "controllable". It will interact in the world, affecting its environment as natural things do – with impacts so profound we barely comprehend them. Its chemistry will affect the chemistry of the world. Its wings will create hurricanes. In fact, the more artefactual entities successfully mimic their natural counterparts, the less control their designers have over them. Hence the significance of concerns, such as those expressed by Bill Joy, Chief Scientist at Sun Microsystems in "Why the Future Doesn't Need Us" (*Wired*, April 2000), about self-replicating, mutating biological or mechanical plagues causing a final extinction of the human species.

Wild nature does exist, if only in tattered remnants, and it is wild in the most commonly understood meaning of the word. It is independent, genetically intact, highly boundaried, dynamic, self-determining, and self-organizing. And contrary to much of postmodern thought, which seeks to extend and democratize values, the existential values of natural and artefactual beings are not relative. Natural beings are vulnerable in relation to artefactual beings, and, as Bill McKibben points out, it is inevitable that as artefacts interbreed with natural kinds, there will come a point where natural kinds cease to exist. Genetically engineered rabbits will be the existential equivalents of Coke bottles.

Thus we must now ask on behalf of most of western-going-global culture: if our realities are increasingly urban and almost exclusively artefactual, what risks do we run of an "extinction of experiences" previously bound to and made real by the natural world? Do we lose a responsiveness to all that is not ourselves, all that is *not* the sum total of our manufacturing? Are we to lose forever the very stuff and scale and discovery of being alive amidst a creation of four billion and more years?

And, if we were to usher in a world constructed by intentional design – with imperfections "deleted" and perfections "selected" for humans beings and the rest of the living world – what implications would such a world carry for existence? In a world constructed to specification, what happens to human perception of all that must be experienced and cannot be specified – and thus to human cognition, to consciousness, to the ethical regard for self and other?

Along these lines, pediatric neurologist Martha Herbert and cognitive scientist Francisco Varela have responded to an article that describes a reduced capacity in a significant number of people to perceive subtleties and nuance in smell, taste, sight, hearing, and touch. In the studies, urban children had a diminished ability to hear the range of sound contained in a classical symphony. The sheer load of information in urban lives is apparently so rapid and intense, so sensorily overwhelming, that the contemporary brain is "adapting" by storing information in larger categories without cross-indexing and without synthesis. The implication? Less perception of discrete entities, less affect for those entities, and less ability to care: less consciousness.

As Martha Herbert's work also points out, we are already experiencing neurological change at population levels in the United States. Nearly one in five children exhibits neurological, cognitive, learning, and behavioural disorders. Many of these disorders are attributed to chemical insults *in utero*, with profound developmental effects on the brain and nervous system. In addition, social/emotional stresses and derailments in children's daily lives appear to affect their nervous systems in ways that are enduring. Human potential for consciousness, as we know it, is ineluctably situated in our minds and bodies as evoked by the places we live in and the people we live with, yet full-blown biological engineering may irrevocably change its interior and exterior conditions and shift the course for human potential.

In the work of Francisco Varela, notably in his books *Ethical Know-How: Action, Cognition, and Wisdom* and *The View From Within*, we see the discovery of consciousness – of being – as an embodiment of the cognitive structures made possible by the interactions available to us, and not by the mechanisms with which we choose to equip ourselves. In a fundamental way, the substance of our experience both motivates and constrains all rational thought. The kind of life we lead shapes us at the structural level. Should we deprive ourselves of an environment that would call us forward, we would run the risk of becoming, as Varela says, "solipsistic ghosts".

In their book *Vanishing Voices: The Extinction of the World's Languages*, linguists Suzanne Romaine and Daniel Nettle demonstrate that the loss of human languages, which are the richest and most diverse expressions of human nature, is tied to the loss of wild nature. Linguistic losses and biodiversity losses are inextricable phenomena. As Suzanne Romaine remarks, "With the death of each voice, we lose a little more of who we were and are and what we may become." Pluralism in its deepest sense – as a value of difference that is resistant to conformity or flattening – can exist only in a world in which biological diversity thrives. We cannot have different sets of knowledge, languages, or cosmologies if we do not also have an Earth with ecological differences; hence Jim Dodge's observation that metaphoric capacity is always "better" when it is bioregional – it is specific, layered, and resonates from experience.

Finally, an underlying theme of the above is that there is a price to be paid for the loss of "context". It is an existential price – a price of consciousness. Just as an eye cannot see itself, we cannot engineer a world as deep as the one we have. Or, if we knew love for children we would not design children to love. And, if we understood life and death for ourselves, we would not seek immortality. Intuitively we know, and as our various sciences are just beginning to explore, there is a threshold at which we fall into our machinations and out of the living world, and having fallen, lose sight of all that pulls us forward – what Ernest Becker called the "lived truth of creation". May it become an intellectual embarrassment, and a form of easily recognized sadism, to think we can or should design human or wild nature. And may that embarrassment and ethical consciousness rise forcefully from a world of ravaged but still infinite possibility for each of us.

FALL OF THE WILD

The debate over the biotech industry ignores the central dilemma:
What does it really mean to engineer ourselves out of existence?

Each of us could, as many do, dismiss the spectre of human genetic engineering as overblown – the *subjet du jour* of alarmists adrift in dystopian novels or of techno-fabulists afloat in ever-everland. The cultural rage, but ultimately "fringe". After all, in country after country, people consider the cloning of humans repugnant, and genetically engineered crops are not bearing up well under public scrutiny, nor is aggressive corporate ownership of over ninety percent of the world's food germ-plasm. So why not believe reproductive cloning will fall off the radar once it's regulated as a "last resort" fertility therapy for a minor fraction of humanity? Or, that cloning and embryonic stem cell techniques will simply yield pharmaceuticals, tissues, limbs, and organs unavailable or too costly by other means? Why not believe ownership of the human genome will settle into industries, as all new and useful discoveries do, and provide the basis for curing disabilities and disease for each of us and succeeding generations? This too will work itself out, the reasoning goes. The dust will settle.

Already we see it coming: prolonged battles of months, maybe years, but battles with beige and not-too-bloody outcomes after NGO campaigns, corporate PR campaigns, legislative hearings, institutional and professional turf wars, dizzying media, the divvying up of funding, regulation, and enforcement at state and federal levels, lawsuits of antitrust and individual rights, judicial decisions, and a parallel track of presidential pressure for international treaties and trade agreements. So why get riled up, why get interested?

The questions are wrong. The language is inadequate. We need to start over.

It doesn't take too supple a wit to see the gap between any urgent public health need for human genetic engineering and the astounding amounts of money, expertise, and patenting currently being devoted to its discoveries and inventions. Medical need is not the driving question for the new biogenetic engineering industry – unless we agree to redefine medical need to include any and all consumer options for altering bodies and extending lives beyond the body's natural limits. The industry has hit a gold mine, and knows it. Who wouldn't opt to stave off death? Choosing *not* to purchase or assert entitlement to new tissues and organs when various body parts become damaged, diseased, and worn out over time is next to impossible to imagine. The chemistry between a potential market of six billion and the greed or altruism (it doesn't matter which) of corporations would, without doubt, change forever what it means to be a human being.

Human genetic engineering isn't going to go away, but few are asking the questions that will bring us closer to the momentous, radical public debates such momentous, radical ideas about human life deserve. This is a tender point, an important point. To address it adequately, we'll have to get beyond issues of engineering defined by the categories of public politics and public journalism – debates of safety, efficacy, and rights – and begin to wonder at the ways in which engineering human life forces us to contend with matters of existence. If we want to think intelligently, debate intelligently, we must ask ourselves this: is there a threshold where intentionally changing the biology of a human being violates that life and those around it irrevocably?

Extropians, a Los Angeles-based group of wealthy transhumanists, invest over ten million dollars of R & D annually in a future that does not include natural human aging and death. Members refer to those who accept death as essential to life as "deathists". Currently, by purchasing cryogenic services provided at Alcor Life Extension, Extropy Institute members count on the day future biotechnologies will regenerate new bodies from neurals (heads only for $50,000) or full bodies (bodies intact for $150,000), each frozen upon death and stored in liquid nitrogen. Shocking as the idea may be, the possibility of a "post-human" future can no longer be dismissed as the wacko imaginings of privileged Californians. A 2000 *New York Times Magazine* cover story by Stephen Hall, "Racing Towards Immortality," details the history and promise for what *Science* magazine calls the "breakthrough of the year": embryonic stem cell technologies.

Enthusiastically dubbed "the mother of all cells," a pluripotent, embryonic stem cell has the potential of growing into anything you and I may someday require: new brain, heart, retinal, skin and nerve cells; or whole hands, arms, livers, or hearts. Grown from our own biopsies, these tissues would also have the inherent advantage of sidestepping "mismatch" and immunological rejection – stumbling points for transplants thus far. Notably, Geron Corporation, upstarted as an "anti-aging" company in Menlo Park, California in 1992 with $7.6 million, has privately funded such university research or acquired it.

In May 1999, Geron bought Scotland's Roslin Bio Med as a subsidiary in order to own Dolly-the-Sheep's nuclear transfer technology. Today, Geron owns a stunning corporate portfolio: the patents and licensing on the exact three technologies poised to revolutionize the consequences of accident, disease, and mortality (telemerase enzymes, nuclear transfer technology, pluripotent stem cells). Posted for the public on its website, Geron already envisions stem cell treatment for some of the largest medical markets: "Such cells could be used to treat numerous major chronic degenerative diseases and conditions such as heart disease, stroke, Parkinson's disease, Alzheimer's disease, spinal cord injury, diabetes, osteoarthritis, bone marrow failure and burns."

In one swift upping of the human engineering ante, stem cell technologies trump the "spectres" of human engineering argued pro and con in recent years. No longer are we *merely* contending with the obvious morass of human rights, social relations, and fiduciary assumptions for clones as children or as organ factories, or with the morass of inhumane societies rising from new, genetic lines of designer babies (germline manipulations). Now, quite literally, we are speculating about a world in which "normal" human beings never grow old and die. You and I and our loved ones would become the living sum of our replacement parts, forever.

If the old philosophical conundrum of whether an axe is still the same axe if you've replaced its axe-handle seven times and its axe-head eight times isn't enough to ponder, add to it the conundrum of enhancing our bodies with high-tech, superhuman abilities and ask whether you and I would still be human – or would become merely human or even "subhuman". In 1999, Extropians organized Extro 4, "Biotech Futures: Challenges of Life Extension and Genetic Engineering," a conference at University of California, Berkeley. Featured speakers included Calvin Harley, Chief Scientist at Geron Corporation, and Judith Campisi, a scientific advisor to Geron. The Extro 4 conference drew other speakers well-known in the biotech field such as Gregory Stock (University of Califorinia, Los Angeles), Roy Walford (physician at Biosphere 2, named by *Time Magazine* as one of 100 most influential Americans) and Cynthia Kenyon (University of California, San Francisco), all of whom gathered to seriously discuss state-of-the-art technologies, legal problems, and public relations strategies.

The most telling vision came with Saturday evening's keynote address, "The Ultrahuman Revolution: Amendments to the Human Constitution," by Max More, president of the Extropy Institute. In it, he asked participants to stretch their imaginations beyond biological problems to achieving the ultimate human achievement: the creation of "ultrahumans" with metabrain processors and emotion modulators, supraorganic perceptual abilities, bodies integrated with non-carbon compounds, and immortality guaranteed through genetic, cellular, or synthetic means.

Acknowledging the vast amount of time, energy, and money Americans already spend on looking and feeling younger as they grow older, and reviving energy as they lose it, engineering our bodies to achieve results would only ratchet up spending along the present path. Marketing would have a heyday in goosing up all-American, "made-for-success" bodies in the belief that it is good and right for citizens to be freed from "suffering," and, even more, to become physically, mentally, and emotionally "high and higher functioning". And, to fight for equal access to bodily "upgrades and endowments," which, just like computers for every school-aged child, are deemed basic by conservatives and liberals alike to living in a world of information, communication, and competition. Without a radical return to questioning the biology of human nature, it's impossible to imagine what lines we would draw against "ultrahumans". After all, America already tacitly blesses the humanist dream getting a quantum, transhumanist boost, with the fortunate among us becoming "persons of unprecedented physical, intellectual, and psychological ability, self-programming and self-defining, potentially immortal, unlimited individuals."

We are indeed up to our chins in the snarling beauty of the Chinese proverb, *may you live in interesting times*. Existence, the matter of it – our bodies, our being, the living world around us – is on the line as it has never been before, and never will be again. Which is *good*. Our moment in history is, by many accounts, long overdue. Setting aside our startlingly bold and pyrotechnic abilities to fund, research, design, and market creative new ideas for our bodies, let's return to our original question. Let's ask, as researchers do in the organismic, somatic, cellular, and cognitive sciences: how does any creature, particularly a human being, live through time and space, and is that process violable?

Any organism is an amalgam of wily, fluidly constituted and evolving moments in which it is primarily making do alongside all other creatures likewise making do with the particular materials, temperatures, fluids, surfaces, and interactions at hand. As cognitive and cellular scientists have found over the last thirty years, the mind and the body cannot be explained either as a construction of one-to-one, cause-and-effect correspondences, or as a construction made from a series of sophisticated, selective functions. Instead, we see a profound fragility and transience to organismic life, from which we ourselves experience constantly emergent and coherently distinct points of view. Our body "parts" are not so much obtained as exercised.

We become who we are by the world that calls us forward and by our capacity to respond, each in continual "creation" of the other. In this sense, existence becomes a function of tension between differences in kind in context, not of more or less omnipotent creators and creations.. Andy Clark observes in *Being There: Putting Brain, Body, and World Together Again*, "If the brain were so simple that a single approach could unlock its secrets, we would be so simple that we couldn't do the job!"

In concrete terms, we know that what our eyes and ears can do is not based solely on their mechanical capacity, but on the will that drives them and the context which calls them forward. An eye that can see, for instance, is not necessarily an eye that looks. An ear that can hear does not necessarily listen. It is only in the acts of looking or hearing, that we physically build the neurological couplings that functionally contribute to an ongoing embodiment of actions, skills, and inspired intentions – none of which could exist alone; in isolation, as "given". This is extremely important. As Francisco Varela writes in *Ethical Know-How*, "The cognitive self is its own implementation: its history and its action are of a piece."

Likewise, Varela scoffed in a discussion he and I had at the idea we can outfit ourselves with "infrared-seeing" equipment and suddenly see the infrared spectrum. A classic study on perception with kittens, by Held and Hein, demonstrates that the physical rise of perception is always relative to activity. Raised together in the dark with their exposure to light tightly controlled, kittens were separated into two groups – one in a basket on a carriage being carried, the other harnessed and pulling the carriage. When the kittens were released into light, the passively carried kittens stumbled about as if blind while the actively pulling kittens walked about normally.

In a second dimension, Varela identifies the environment as essential to evoking perspective – not so much by providing the field in which we play out our plans, but by supplying the conditions which demand an active, ongoing assemblage of what counts to us. Varela points to moments of "breakdown," as the hinge moments in which our previously constituted micro-worlds come up against new situations demanding new assembly and new action. It's in these moments our bodies and minds must find their way, quite literally, by coming forth with appropriate conceptual and behavioural creativity. In those moments, new couplings are made in mind and body, and the concrete is born. For Varela, the environment as essential *evocateur* to ethical expertise – knowing how to act – is crucial. If we lacked – or if our world failed to call forward – the ability to "couple activity," the cognitive self could not physically incorporate and would become, in his words, a "mere solipsistic ghost".

It is here that we return to defining the threshold of life: there is no way that obtaining "wares" for the human body that will somehow make us more alive, more *us*. We live first and last as organisms, with unique points of view that organize and articulate themselves throughout our lives. We literally learn ourselves into being by pulling ourselves upright, freeing our hands and walking around, by hearing, speaking, reading, and writing a language, by playing between imagined and real worlds, by testing our desires, as they are made possible and constrained, situation by situation. The more conscious our points of view are, the more we yearn to live exposed, incorporating ourselves authentically not derivatively, by our own constitutions and not by the conventions and ideas of others. When we forget this, we exclude ourselves absolutely from our own distinct incarnation, which, in turn subtracts from our own impact on an equally distinctive world.

Which isn't to say it doesn't come as any surprise that our hearts leap at the promise of avoiding the *praxis*, or *doing* of life, by transcending it. It's easy to wish for mechanical assembly, but it's a seriously misguided wish – a wish born of seduction not wisdom – that rises from a tragic confusion between what we can make and what we cannot.

Artifice invariably disappoints us when it substitutes for an organic self or for an evocative, grounding environment. We can define, as Keekok Lee has in *The Natural and the Artefactual*, a threshold for artifice based on the intent we impose on our creation's being. If we strip any form of life, any creation – including our own – of its own self-organizing, self-willing capacity simply to further ideas and ends of our own, that life is no longer wild. No wonder the yields of "breakdowns" prompted by artifice are more ghostly than the corporeal "breakdowns" of real, living things. The ability to recoup will and purpose is nil. Akin to Kafkaesque bureaucracies or human hives, an increasingly constrained, artificial and managed world, is in itself an exercise in solipsistic, infinite regress. We can sense ourselves becoming smaller, insect-like, reduced to moving in four directions, locked out of recognizable selves and locked out of a world that would call us forward.

There's an immeasurable relief to admitting life is fearsome, is ecstatic, and is what it is because we live in a time, a place, and are mortal. There are no shortcuts, no received wisdoms worth their promise and price. Ernest Becker said it beautifully in *The Denial of Death*, "I think that taking life seriously means something like this: that whatever man does on this planet has to be done in the lived truth of the terror of creation, of the grotesque, of the rumble of panic underneath everything. Otherwise it is false. Whatever is achieved must be achieved from within the subjective energies of creatures, without deadening, with the full exercise of passion, of vision, of pain, of fear, and of sorrow … Manipulative, utopian science, by deadening human sensitivity, would also deprive (us) of the heroic in (our) urge to victory. And we know that in some very important way this falsifies our struggle by emptying us, by preventing us from incorporating the maximum of experience. It means the end of the distinctively human – or even, we must say, the distinctively organismic."

Nor does is come as any real surprise that organismic life moves contextually. It couldn't be otherwise for creatures living through space and time in a world that is also living through space and time. No recall, clean-up, or restoration is truly possible, ever, when the living context has already changed. Instantly, the idea of resurrecting ourselves or woolly mammoths from icy tombs generations or centuries later, or changing the genetic lines for future human beings, ignores something so basic to the way life *is* – the way any individual or any whole system actually *lives* – that our "victory" over the transiently fragile, evocative milieu of a world living in time and space rings without conviction, as hollowly as an outright denial of a living world.

Thresholds of the biological world, ourselves included, are crossed when we willingly create the fall of the wild: a world that fails to call all intelligence forward into a point of view. A world stripped of nuance, its own systemic wildness, would impoverish and diminish our bodies and minds absolutely. Again, it doesn't require too supple a wit to imagine an engineered world whittling us down. In fact, some research suggests we can see it already.

Recent studies out of Germany – from Tuebingen University and Gesellschaft fur Rationelle Psychologie in Munich – show that our contemporary environments have in fact already changed our biology. In the last twenty years, from repeated testings of 4,000 participants, the senses of smell, taste, touch, sight, and hearing have *decreased* at a rate of nearly one percent per year. "15 years ago, Germans could distinguish 300,000 sounds. Today, on average, they only make it to 180,000. Many children stagnate at 100,000. That is enough for hip hop and rap music, but it is insufficient for the subtleties of a classical symphony." And, GRP studies showed "generation gaps" between brains formed before 1948, brains formed between 1948 and 1968, and brains formed since. The newer the brain, the more "dissonance" it can tolerate. New brains accommodate floods of contradictory information as data without, apparently, fighting the crush of time for synthesis – a neurological process amounting, in the researchers' view, to a loss in what the brain can bring to consciousness. Data shows that the unconscious has risen from 87% of total brain processing to 94%. Dr. Henner Ertel says, "We are seeing the largest and fastest breakthrough since the dawn of consciousness. Our brain is not adapting. It is rebelling against the world and changing it (the world) by changing itself. Red is no longer red. Sweet smells begin to stink. In the next century, different people will be living in a new world."

The debate I'd like to see recognizes that even our best case scenario of debating technological efficacy, safety, or rights won't work. *Even if* each new human engineering technique were guaranteed to do its job precisely and accurately; *even if* each were deemed safe to all donors, recipients, and succeeding generations; and *even if* all concerns for democratic process and equal rights were met and approved by an overwhelming and global majority, these standards of proof won't in themselves prevent an American-going-global civilization imagined and created by bioengineering technologies. The debate would return us to life as experienced organismically, within parameters of what it means to be alive in space and time. The debate would insist on understanding human nature as wild, and it would begin with this premise: we refuse to become engineered ghosts, a species of the walking dead.

REAL NEWS

The failure of the fourth estate.

I

Over the past few years, an encouraging number of people in an encouraging number of places have resisted corporate interests and agricultural practices producing transgenic or genetically modified organisms. Indeed, several counties in California have pronounced themselves "GMO-free" by popular vote. Yet, the question that disturbs, or ought to, ventures past votes against strawberries engineered with flounder genes or corn with pesticides, and forces us to answer whether we know anything new for all of our debates on biotechnologies and are in fact any wiser. Do we recognize other potential abuses coming from the scientific and technological enterprise and anticipate them with knowledgeable arguments that will constrain and direct its power, not simply object to it? Not yet.

II

In November Californians will vote on Proposition 71, which directs three billion dollars from the general fund to stem cell research that emphasizes the production of embryonic stem cells from clonal embryos – research that has been restricted by federal law. Unfortunately, as far as most people continue to perceive it, the embryonic stem cell controversy remains a bastardized extension of the Supreme Court case *Roe v. Wade*: is it better or more right to engineer nascent human life in the pursuit of scientific questioning and new medical cures – or, is it better or more right to protect nascent human life from engineering and redirect science and medicine from these pursuits?

Ironically, many of the same people who are against Genetically Modified Organisms actively support the cloning of embryonic stem cells in the belief that such research is consistent with liberal, secular, "pro-choice" values, and is socially responsive to the rising demand for health care through an investment in research (which promises to cure a range of serious illnesses from diabetes to Parkinson's disease to cancers). Additionally, supporters welcome the economic boost that comes with re-positioning California-based research at the international level, securing patents and licensing, attracting investment, and developing new jobs. In a state suffering from its technology sector "crash" of the early 1990's and the cascade of events leading to a staggering budget deficit, an investment of public funds in new scientific and technological research appears as a win-win proposition. Few supporters question why various interested parties – primarily biotech and venture capital groups – have raised a reported 20 million dollars to place Proposition 71 on the ballot and conduct a massive media campaign to ensure its victory. Or, question why Proposition 71 establishes an independent institute that will be responsible for all funding decisions and oversight, to be run by persons from universities, corporate research centres, and advocacy groups with financial and proprietary interests.

Among those who oppose Proposition 71 are fiscal conservatives who object to its three-billion-dollar draw from the state's general fund (which doubles to six billion, including interest), further compromising the state's ability to meet existing obligations to schools, roads and infrastructure, and other health care programs. But the opposition that argues most vocally against what Proposition 71 seeks to accomplish is the loose association of those typically allied against *Roe v Wade*, such as members of the Catholic Church and fundamentalist Christian Right, who tend to believe that opposing Proposition 71 enacts conservative, religious or spiritual, "right-to-life" values in its protection of human embryos. Indeed, a recent lawsuit paid for by supporters of Proposition 71 tried (albeit unsuccessfully) to bar California's Secretary of State from allowing the controversial language of "embryonic cloning" to appear in voter literature and, instead, force the less evocative semantics of "nuclear transfer."

III

But in today's world of big business, the language games reminiscent of *Roe v Wade* and the usual political positioning evoked by them does not apply. In fact, none of the usual divides that create public discourse – liberal versus conservative, secular versus spiritual, pro-choice versus right-to-life – can intelligently direct a scientific and technological enterprise that is indifferent to the commitments of non-business values or the fierce contention that occurs between them.

IV

What is at stake for citizens on Proposition 71 remains, therefore, at stake on many newly emerging biotechnologies, and/or technologies with biological effects.

If we expect to become a society in which rational inquiry, creative speculation, and ethical choice is made possible to all its members on issues of greatest consequence, an immediate and concerted effort must be made to understand the extent to which today's scientific inquiries have been and continue to be directed by business interests toward profitable products and procedures. Furthermore, an immediate and concerted effort must be made to understand the extent to which those same interests have, in turn, constrained creative speculation and ethical choice.

Missing from science and public discourse are those inquiries that receive little to no funding – yet, by their very nature, serve to open society to new knowledge and ideas that are non-conforming, non-complacent, and make profound change possible.

At any moment in human history, rational inquiry – including scientific inquiry – is perhaps best described as questioning that makes good sense in relation to the reality it perceives. Its questioning draws us closer to truths that, if we were to ignore them, would place all that we cherish in peril; and, if we were to attend to them, would advance our knowledge and understanding for all that we cherish.

Given the most crucial truth of today's world, in which nuclear, chemical, genetic, and electromagnetic technologies (with military, pharmaceutical, agricultural, transportation, Internet and telecommunication applications) are reaching directly or indirectly into the substrate of physical and biological structures and creating changes that affect human health, ecological health, and the evolutionary direction for life on earth, we are forced to discern which inquiries – including which scientific inquiries –make good sense. And, forced to discern which speculations are creative, and which choices ethical.

V

Among those who oppose Proposition 71, in substantive terms, is another loose-knit group of scientists, bio-ethicists, social scientists, philosophers, environmentalists, *et al*, who are attempting to look beyond the medical and economic hype in judging which scientific inquiries make good sense, and which inquiries do not. Yet, these voices stand well outside and off the discursive map as it is known to the public.

One of their key arguments is that human health is directly tied to environmental health. Given the sudden rise in and concentrations of human population centres, environmental toxins, radiation, transgenic foods, zoonotic and cross-species diseases, and so forth, it is more rational to pursue scientific inquiries that allow us to understand what human health means in relation to the environments we are actively creating, and less rational to pursue medical "cures" in the form of new products and procedures. Not only are such medical solutions palliative, and not only do they actively ignore the wider biological context in which medical products and procedures are situated, but, as we know from experience, they are likely to further exacerbate existing biological problems and/or create wholly novel biological problems.

While many support stem cell research in principle (from other sources such as umbilical cords, brain ventricles, or fat), those who oppose embryonic cloning techniques in particular argue that such techniques are neither justified, nor justifiable. Given the abyss that exists between our technological abilities to engineer life at structural levels, and our discursive inabilities to know which structural changes are desirable (for humanity, ecosystems, and the evolutionary direction for life), it simply does not make sense to embark, with public funding, on the exact technology that most distinctly enables human engineering at its source – the human embryo.

When medical science does not account for phenomena that drive our discontents, injuries, and diseases, and its treatments and cures are effective only insofar as they change our internal responses to them, a critical loss in our relationship to reality occurs. Not only do we deprive ourselves of feedback – that our stresses, depressions, sleep disorders, cancers, attention deficit disorders, auto-immune diseases, neurological diseases, and so forth, are *bona fide* responses to larger socio-ecological contexts – but we prevent ourselves from coming into direct relationship with the terms and conditions of our own existence. And it is this distancing from existence, this proclivity for medicating and engineering, that makes us less human, not more.

Our answer to the rising costs of protecting public health is less likely to come from stem cell research and regenerative technologies than it is from research that establishes clear requirements for environmental and public health – in terms of water, food, air, toxins, endocrine disruptors, radiation, climate change, and so forth – and makes those requirements both self-evidently desirable and enforceable.

VI

As America drifts toward its November ballots, there is perhaps nothing more galling to its thinking people than the open drift of public opinion in the wake of media that cannot or will not represent the most consequential issues facing humanity, conduct rational inquiries, and hold both business and politics to their findings. Above all, we are witnessing an excruciating failure of the fourth estate – journalism and media – and with it an excruciating failure to respond to reality.

What can be done? The news can be changed. In fact, the momentous "zeitgeist-ness" of changing the news, *post haste*, acknowledges that most adults do respond to the kinds of knowledge and understanding that make choice and action self-evident; that allow them to exercise responsibility; that infuse their lives with meaning and purpose; and that allow them to experience, as well as refine, intimate relationships with other people, the living world, and the cosmos. Indeed, intractable levels of stress and anxiety experienced by many talented and intelligent adults today may be directly attributable to the abyss, albeit dimly perceived, between what rivets our collective attention and what should.

VII

Let us assume a healthy conceit: how can Americans come to see their true position as the most powerful actors currently acting with the most powerful consequences for the earth and humanity? By making such news *the* news, implicitly and explicitly. By making the evolutionary-scale events occurring within nature and within human existence the news deemed worthy of our best reporting, analysis, and commentary.

VIII

Cell phones, WiFi, SUVs, molecular electronics, brain implants, and clonal embryos do not call for the usual news by news release and ideological war, but call for deliberations over the best knowledge available to us of what biological and existential conditions exist and what these innovations mean to them. How does the electro-smog associated with ubiquitous cell phone use, for example, change biology in one direction rather than in another? How does the constant use of wireless Internet connections change communication, the context of cognition, and consciousness in one direction rather than another? How do changes to nature and human existence rapidly foreclose upon the base knowledge of life as it can be known *now*, and critical to discerning what humanity intends to conserve, change, or invent?

IX

To produce such "news," a model of serious, open-ended inquiries ought to be created that has nothing to do with endorsing or condemning technologies (or the economics and politics that drive them), and everything to do with revealing "how life works" at physical and biological levels, and "what the human experience means" within varying existential conditions. These pursuits are not alien or obscure. They are, in fact, what should be occurring within the sciences and humanities if each discipline were free to conduct itself according to its highest purpose. In fact, a concerted drive toward disciplinary and trans-disciplinary, cultural and trans-cultural knowledge, would be of incalculable benefit – not only to informed decision-making but to public regard for the actual worth of such intelligence in response to reality. If only media-makers were free to imagine it.

California, 2000-2004

Casey Walker founded Wild Duck Review *in 1994 and has edited twenty issues to date, featuring essays, poetry, book reviews, memoirs, and over eighty interviews with literary artists, scientists, cultural critics, activists, and political leaders. She was educated at the University California, Davis and the Institute for European Studies in Vienna, Austria. She now lives in Santa Cruz, California, where she directs the Institite for Inquiry.* Wild Duck Review *takes its name from a passage by Henry David Thoreau:"In literature it is only the wild that attracts us. Dullness is but another name for tameness. It is free and wild thinking in* Hamlet *and the* Iliad, *in all the scriptures and mythologies, not learned in the schools, that delights us. As the wild duck is more swift and beautiful than the tame – so is the wild – the mallard – thought."*

IN CONVERSATION

Four Critics of Biotech.

The following four interviews – with two distinguished biologists, one expert on genetic technologies, and one lawyer and author – are reprinted courtesy of the American journal Wild Duck Review *(Vol VI, No 1). They were conducted in person and/or through correspondence by the journal's editor, Casey Walker, whose own four-part reflection on biotechnology begins on p. 133.*

STUART NEWMAN

Stuart Newman is Professor of Cell Biology and Anatomy at New York Medical College. He directs a laboratory in developmental biology and is a founding member of the Council for Responsible Genetics, an American public-interest organization opposing the misuse of biological science and technology. In addition to many scientific papers, he has also written on the cultural background and social implications of biological research.

As a cellular biologist, where do you see poor assumptions and bad theory playing themselves out in biogenetic engineering?

It begins with the false idea that organisms can be designed to specification, or corrected by popping in new genes and popping out bad genes. We see these assumptions in agriculture with genetically engineered foods, and with practices such as inserting naturally occurring insecticide proteins into crop plants like corn. There is a prevailing and, in my view, incorrect idea that genes are modular entities with a one-to-one correspondence between a function and a gene. My particular interest is in how these ideas are being played out in human biology, where we see the same kind of genetic reductionism justifying attempts to assign genes to complex conditions such as schizophrenia, intelligence, homosexuality, and so forth. Definition of problems in genetic terms obviously leads to calls for genetic solutions with profound consequences for human beings and evolution.

Although it's unquestionable that every complex biological condition has a genetic component to it, the mediation that occurs between the genetic component and the actual behaviour or feature is typically quite complex and should militate against taking the reductionist approach. Frequently, a gene in one context will influence a condition in one way and in a different context will influence the condition in a completely different way. There's simply very bad theory behind a lot of the genetic interventions now being proposed. In particular, bad theory (tied to commercial interest) is at the root of proposals for human germline modification, which would take a human embryo on the path to developing one condition or another, perhaps a disease, and modify its genes.

Is it misleading to perceive genetic expression and environmental influence as two discrete processes?

Yes. There's a genetic component to an organism's susceptibility to environmental effects and there's an environmental component to its expression of genetic effects. Thus, there's a composite of interpenetrating genetic and environmental processes that give rise to every organism during development. Another very common misperception comes with the conclusion that anything congenital – inborn – is inherited from the parents' genes. There are many studies currently attempting to tie personality traits such as shyness or aggression to genes. While people do recognize that various traits seen in their children were there from the very start, they need to also recognize and understand that the developmental processes of that child were far more complex than a playing out of its inherited genes. There are infinitely complex processes during development that make each outcome unique. Features in a newborn that are undeniably congenital and could even be said to be "hardwired" into the biology of that person may have very little to do with either parent. Thus, to say something is "congenital" does not mean it can be deconstructed and attributed to inheritance from one or the other parent.

Will you describe those processes that influence various outcomes during development of the human embryo?

At the start of development, the fertilized egg has all the nuclear genes contributed by its parents, and also the separate mitochondrial genes from the mother in the cytoplasm of the egg. The egg's cytoplasm also contains protein and RNA products of some of the mother's genes that are not part of her genetic contribution to the embryo. At first, the genes in the nucleus of this newly fertilized egg start to be activated and cause proteins to be made. But that's not the only thing that's going on. There's the mother's uterine environment that this organism is exposed to, and there is an "intrinsic plasticity" that allows the embryo to readjust and recover from perturbations or disturbances. For example, if you have a two-cell embryo and somehow the cells get detached from one another, each of those two cells – even though both were originally one-half of an individual – will go ahead and become a separate, complete individual. This of course is the basis of twinning. Mouse embryos at the two-cell stage can be separated and each of the cells will make an individual, even though under natural circumstances they wouldn't have done it. Through this kind of plasticity, a species-characteristic outcome is achieved even if it now takes the form of two organisms.

Something even more unusual can be done experimentally that may never or only rarely happen in natural circumstances, which is to take two embryos that are separate from each other and jumble the cells together. Again these cells will readjust their fates to create a complete individual. You can show this by taking organisms of two different strains, or two different species, and creating one single organism from them. You can make a chimera – which is what these combined embryos are called – between a sheep and a goat (a "geep"). Of course, that would never happen in nature, yet we do get a composite individual with all the normal parts.

Which implies a kind of strategy or will within embryonic cells?

It's a subject of major scientific debate as to what it implies. Some say that throughout our evolution embryos and organisms have been subjected to so many different stresses and strains and aberrant environments and strange conditions that we have within us a completely hardwired set of programs to get us out of all of these things that might happen. This notion has been put forward by some prominent developmental biologists recently and called "adaptability". They say this developmental plasticity is a very sophisticated product of our evolutionary history, and is dependent upon highly evolved genetic circuits and programs.

That's not the view I take. I see plasticity, or the ability to readjust in the face of environmental change and to take on characteristic forms despite all the vicissitudes of the developmental process, as a property intrinsic to the materials that make up organisms. An analogy may help here. If you look at rain, you'll see that every raindrop falling through the air has the same shape. Why is that? Not because a raindrop has genes to develop its shape, but because it's a piece of a particular kind of matter, a drop of water being subjected to certain external, physical processes. If you take a still body of water and agitate it, you will always make waves; if you swirl it, you will always make vortices. Here too, a particular material will do a certain set of stereotypical or "generic" things because of its composition and the forces to which it is susceptible. There are many more sophisticated properties that certain materials can exhibit – even if they're not alive – that support this view. There's a whole class of materials called "excitable media" that are studied by physicists and chemists. These are things that will give you back more than you put into them because they contain stored energy and have a stored ability to react chemically. For example, chemical reactions of diffusing molecules can spontaneously produce stripes or spots or spirals of chemical substance arranged across a spatial domain. Since this occurs with nonliving materials, we know there's something characteristic about excitable material itself that is not simply the result of a list of ingredients (which is what the genes provide). Instead, the composite materials formed from those ingredients will exhibit certain generic physical behaviours.

Now, embryos are excitable media. They inevitably do certain things because of their physical and chemical properties. This opens up a whole new set of causalities in the formation of an organism. It's not simply tracking the playing out of genes, but, rather, recognizing that there are physical and chemical properties that arise as the products of genes interact with each other within cellular and multicellular contexts that also contain non-genetic substances – water, ions, and so forth.

Is there a threshold, a critical mass of cells, where an embryo becomes an "excitable medium"?

The excitability is there from the start because each individual cell is excitable. It's metabolizing, it's exchanging matter and energy with its environment. But individual cells have a limit as to how differentiated each can get. Even though a single cell has many substances in it and these substances may be produced in one part of the cell and not the other, there will be a rapid mixing and homogeneity will generally prevail because the cell is so small. However, with a cluster of cells, because it is larger, something may occur or be produced at one end and not at the other, and create the gradients or inhomogeneities which provide the basis for cells to differentiate and take on distinct roles. Increased size brings several new physical factors into play that affect cellular development. In addition to the role of diffusion just described, surface tension begins to play a role in embryo shape and tissue-boundary formation. This is another factor which is not relevant at the scale of the individual cell.

Now, if it is the case that in embryogenesis of a contemporary organism these physical processes have an importance that is neglected by concentrating solely on genetics, I will also tell you that evolution has also utilized the outcomes of those physical processes. In certain cases, the outcomes were adaptive – they led to organisms that were functionally adequate in certain environments – and those outcomes were consolidated by additional processes, often genetic, that built upon and stabilized them. If a physical process led to an outcome that worked in nature, then, after a great deal of evolution, we find there are ways of achieving that endpoint independent of the originating, physical process. This is important because evolution away from strict reliance on physical processes makes morphogenesis more robust and reliable.

When we look at modern organisms, we can see the imprint of these physical processes along with the genetic processes that support and reinforce them. The process of evolution opportunistically consolidates certain outcomes that may have originally arisen as a result of completely different causes. At the end of a long period of time, you have many parallel processes directed toward the same endpoint. In short, the modern organism which the embryo develops into is a very, very sophisticated structure that makes use of genetic processes, physical processes, and genetic processes that have co-opted the outcomes of physical processes in ways that physics alone can't do.

If we look back at the raindrop analogy, we see that the raindrop has a head and a tail because of the physical medium it's falling through and the material it's made of. But you can imagine that if the raindrop had genes as well and those genes were subject to evolution, you might find that after a half billion years that particular shape wouldn't necessarily depend on the continuous falling through the air in order to be maintained. You might get other ways – genetic ways – of getting that shape to be established. It is also clear from this that structures may arise for physical reasons that are not for anything and later become consolidated by genetic circuitry. These features, which may be as profoundly part of an organism's identity as body cavities or segments, may ultimately have little or nothing to do with adaptation.

When you write of the conceptual gap occurring today in evolutionary theory, is this it?

Yes. If we go back in evolutionary history, before genetic integration and consolidation took place, the interactions between the material of the organism and the external world were very conditional, very context-dependent. Such interaction-dependent causation is called "epigenetic". With virtual certainty, those processes were very important in early evolution. As evolution progresses, the genes capture some of these outcomes and integrate them into the repertoire of the organism, so that what previously depended upon organism-environment interaction is internalized and part of an intrinsic program in the system.

Yet we commonly assume genes generate rather than support various physical features?

Exactly. Even if a feature becomes genetically prescribed, its origin was most typically in an interaction. We can look at the outcome, the end products of evolutionary processes, and appreciate the ways in which genes latched onto all sorts of things that originated through epigenetic mechanisms. However, if you try to understand the structure of the system by just looking at the genes, you will be terribly confused. Life forms did not arise from incremental pathways of small genetic changes. Instead, genes basically insinuated themselves into processes that genes themselves did not originate – a phenomenon ignored in the neo-Darwinian notion of the incrementally achieved "genetic program". In other words, genetic integration is a post hoc scaffold that stabilizes life forms, but is very different from a program. Looking at organisms this way allows us to appreciate the fact that there are aspects of our biology that have been consolidated by genetic evolution even though genetic evolution did not originate those aspects.

This becomes interesting when we look at humans and consider our biological repertoire. Even if certain aspects of our biology are completely settled – as in the case of the general form of our body – that doesn't mean other aspects are. Our brain's physical form results from relatively programmed morphogenetic processes during our development, and yet its cognitive potential remains subject to interactions throughout our lives. New thoughts are not dependent on remoulding the brain's morphology, but depend upon connections, many of which are conditional-epigenetic. Our brains are not finished products of evolution. The topology of the neuronal connections in the brain is plastic – fluid in the metaphorical sense. The ideas and values we hold are based on social interactions and interactions with the outside world.

That's not to say that genetic evolution may not eventually consolidate some of these aspects as well. For example, some species of birds learn who their predators are because their parents will squawk when predators come by and they learn to recognize certain silhouettes as hostile. Other birds have an inborn propensity to react very strongly against certain silhouettes. In some lineages of organisms, certain things result mainly from epigenetic interaction and in other lineages they result mainly from genetically-based propensities. Now, if we want to interpret what's going on in a reasonable way, it seems as if interaction plays the originating role, and genetics only captures and consolidates the behaviours under certain evolutionary circumstances.

Does this imply that evolution consolidates a certain taken-for-grantedness, a genetic wiring for survival?

It depends on the social and ecological setting any lineage finds itself in. It may be that under certain evolutionary circumstances things in the experience of that lineage get consolidated into the genome, but it's important to note that consolidation also leads to rigidification. If certain nonhuman species have a hardwired set of behavioural capabilities, they have thereby lost the plasticity that human brains still retain. I would suggest that cognitive plasticity is really, in some sense, a primitive feature that never got rigidified in the human lineage. Although our bodies have become evolutionarily stereotyped, our cognition has not. We've retained the interactive capacity that is probably at the origin of all cognition and behaviour, but we've made use of that "primitive" plasticity to a much deeper extent than other species.

Is higher plasticity true of sentient organisms in general?

Humans and dolphins seem to have retained this much more than other organisms, and there's novelty that comes into play with it as well. If primordial organisms indeed had brains that exhibited a lot of behavioural plasticity, they were also very small brains which weren't capable of very high levels of cognition. But if you simultaneously have a large brain and one which has retained behavioural plasticity, you are in very good shape for interacting with your environment in novel and productive ways. Thus our behaviour, thoughts, and imagination all depend on organism-organism and organism-environment interaction.

I also must say that this is an area in which I think the evolutionary psychologists and sociobiologists draw incorrect conclusions. Many look at primate species that are supposedly "lower" than we are or more "primitive" evolutionarily – which I think are incorrect ideas – and say that because certain stereotypical behaviours are found in both primates and human beings, these behaviours must be deeply embedded in our genes. I think this is totally wrong. Many behaviours – aggression, territoriality, sexual roles – may arise from circumstances in particular social settings, and initially depend on those social settings for their perpetuation. They may work in allocating resources in a successful fashion under certain constrained conditions. Those circumstances may pertain to certain human societies in our history, as well as to chimpanzees and baboons and so on, yet it's very reasonably the case that whereas these conditional outcomes may have become genetically integrated, consolidated, and hardwired in certain species – rats, baboons – they may still remain dependent on circumstance for humans. Even if a genetically-fixed behavior in an ant or a rat looks like a behaviour we see in people, it doesn't mean that it's associated with particular genes in a person. This is a common fallacy and, again, comes from not appreciating the role of epigenetics and plasticity in evolution.

Will you address the concept of the "intensification of uniqueness" as opposed to "open-ended production of difference" as another way of looking at evolution?

The standard view of how organisms have evolved, which is the Darwinian view, assumes a general correspondence between genetic change and phenotypic change. There's a kind of uniformitarianism embedded in

Darwinism that says that the general progress or alteration of phenotype is correlated with the general rate of alteration of the genotype. If you take that point of view, organisms are always on their way to becoming something else, and any boundaries between species are incidental. In Darwinism there's a general propensity to think that species identities are transient, temporary distinctions. They look like natural groupings, but the boundaries are always blurry because there's always the possibility of moving outside that perimeter through successive genetic change.

From which transgenics follows easily?

That's right. Darwinists say the idea that species are discrete, separate entities with species boundaries that are not crossed naturally is a remnant of biblical creationist ideas. The point of view that I'm describing, which is based on epigenetic causality, says that at the time the major differences between organisms arose, they did so on the basis of epigenetic changes – what I've also been calling plasticity or conditional and interactive processes. A given genotype would have exhibited a range of phenotypes, depending on the circumstances. In other words, there was no necessary connection between what the genetic content of an organism is and what the organism looks like. Physical and epigenetic determination may have been so important at these early periods of evolution that if the temperature, salinity, or some other aspect of the environment was changed, you would have gotten a very different looking organism. Now, if the origin of organismal diversity was in epigenetic processes, and if genetic evolution acted upon those dramatically divergent forms and consolidated them under various conditions of life, then after vast amounts of time you would have organisms that were no longer malleable or interconvertible. They would become walled off from each other by the genetic consolidation that evolution produces. Over time then, organisms stop changing into other kinds of organisms; they're becoming more themselves. Their characteristics are becoming more and more integrated and intensified so that at the end of a long period of evolution the boundaries between species have become much sharper. This view basically turns neo-Darwinism on its head in its proposal that phenotypic change precedes the genetic evolution that consolidates it. This is possible because most phenotypic innovation results from epigenetic processes. These processes can be mobilized by either environmental alteration or genetic mutation, but any new character that results will be subject to a more gradual cooptation by subsequent genetic evolution. This implies, contrary to neo-Darwinism, that most genetic change doesn't play an innovating role, it plays an integrating and stabilizing role. If you go back to the earliest history of organisms, I think it's inescapable that there was much less genetic integration, much less resistance to perturbation, and you had organismal forms that were malleable and polymorphic, because phenotypes were more dependent upon circumstance.

Such organisms differed from modern ones – their capacity to undergo phenotypic change in response to altered conditions having been virtually Lamarckian. After time, with genetic consolidation, organisms evolved into the Darwinian entities that populate the contemporary biosphere. However, the high degree of genetic integration means that the period of large-scale evolutionary change is over – Darwinian mechanisms of small phenotypic alterations due to small genetic changes will never result in a new genus, class, or phylum.

Along these lines I appreciated the analogy, in your chapter "Carnal Boundaries," that the organic possibilities of life are as distinct as the elements found on the periodic table.

Right. The periodic table displays the 110 or so stable "types" (elements) that are possible given the physics of the fundamental particles involved. This is all you can get, regardless of how much time elapses. I would suggest that in an analogous fashion, the pertinent physical and other epigenetic process acting upon aggregates of living cells can only give you a predictable, limited array of body types – the core of the taxonomical chart – regardless of how much additional evolution occurs. Of course, living systems are more massive, complex, and multifaceted than atoms, so you can get more subtypes within the major themes as organismic evolution progresses.

When the Darwinian model is upended, what does this imply for human potential?

It does imply a different way of conceiving of potential. I should say that in substituting an alternative view for Darwinism, it's important to utilize and appeal to concepts that are as rigorous, or more rigorous, than those identified by genetic determinists. Genetic determinism has claimed the scientific high ground because it deals with the very specific, measurable, quantifiable, tangible entities of genes. I would not want to supplant Darwinism with a paradigm based in the metaphoric or metaphysical. The epigenetic view brings in other causal modalities that are neglected in the standard picture, partly because of the training of biologists. Today a student can go through a university biology program through the PhD without ever taking physics, and miss out on this whole level of causation. The concept of epigenetic-genetic interplay is scientifically more complete than genetic determinism, and genetic determinism is actually obscurantist because it tries to explain things by genes that are genetically inexplicable.

So, to return to your question about human potential, which takes us into the realm of art and poetry, we must recognize that we're dealing with a human brain that, on a physical level, is a highly interactive system in which multiple causalities are brought to bear. To acknowledge this is to be more, not less, scientific. Evolutionary psychologists such as Steven Pinker aspire to rigour by saying it's all in the genes. But if you consider how the evolution of the body occurred over vast amounts of history, and how the outcomes of epigenetic processes have been genetically co-opted and assimilated in certain lineages and not in others, you can understand that neural connectivity in the brain has been subject to the same kind of thing. Even though we are partly the product of an immense period of genetic evolution, it does not follow that our thoughts and our ability to imagine are the products of genes. Analysing the human mind genetically is like trying to interpret *The Divine Comedy* by chemically analysing the ink it's printed in.

Based on this view of evolution, species boundaries, and epigenetic influences on development, how do you establish lines for what is appropriate or inappropriate in biogenetic engineering?

While it is true that certain versions of genes are associated with certain disease conditions, this is only part of the story. We know the gene and exact site of mutation in sickle cell disease, for example, but we don't know why this disease is mild in some individuals and fatal in others. imilarly for cystic fibrosis and phenylketonuria, the diseases are far more complex than the designation "monogenic trait" would imply. I would say it's rational to use genetic information in a very conservative way – as a prenatal diagnostic. But, the idea of using genetic information as a tool to go back to the embryo and start tinkering with it is not rational at all.

How is the cherished goal of biological perfectibility and the eradication of biological defects through genetic engineering a misguided goal for humans and for evolution?

First, it's easy to fall into language that looks at all deviation from certain norms as being a "disease" condition. For example, it's been noted that if everyone were genetically engineered to be six inches taller, there would still be the same number of people in the lowest quartile of height. I'm on the Board for the Council for Responsible Genetics, Cambridge, Massachusetts, which has been considering the social implications of genetic technologies for the past two decades. Although we started with the perspective that the use of genetic information should be left to individuals, we have grown to appreciate how deeply individual thinking about biological variability is influenced by the prevailing eugenic ideology. Even the concept of a birth defect is a relative concept.

It's also pretty clear that our germline and somatic cell genes are under assault by environmental pollutants and the thinning of the ozone layer, and that some birth anomalies are tied to environmental toxins and prescribed and over-the-counter medications. Particular cases of this have often been difficult to establish because it is frequently impossible to distinguish statistically real effects of known toxins from clusters of cases that are randomly occurring, or due to unknown agents. Furthermore, our knowledge of the basis of vulnerabilities to toxins, or synergistic effects among them, is quite primitive.

In any case, because of the interplay of epigenetics and genetics it may be impossible, even in principle, to determine if an abnormal developmental outcome was "environmental" or "genetic" in certain cases. (Many cases, of course, will be less ambiguous). It should be recognized, however, that even if epidemiology does not disclose a clear-cut relationship between a chemical and a type of defect, that does not mean that the chemical did not contribute to the defect. Polluters and manufacturers of suspect drugs will typically want to blame the victim – saying that "bad genes" were the cause of an individual's birth anomaly. Since genetic background influences susceptibility to toxic substances, the logical consequence of genetic determinism will be to screen people's genes and tell them where they can work or live, rather than clean up the environment. In the future, we can even genetically engineer them to have an improved capacity to repair environmental damage to their DNA, a proposal actually made by a well-known Human Genome Project program director at a meeting I attended.

Can we say that the set of problems addressed by genetic engineering is not well-posed – that the causes of human suffering have cultural and societal, rather than genetic sources?

Exactly. Right. People being outside of the norm one way or another is not the problem. My colleague Gregor Wolbring, a professor of biochemistry at the University of Calgary, was a victim of prenatal thalidomide exposure, but does not consider himself to be a person with birth defects. There's an interesting connection here with the evolutionary ideas I was discussing before. The way that Darwinism accounts for structural innovation is by the accumulation of many incremental changes that are tested at each step for functional advantage or improved adaptation. But people with congenitally missing limbs and other birth anomalies typically reject prostheses and find a way of operating in the world that suits their biology. When we see how thalidomide people relate to the world, and other people with so-called birth defects, we see they typically find a way of operating that suits them. Organisms don't relate to their environment because they've been evolved to match with that environment more and more perfectly, but because they figure out how to make what they have work. For example, there's a community on Martha's Vineyard in Massachusetts in which almost everyone is deaf. Deafness is not considered a defect because that's the way the people there are. So, with epigenesis and creative survival (followed, in many cases, by genetic consolidation) driving evolution, we can throw out the incrementalist perfectionism of Darwinism – it's not needed.

Will you comment on the distinctions to be made between a wild system and one that is biogenetically engineered? At what point does engineering usher in irreversible artifice or domestication for a species and a system?

The idea of the "natural" and the "wild" is out of fashion with many geneticists and evolutionary biologists who see evolution as pure opportunism, lacking any inherent direction. Short of inducing an overt pathology, genetically engineering an organism in this view yields a product with no ontological distinction from a naturally-occurring organism. While I resist romanticizing the "wild," if evolution proceeds in preferred directions, as I have suggested, it becomes harder to sustain the notion that arbitrary genetic changes are as natural as evolved ones. Domestication of animals has been pointed to as an example of human-guided deviation from the wild. I suggest, however, that like natural evolution, but unlike the results of genetic engineering, the phenotypic changes induced by domestication have proceeded in "natural" directions.

There have been some studies going on for over a half-century in Siberia on the domestication of foxes. The geneticist Dmitri Belyaev, who started the whole enterprise, looked at different domesticated animals and saw commonalities among even widely divergent species that had been domesticated, such as dogs, cattle, and pigs. There was a common reshaping of the skull, and even in the pattern of coloration there was a convergence to certain recurrent themes. Belyaev and his colleagues decided to try it with foxes, a species that had never been domesticated before. They found that in just a couple of generations the same changes occurred that had occurred in other, unrelated lineages. They found that if animals are selected for docility – a common mode of domestication – then the maternal environment of the embryo contains decreased levels of aggression-associated hormones. This in turn affects the course of the embryo's development, delaying certain processes and accelerating others, altering foetal form and physiology. While the investigators have hypothesized that their initial selection for docility was a selection for genetic variants, this is just a speculation, although one that is understandable from Russian biologists eager to avoid a Lysenkoist taint. It is also known, however, that phenotypic differences may even exist between genetically identical individuals. What is clear is that the motive force of the morphological changes observed in this study was epigenetic – a changed gestational environment. Moreover, common epigenetic processes seem to be involved in the convergent effects of domestication of genetically divergent species. It is not too much of a stretch to imagine that the transition from ape to human occurred through such epigenetic causation, brought about by self-domestication. After all, we share more than 98 percent of our genetic sequences with chimpanzees. The standard idea, of course, is that the unshared two percent is what makes all the difference.

It seems to me most critical to consider how biogenetic engineering will contribute to an increasingly artefactual world and to draw the lines for its implementation on those terms.

From what I have described above, wild and domesticated forms are both varieties of the "natural". The writer Paul Shepard has discussed many reasons to value and preserve wild forms, which of course are different in profound ways from their domesticated counterparts. But from a strictly biological point of view, according to which even the human species, at least up till now, is "natural," I would counterpose wild and domesticated species on one side to genetically engineered forms, which I see as tending toward the status of artefacts. Advocates of genetic engineering claim that it is no different from what evolution has done, and that it is in fact a new form of evolution. But genetically engineered crops are not analogous to products of normal evolution. If epigenetic causation is the motor of evolution as I have proposed, and genes play a subordinate, consolidating role, then going at the properties of an organism by manipulating its genes is not even really "engineering". It is the hit-or-miss production of potentially useful monstrosities.

The current period is characterized by a growing drive to turn the living world into a collection of manufactured artefacts. Already the legal system says that if you make a genetic modification in an organism it's a human invention, it's not part of nature. This was the stated majority opinion on the Supreme Court in its 1980 Chakrabarty decision, which affirmed the right to patent organisms. I don't have anything against manufactured items, and will even acknowledge that genetically modified micro-organisms may be useful. I use them in my own research. But I am dead set against patenting them. This takes the threat of blurring the distinction between organisms and artefacts that is implicit in genetic manipulation and turns it into a legal and cultural reality. The Chakrabarty patent was for an oil-eating bacterium. Since then it has served as a precedent for the issuing of patents on mice, pigs, and cows, some containing introduced human genes, as well as naturally occurring human bone marrow cells. There is no US regulation that would forbid a patent on a genetically modified first-trimester human embryo – and such things would indeed be useful and commercially viable.

Do you see an irreversible threat to natural systems and evolution with transgenic introductions?

I do. There's a thicket of ideology that surrounds all of this that is important to understand. The biologist E.O. Wilson and his followers say that evolution is totally opportunistic, based on the harshest of organism-organism and organism-environment interactions, but, at the same time, the products of evolution are love-inspiring. They speak of "biophilia," our love for the living products of nature. Yet, as the philosopher Hans Jonas notes, from a Darwinian viewpoint evolution is nothing but the successive elaboration of "pathologies". In my view it is not enough to say that although life is the result of arbitrariness and opportunism we should love it just because that's what we happened to get. Of course many modern Darwin-influenced thinkers aren't as ardent as Wilson – they just think it's all meaningless. Another somewhat one-sided view of living organisms has arisen with applications of the mathematical field of complex systems theory. Although this approach seeks to identify living processes with dynamical phenomena neglected by genetic reductionism, it in turn ignores an organism's accumulated legacy of jury-rigged gene-based stabilizing mechanisms. If we look at a modern organism, we see that it is a composite system that bears the stamp of originating, self-organizing processes, but also exhibits the incredible integration and consolidation that results from vast periods of genetic evolution. As a result, the living systems that we are familiar with are very different from nonliving systems – even self-organizing dynamical systems.

How can we understand the question of what life is in a way that enables us to put biotechnology into perspective?

Biology or at least biology as a traditional vocation – which is to understand what life is and how it works – is very different from biotechnology. Now the distinction has become blurred because of the commercialization of organisms, and because the ideology of the gene collapses everything into a single thing that can be sequenced, modified, bought and sold. People too easily confuse the manipulations technologists can do for the types of things that evolution has done. Darwinists will say evolution isn't wise, it's just whatever works. I wouldn't want to anthropomorphize evolution and say it is wise, but neither is it arbitrary.

RICHARD STROHMAN

Richard Strohman is Emeritus Professor of Molecular and Cell Biology at University of California, Berkeley. One of the leading figures in the theory of living systems, and the author of many articles, he has also served as the Research Director for the Muscular Dystrophy Association's international effort to combat genetic neuromuscular diseases. He is currently writing a book on the growing crises in theoretical biology.

Will you begin by describing the properties of a scientific Kuhnian Revolution, and why Kuhn's understanding of paradigmatic shifts is key to a deeper critique of current developments in biogenetic engineering?

A scientific revolution is one in which a prevailing, dominant paradigm – one that defines a scientific worldview, together with the methods of achieving research-based understanding and technological utility – is replaced by a contending paradigm. The revolution, according to Kuhn, has several properties. One is incommensurability, where the scientists on either side of the paradigmatic divide experience great difficulty in understanding the other's point of view or reasons for adopting it. Second is the accumulation of anomalies, wherein "normal science" of the current paradigm unintentionally generates a body of observations which not only fails to support that paradigm, but also points to glaring weaknesses in its method and theoretical outlook. The paradigm, under the weight of accumulated anomalies, loses the confidence of scientists in a minority sector and is ripe for overthrow. Third, paradigm shifts encounter resistance to change from the old guard, which is based not only upon a scientific incommensurability but on traditional ways of teaching and training the new generations in the (old) ways of research. Finally, there is enormous inertia based on the inability of a challenging paradigm to be fully capable of assimilating the accumulated anomalies and to provide a thoroughgoing scientific analysis and methodology capable of spelling out future programs of research and technology. The old paradigm may be a "scandal" of mistaken assumptions and failed predictions but if there is no fully competent paradigm ready to take its place, the scientific establishment must, by definition, remain loyal to it. As Kuhn compassionately noted, scientists cannot at the same time practice and renounce the paradigm under which they work. Thus, because of incommensurability, resistance to change, and inertia, the discovered accumulation of anomalies will be ignored until a new and competent paradigm is capable of replacing it.

In the present climate of biogenetic engineering, which is based on the dominant paradigm of molecular-genetic determinism, Kuhn's critical analysis allows us to recognize features of the paradigm's relative success and failure over time. These features might not otherwise be noticed or, if noticed, might be forgiven for a host of reasons having to do with the belief that science is always an accumulative process, and, presumably, given enough time, any anomalies would be assimilated by progress within a "more of the same" pattern of research development. But in today's setting, where vast sums of intellectual and monetary resources and power are devoted to the genetic determinist paradigm and its application in fundamental biology, in biomedicine, in agriculture, and bio-warfare, we need to exert every opportunity to examine our paradigm lest it be found, too late, to harbour anomalies that may turn out to be irreversible in the long run. Granted, it is not always a good idea to prejudge the performance of an ongoing paradigm since it may indeed be self-correcting. But our dominant paradigm in biology has accumulated many anomalies, errant predictions, proven false assumptions and outright errors of application in basic research and in biotech application in medicine and agriculture. The question is: can biogenetic engineering in its present mode be dangerous to the public health?

Kuhn's normal science in today's biology discovers its own flawed assumptions but this does not lead to further insight. It reveals a complexity more grand than that imagined – but a complexity revealed is not the same as a complexity understood. The fact that we have discovered more than we understand – including the overwhelming databases of the various genome projects – suggests that our present paradigm is missing something essential. We need to recognize this incompleteness before going further with genetic engineering that will also produce unforeseen events in the Earth's populations of animals and plants.

In "The Coming Kuhnian Revolution in Biology," you wrote "We have taken a successful and extremely useful theory and paradigm of the gene and have illegitimately extended it as a paradigm of life." How did this illegitimate extension occur? Why did genetic determinism win out over systems theory, holistic biology, or areas of research in the complexity and non-linearity of life?

The revolution in biology is all about the failed theory of genetic determinism. At the level of coded information in DNA – of replication, inheritance, and decoding of DNA messages – the theory of the gene is elegant in a simplicity accurately captured by what has come to be known as the central dogma of molecular biology:

$$DNA \longrightarrow\!\!>> RNA \longrightarrow\!\!>> Proteins \longrightarrow// \longrightarrow\!\!>> Functions$$

At this level the gene theory is complete or nearly so. However, this theory of what genes do and why genes are important has been extended to a theory of life which states that genes determine more than local function defined by individual proteins (and even this is exaggerated). Extended, the theory of the gene is a theory in search of ways in which genes determine complex functions like normal or super intelligence, disease states, psychological states, and so on. It is this extension – from understanding inherited DNA as determinative of local protein functions to DNA as determinative of complex functions – not only of cells but of organisms of trillions of cells – that is illegitimate. It is this extended theory and paradigm of the gene that is in trouble, and where the revolution in biology is brewing.

It is easy to see how this illegitimate function was assigned. The structure of DNA as given by Watson and Crick was such a powerful insight about biological information and generated such a productive wave of discovery and understanding at the molecular level, there was every reason to think that this information somehow extended beyond proteins to programs of behaviour. However, no genetic programs have ever been found, and here is our dilemma. We organisms are certainly "programmed" in some sense of that word, but if the program is not in our genes, then where is the program? We have no answer to this question and, according to Kuhn, without a paradigm capable of addressing the mystery of the missing program, we will have to hang on to our incomplete paradigm of genetic determinism. Current references to non-linear dynamics or complexity theory or chaos are all interesting starts at contributions to a new theory, but they remain as starts. That is our situation as we enter the new century. Our view of life is incomplete by half – at best.

For now, we adopt the shorthand expression for these alternative approaches and group them under the heading of "dynamics," the science that studies time- and context-dependent change in simple and in complex systems. In life, both genetics and dynamics are essential. They are also irreducible, meaning that one cannot be derived from the other in any formal way. In life, genetics and dynamics are irreducibly complementary. In the last 100 years we have had science based mostly in genetics, but mostly without dynamics. Dynamical systems science offers many possible approaches in which genetics may be complemented so as to provide understanding of complex organisms.

Neither genes nor environments "cause" complex traits. If a word be needed here then "cell" will name the cause. It is the cell, and the body of cells as a whole, that selects from the dynamical interactions inherent in its physical and chemical pathways and responds formatively and adaptively to the external environment. We have mistakenly replaced the concept and reality of the cell as a dynamical center of integrative activity with the concept of gene causality.

Will you describe the anomalies discovered for genetic determinism? What doesn't genetic sequencing or complexity alone account for?

At all levels of life's organization – the evolution of populations, individual development, physiology, cell and molecular biology – and in applications in biotechnology and biomedicine experimental and field studies, we are discovering new facts that cannot be explained easily and sometimes not at all by the current theory. In many ways these discoveries are merely modern versions of old but forgotten aspects of elementary (non-linear) dynamic genetic processes, such as epistasis (gene interactions) and pleiotropy (one gene or protein with multiple effects). At all levels, one detects lack of correlation of genetic complexity with morphological complexity (an organism's structure and behaviour). So, for example, differences in genome size and complexity between species are often much smaller than the differences in structure and behaviour of those species (humans and chimps, for example, have DNA that is roughly 98 percent identical). Errant predictions based on genetics and the notion of specific cause and effect are turning up everywhere.

Development is a process in which identical genomes produce, in the case of humans, over 250 different cell types! In molecular and cell biology, one can delete genes with no apparent noticeable effect even though the deleted genes were thought to be essential. Once again, genetics alone fails to predict the correct outcome in these experimental settings. There are many other examples of anomalies.

On the other hand, complex dynamic processes do not account for the discrete informational bits in DNA and the syntax rules by which that information is encoded and manipulated. Genetics and dynamics are complementary – both are needed.

Is it possible that the scientific proof for a new paradigm will not come from any kind of determinism but from a description of motive, strategy, interactive will? If so, would theories along the lines of complex adaptive systems, epigenesis and non-linear dynamics, chaos, or self-organized criticality be grounded in scientific proof?

We are at the beginning of a Kuhnian revolution, and, as Kuhn said, a scientist cannot remain a scientist and at the same time be without a paradigm. The result would be complete confusion. All or most of the candidate theories that I have gathered under the heading of dynamics do contain references to motive, purpose (*telos*) and will as needing to be included as essential irreducible facts of life, and all, in one way or another, address this necessity without needing to throw out reductionism or genetics, but to complement these with dynamics. It is much too early in the game to even guess how this is going to work out.

For now, pragmatics dictate a loosening of the theory of genetics to include dynamics. Biology needs more work, not less. While calls to abandon biotechnical applications based on incomplete science are not only pertinent but essential, such calls should not be misunderstood as being anti-scientific – it is quite the reverse.

Will you explain epigenesis as an alternative to genetic determinism and describe the levels of dynamic organization it contends with? Further, will you speculate on the full import of understanding boundary conditions as key to the laws of living matter?

Epigenesis is the historical alternative to biological (genetic) determinism. It emphasizes a science of processes over objects, of order over heterogeneity and has, from the beginning, talked about the necessity of developing a science of qualities, purpose, and intentionality. The *telos* emphasized here has nothing to do with metaphysics or vitalism but everything to do with finding scientific laws unique to these qualities of life. Epigenetic process has been ignored for hundreds of years but has now been thoroughly revived – first as a necessary assumption to explain anomalies, and now as a description of regulatory (dynamical) processes that serve to regulate patterns of gene expression in a context-dependent manner. These networks are open to the world and provide the sought-after link between the environment, experience, and management of genetic information.

I wrote about boundary conditions as key to laws of life and I also spoke about epigenesis as able to provide only partial answers. Epigenetic processes are a class of dynamical processes operating in living systems. For example, they operate at the level of the genome to regulate patterns of gene expression – how signals from the world are integrated to turn genes on and off in an adaptive manner. But this is only one level of epigenetic regulation. There is a kind of infinite regress here since we now have to ask: what controls the control of gene regulation? The answer we might have to settle for is the cell. Then what controls the cell? And so on. Here we have to talk about boundary conditions. Michael Polanyi, the late, great professor of physical chemistry and of social studies at the University of Manchester (those were the days!) said the following: "Live mechanisms and information in DNA are boundary conditions with a sequence of boundaries above them" (see *Science*, 160:1308-1312 for 1968). He means that, in life, there is a continuous complementary relationship between genetics and dynamics from which comes the adaptive qualities of life. If we start with DNA, then the first, innermost, of a sequence of boundaries moving out to the cell as a whole is the epigenetic control of gene expression, and this boundary moves outward to populations of cells, to the whole organism and beyond to communities, populations, and, of course, to the world, natural or otherwise. They are all connected. And the idea of boundary conditions gives us a scientific way of understanding the connections. As Polanyi put it, "...The outer boundary harnesses the laws of the next inner one." To which one might add, "Or is it the other way around?" By partial answers from epigenesis, I mean that at some point we have to stop calling these levels epigenetic and call them something else. Polanyi's discussion reminds me of Wendell Berry's essay on the "system of systems" in *Standing by Words*.

What perspective do you hope society will gain, finally, on the usefulness of biogenetic engineering?

Biogenetic engineering, when faced with the limits and dangers of an incomplete genetic science, will have to conclude that engineering the human genome is – for 98 percent of our problems – facing an overwhelming complexity. That is the message from recently discovered anomalies and from experiments pointing to epigenetic, context-dependent regulation of the genome.

What then? Is that the end of genetics or of biological engineering? Certainly not. Biological – not biogenetic – engineering, through dynamics will, or may, expand outward to include the organism and the natural world – the system of systems of the philosophers, poets, and scientists of the land, such as Wendell Berry, Wes Jackson, and many others. The human genome is ancient, conserved, difficult to improve upon most of the time and for most people. Biological engineering may use its databases not to engineer genomes but to understand the requirements of genetic agents and epigenetic processes in the world. Biotechnology and engineering would then be devoted to a restoration of the world to reflect the conserved genomes of organisms – human, non-human animals, and plants – that must occupy the land in common.

Biogenetic engineering assumes that organisms may be improved through genetic information almost exclusively. Biological engineering looks at the boundary conditions between genetic and other kinds of information and at the boundary conditions at all levels of living things, including the interface between the individual and the environment. As an example of the latter, elimination or reduction of human health risks (malnutrition, contaminated water and food, and tobacco smoking) has been the single most effective biological engineering in human history. We have already used it to gain 35 years of life expectancy just in the last 100 years. We have done this without engineering any genomes but have instead provided those embodied genomes with a proper world, one that reflects their evolved limits and capacities. In fact, further improvements in life expectancy are expected not from eliminating diseases associated with old age, or from genetic breakthroughs, but from further improvements in eliminating environmental risks and in greater access to improvements for those who suffer premature morbidity and mortality. For example, people suffer from their lack of access to the food we can provide, not from our lack of ability to provide that food. However, as our world continues to suffer the disasters of our other technologies (land, water, air degradation), and as we continue in the futile hope of being immunized to the consequences of this suffering by genetic engineering – of ourselves or of the animals and plants – we will surely begin to lose the gains in health and life expectancy we have achieved this century.

In sum, several conclusions concerning the future of biotechnology seem inescapable. First, in the science of molecular genetics the fundamental assumptions about specific genes and their specific "causal" effects on organisms are deeply flawed. As one recent paper in a major journal noted, there is now every reason to believe that it will not be possible to carry out genetic engineering (transfer of specific genes to a host cell) in the hope of achieving a specific effect. The normal complex interactions between genes and molecules in cells will be distorted by the presence of even a single transferred gene yielding unpredictable and therefore potentially dangerous results of unknown dimensions.

Therefore, biogenetic engineering of humans and of plants where unanticipated results could cause damage to individuals or to millions of acres of cropland will have to cease except under tightly controlled laboratory conditions and until the time when the complexities are understood and the dangers eliminated. Controls here would include concerns of ethical, legal, and social dimensions. These concerns must reflect the "ethics of the unknown" of the incompleteness of the science being applied, and not just the ethical concerns growing out of a "successful" technology.

There is, after all, an ethical component built into the structure of science itself, one that is often ignored by governmental and corporate structures as funders of research. This component includes the imperatives to seek evidence for disproving one's hypothesis (Popper), and to consider all, and not just selective evidence (Whitehead). It includes also the historical record showing the capability of "normal science" to uncover the flaws and misconceptions of a prevailing paradigm (Kuhn). These imperatives and demonstrated long-run capacities are inconsistent with modern corporate technology, which is based on the need to produce marketable results in a cost- and time-effective manner and in a manner that deflects anomalies from consideration. Government support of "basic" research is all too often heavy-handed in insisting that all efforts be "sold" under the heading of being able to solve key problems or address other issues reflected, as Whitehead pointed out, "…in the fluctuating extremes of fashionable opinion." Science is mostly a long-range affair while technology is not. The question remains: who will pay for the long-range need to know?

Second, the flagship of biogenetic science is the human genome project, and similar projects involving other animal and plant genomes are themselves squarely facing the anomalies discovered by their own scientists. Leaders of these projects are now increasingly aware of the flawed assumptions just discussed, and these projects are all now actively seeking to place their genetic findings within a wider physiological and ecological context. The search is on for the "meaning" of life that is now acknowledged not to be simply genetic in nature. The context has progressively shifted from epigenetic levels of genome control to a hierarchy of control extending to the cell as a whole and beyond the cell-to-cell populations, to organisms, and to the interactive and mutually dependent communities of life. The revolution against a preordained genetic determinism has discovered a complexity from which there is no turning back. However, without a fully developed paradigm of complexity as robust at the higher levels of biological organization as the Watson-Crick theory has been at the level of the gene, further progress will, predictably, be ruled by conservative forces. Therefore, in the interim, all caution must be exerted to guarantee that those forces also tightly regulate the old incomplete paradigm while we await its complementation with a science we have here called simply "dynamics".

This is the first time in the history of the life sciences that a single generation has been able to live through the rise and fall of a single dominant paradigm. It is a deeply disturbing experience, especially for those who have followed the radical change from a distance, and especially given the enormous investment our culture has made in ideas tied to a hopelessly ineffective, linear causality and determinism. Of course, from my perspective as a biologist, all this is wonderfully exciting: science can and does work in a free society. As the great astronomer and cosmologist Sir Arthur Eddington has said of basic science, "We must follow science for its own sake whether it leads to the hill of vision or the tunnel of obscurity." Today, with the obvious link of science and society, there are many opportunities ahead – having to do with those as yet unexplored boundary conditions and mysterious spaces between hierarchical levels where "emergent" qualitative features arise from quantitative interactions below – to understand biology as the most complex of all sciences, and to understand the equally complex impacts of its applied technologies.

RICHARD HAYES

Richard Hayes is the Executive Director of the Center for Genetics and Society, in Oakland, California, a non-profit organization supporting responsible social governance of the new human genetic technologies. He received his doctorate in Energy and Resources from the University of California, Berkeley, and formerly worked for the Sierra Club, the oldest and largest conservation organization in the Unites States.

Will you describe how you came to realize the significance of developments in human genetic manipulation and why you consider public involvement a matter of urgency?

As part of my dissertation studies at Berkeley I wanted to learn about the new human genetic technologies and their social implications. I did course work in genetics and began attending conferences. I was stunned by what I discovered. We are very close to crossing technological thresholds that would change forever what it means to be a human being. The most consequential of these involve the modification of the genes that get passed to our children. In addition, there's human cloning, artificial human chromosomes, bovine/human embryos, "reconstructed" embryos using genes from three adults, and more. It sounds like science fiction, but it isn't.

These technologies are being developed right now in university and corporate labs, and neither policy-makers nor the general public have any idea of what's going on. These technologies are being promoted by an influential network of scientists and others who truly believe that they are about to usher in a new, techno-eugenic epoch for human life on earth. They look forward to a world in which parents design their children quite literally by selecting genes from a catalogue. This would change everything we understand about what it means to be a parent, a child, a family, or a member of the human community. We'd come to see people as artefacts, collections of parts assembled to achieve a particular result determined by someone else. Once we start genetically engineering our children, how would anything less than the "best" be considered acceptable? Once we start, where do we stop?

Until recently these sorts of questions could be dismissed as speculative and far-fetched, but no longer. As far back as 1998 a major conference was held at UCLA to promote the idea of how wonderful it's going to be when we can manipulate our children's genes and finally "seize control of human evolution." One thousand people attended and press coverage was extensive. Just a few months later, one of the noted scientists at the conference submitted the first proposal to begin experiments involving the modification of heritable genes. Things are moving very fast.

Mind you, some of these technologies hold great promise to relieve suffering and prevent disease. But we can draw bright lines to separate benign applications from those that are likely to set the world on a slippery slope to a horrific future.

Will you describe current genetic engineering technologies and those lines you believe can be drawn?

First, what's a gene? A gene is a string of chemicals that codes for and enables production of a particular protein, and proteins are the building blocks of our entire bodies. Genetic engineering is the process of adding, deleting, or modifying specific genes in a living cell. If your lung cells, for example, are missing a gene that produces an essential protein, you can use genetic engineering to try to acquire that gene. To do this you attach copies of the needed gene to harmless viruses, and let the viruses penetrate the cell walls and nuclear membranes of your lung cells. The needed genes are released into cell nuclei, incorporated into chromosomes – which are just long strings of genes – and, hopefully, begin producing the needed protein. That's genetic engineering.

However, an important distinction must be made between "therapy," which refers to gene modifications intended to address a medical condition, and "enhancement," which refers to modifications intended to improve some aspect of normal appearance or performance. Treating or preventing sickle-cell anaemia or cystic fibrosis would be therapy. Attempting to modify stature, agility, cognition, personality, or life span of a healthy person would be "enhancement."

A second important distinction must be made between gene modifications that have an impact solely on a single person and those that have an impact on a person's children and subsequent descendants. This is the distinction between "somatic" and "germline" genetic manipulation. Somatic manipulation seeks to change the genetic makeup of particular body (somatic) cells that comprise our organs – lungs, brain, bone, and so forth. Changes in somatic cells are not passed on to one's children. Germline genetic manipulation changes the sex cells – that is, the sperm and egg, or "germ" cells –whose sole function is to pass a set of genes to the next generation.

The critical question – perhaps the most critical ever posed in human history – is, where do we draw the line? Somatic gene therapy for individuals in medical need is already being tested, and few find it ethically objectionable. Somatic gene enhancement of people without medical conditions raises more concerns. Some somatic enhancements may be no more controversial than rhinoplasty, while others may be profoundly dangerous or otherwise unacceptable. But the effects of somatic enhancements are limited to a single person, so the risk to future generations is nil.

By far the most important issues concern germline engineering. Advocates of germline engineering invariably appeal to our compassionate desire to prevent the suffering often associated with heritable disease, but they're not putting all their cards on the table. Couples who believe they are at risk of transmitting a serious disease can already employ the far simpler technique of pre-implantation screening to ensure that their children are free of the condition. In this procedure, a number of fertilized eggs are created *in vitro* – that is, in a Petrie dish – and are tested to see which ones are free of the disease-causing gene. Only these are implanted. Any child subsequently born will be free of the disease, as will all of that child's descendants. The current aggressive push for germline therapy makes no sense, unless the real intent is to pave the way for germline enhancement, designer babies, and the technological reconfiguration of human biology.

Along the same lines, will you address human cloning and other technologies?

Cloning is the asexual creation of a human being by taking the nucleus from a cell of an adult or child and transplanting it into a woman's egg from which the nucleus has been removed. The resulting embryo would produce a baby that would be the genetic duplicate of the nucleus donor, similar to a twin. If someone cloned himself or herself, it's not clear whether the resulting infant should be regarded as the "sibling" or the "child" of the nucleus donor. In fact, it's neither; it's a new category of human relational identity: a clone.

Over the past century few issues have garnered such immediate and resolute consensus as has the issue of human cloning. Over 90 percent of Americans oppose human cloning. The great majority of industrial democracies, with the US being the glaring exception, have already made human cloning illegal. Human cloning is condemned by every major religious denomination in the world. The United Nations, the G-7, the World Health Organization, and other international bodies have all called for a ban on human cloning.

Despite this, some scientists declare that they're going to do it anyway. Others say that although they are against replicative cloning – the cloning of fully-formed human beings – they support the cloning of human embryos, which can be manipulated at very early stages to produce tissues for treating degenerative diseases. However, success in cloning embryos would make replicative cloning almost trivially easy. Further, the techniques of embryo cloning are precisely those necessary to make germline manipulation commercially practicable. This hasn't been mentioned in any of the media coverage of cloning. It's very difficult to get a desired new gene into a fertilized egg on a single try. To use germline engineering as a routine procedure you'd start by creating a large culture of embryonic cells derived from a fertilized egg, douse these with viruses carrying the desired new gene, and transplant cell nuclei that have been successfully modified into new, enucleated eggs. These clonal embryos are then implanted in a uterus. Without embryo cloning, no commercial designer babies.

Currently at least half a dozen approaches to producing therapeutic replacement tissues, none of which require embryo cloning, are under investigation. There's no overriding reason to develop human embryo cloning techniques, unless the intent is to produce fully formed human clones or to make germline genetic engineering commercially practicable.

What is the significance of artificial chromosomes?

Germline engineering in which the only goal is to change a single gene is technically feasible today. But to engineer a child for more refined enhancements, many genes would need changing and current techniques are too crude. One solution is to build an artificial chromosome that contains all the necessary genes, organized in just the right way. Artificial chromosomes have been successfully tested in mice and in cultured human cells. The cells divide and the chromosomes are replicated intact. Now, human beings have 23 pairs of chromosomes and an extra, artificial chromosome pair would create 24. If you wanted to have the benefits of the artificial chromosomes passed to your children, you could only mate with someone who carried the same artificial, 24th chromosome pair. One of the key characteristics of a species is that members of the same species can only breed with each other. So you see where this is going. In effect, we're talking about the possibility of creating a new human species, perhaps within one or two decades. Few people outside the science and biotech community are aware of this.

If the current pace of research and development continues, there will be an explosion of genetic knowledge and capability over the next several years. We will be able to transform the biology of plants, animals, and people with the same detail and flexibility as today's digital technologies and the microchip enable us to transform information. The challenge before us is to summon the wisdom, maturity, and discipline to use these powers in ways that contribute to a fulfilling, just, sustainable world, and to forgo those uses that are degrading, destabilizing and – quite literally – dehumanizing. Advocates of a full-out techno-eugenic future believe we're not up to that challenge. When push comes to shove, they believe, people won't be able to resist using a new genetic application if it looks like it might allow their children some advantage over other people's children. And they believe that once we allow even a little bit of germline engineering, the rest of the techno-eugenic agenda follows inexorably. I disagree with the first belief – I think we can be wiser than that. But I agree that if the germline threshold is crossed, further control becomes far more difficult.

The infamous slippery slope. Will you elaborate?

Suppose it became permissible to use germline engineering to avoid passing on simple genetic diseases like cystic fibrosis, even though pre-implantation screening could accomplish the same result. What would the argument be against using germline engineering to avoid passing on predispositions to more complex conditions like diabetes, asthma, hypertension, and Alzheimer's – assuming the procedures were judged to be safe and effective? It's not obvious. After that, some scientists might offer gene packages that would endow healthy children with increased resistance to infectious diseases. Is this therapy or enhancement? It's a grey area. Similarly, what if genes that would predispose a child towards being very short could be engineered to predispose the child towards average height? How would you argue that such a genetic intervention be prohibited, assuming it was safe? Once it's accepted that parents have a right to use germline intervention to change a predisposition to shortness into a predisposition to average height, could you argue that they didn't have a right to predispose their child towards above-average height? Or towards above-average performance levels for a variety of simple and measurable cognitive skills? And after that, what about novel abilities that humans have never possessed before? Even if you banned such practices, advocates of germline manipulation say they'll just set up clinics in the Cayman Islands.

Scenarios like this one persuade some people that resistance to the techno-eugenic vision is futile and that we should just accept that it's going to happen. But think of the full implications. If a couple believes that it's desirable and acceptable to engineer their kids to be taller, wouldn't they typically also find it desirable to have a kid that's, say, less disposed to being overweight? Or disposed to being smarter, however they define that? Or more cheerful and outgoing? Or likely to live longer? Once you say "yes" to one enhancement, what rationale do you have for ever saying "no" to any other? If you accept that it's okay to engineer your kid, then doesn't not engineering your kid become something of a dereliction of parental responsibility? Especially when everybody else who can afford it is doing so? There are over 80,000 human genes. How many modified genes do you want to put into your child? Ten? Fifty? Five hundred? Five thousand? Where does it stop?

Imagine explaining to your fourteen-year-old that you engineered her with a set of fifty or five hundred or five thousand carefully chosen genes. Now imagine your child trying to understand who or what she is, and what's expected of her. Imagine her trying to figure out what about her is really her. Imagine her thinking about the children she would like to have someday and of the different ways in which she might like to engineer them.

Let's take it one step further. Suppose you've been genetically engineered by your parents to have what they consider enhanced reasoning ability and other cognitive skills. How could you evaluate whether or not what was done to you was a good thing? How could you think about what it would be like not to have genetically engineered thoughts?

I think the entire scenario of genetic "improvement" is quite literally insane. The fact that so many educated, accomplished people seem untroubled by it is truly frightening. It's the materialist-reductionist-determinist worldview run amok. It's what happens when people become disconnected from themselves, others, and nature. I've been at conferences where participants use phrases like "when we start engineering our children" as if it's a forgone conclusion, with no indication that they appreciate the enormity of what they're saying.

In my opinion, there are clear lines that we can and should draw: no human germline engineering and no human cloning, ever. This is a moderate position, because it doesn't necessarily rule out many forms of somatic engineering, genetic testing and screening. We're going to have our hands full just deciding which non-germline applications to allow; but whatever we decide, we're not putting the future of humanity at risk, we're not eroding the basis of human individuality, self-regard, and autonomy, and we're not undermining the integrity of civil society and a democratic political ethos. But germline engineering and cloning, I believe, would set us on a path that leads in those directions.

I know some people argue that we don't need to be overly concerned about germline manipulation, because, they say, it relies upon the discredited model of genetic reductionism and thus will quickly be found to be ineffective. It's true, obviously, that the great majority of human traits involve complex interactions of genes, epigenetic biochemistry, environment, society, and free will. My guess is that over the next decade we'll find the full spectrum of possible relations between traits and genes: some traits will be strongly influenced by genes, others will have little relation to genes at all, others will be influenced by genes in some environments but not in others, and so on. But in the absence of a ban, researchers will have no problem finding couples willing to run high degrees of risk in order to have a "superior" child. Some procedures will work and others won't. On balance, the techno-eugenic agenda would move forward. If we don't want to go down that road, we need to take stronger steps than, in effect, trusting the market.

Will you describe the world imagined by those advocating a techno-eugenic future?

The key text is Lee Silver's book, *Remaking Eden: How Cloning and Beyond Will Change the Human Family*. It's one of the most pernicious books I've ever read. Silver envisions a world in which the new genetic and reproductive technologies are freely and fully used by everyone who can afford them, in order to give their children a competitive edge over other people's children. He acknowledges that this will lead to deeper class inequities, and then to a system of genetic castes, and eventually to separate human species, which he calls the GenRich and the Naturals. To those who want laws passed to ban the technologies leading to such a world, Silver sort of smirks and says, just try to stop us. He says that today's affluent professionals will develop and use these technologies no matter what the majority of people may decide.

It's difficult to overstate how grotesque a vision of the human future this is. It casually dismisses commitments to equality and democracy and common decency that men and women have struggled for centuries to achieve. It denigrates values of community and compassion as anachronisms ill-suited for the new techno-eugenic era. It celebrates nothing less than the end of our common humanity. Silver and his colleagues are quite aware of all this, but they really don't seem to care; they just want to enable people like themselves – smart, accomplished, aggressive, cynical – to get on with the business of segregating their "high-quality" genetic lines from those of the rest of humanity.

It's astonishing that few leaders in the scientific and biotechnology community have publicly denounced Silver's vision. I've spoken with many, and asked them to tell me how they believe his scenario can be avoided, once we begin germline manipulation of any sort. A third of them avoid the question by making a joke. Another third say, "I don't know." And the final third say, "It's going to happen whether you like it or not."

Some people think scenarios like Silver's are so outlandish that they don't need to be taken seriously. I wish I could agree. It's important to remember that in Germany in the twenties many people dismissed the Nazis as buffoons.

Thresholds can be crossed that change realities of power and consciousness – we should know this by now. I'm not saying that techno-eugenicists are Nazis – in most ways they're quite the opposite, they're radical libertarians. Yet both are obsessed by the idea of the planned creation of biologically superior human beings. This obsession leads in only one direction. What would happen if the elites began engineering their children into a separate human species? There'd be protest, to say the least. Eventually the emerging GenRich would become impatient and start looking for a Final Solution. This is where the techno-eugenic vision leads. It's obscene and needs to be challenged.

Will you speak to the repeated claim that the techno-eugenic future is "inevitable"?

I think it's pretty apparent that claims of inevitability are rhetorical moves to rally supporters and demoralize opponents. Nothing in human affairs is inevitable. Most Americans are surprised to find that in the great majority of industrial democracies – all of Europe, Canada, Australia, and Japan, for example – both germline genetic engineering and human cloning have already been banned. The US is the rogue country on these issues. The claim that people are incapable of agreeing to forgo individual, competitive striving in order to realize a larger social good is simply wrong. Of course, the fact that citizenship values are increasingly and profoundly being eroded by consumer values – in the United States and worldwide – presents a challenge. We're in a classic danger/opportunity situation: if we can't invoke and mobilize a sense of shared human citizenship, it will be difficult to constrain dangerous genetic technologies; on the other hand, the stark danger of these technologies might be just what's needed for the importance of a shared human citizenship to be widely understood and affirmed.

Some say that an authoritarian police state would be needed to enforce a ban on techno-eugenics, because people will do it anyway on the black market. That's hardly reason to accept and encourage it. Rather, we need to say with conviction that germline manipulation and cloning are unacceptable acts of power and domination by some persons over others, and we need to make clear that these technologies are not about curing disease – they're about turning people into artefacts. Strong moral suasion and effective laws can minimize and even eliminate black market abuses.

Techno-eugenic advocates believe they will prevail if they can convince people that bans on germline manipulation and cloning constitute infringements upon reproductive rights. We need to be clear that there's an enormous difference between seeking to terminate an unwanted pregnancy and seeking to manipulate the genetic makeup of a child and all subsequent generations. The great majority of people I work with on these issues support both access to legal abortion and bans on human cloning and germline manipulation. There's no inconsistency in holding both positions.

Will you give a brief chronology of the scientific developments that have led us to where we are today?

Watson and Crick figured out the structure of DNA in 1953, and by the late 1960s the genetic code for all the proteins had been deciphered. The ability to put genes into bacteria was developed in 1973, and transgenic mice were created in 1978. By the 1980s proposals for genetic engineering of humans were being put forth, amid great controversy. A large coalition of religious leaders declared that germline engineering represented "a fundamental threat to the preservation of the human species as we know it," and should be opposed "with the same courage and conviction as we now oppose the threat of nuclear extinction." Germline engineering supporters decided to lay low and work instead to ensure approval of somatic therapy. In 1985 the Federal government gave somatic therapy the go-ahead, and banned germline engineering "at this time". The ensuing race among researchers to be the first to "do somatic" was won in 1991 by W. French Anderson, who inserted genes into a young girl to treat an enzyme deficiency disease.

By the mid-1990s, articles began appearing with titles such as "Germline Therapy: The Time Is Near." In March 1998 the University of California, Los Angeles conference, "Engineering the Human Germline," was organized by a vocal techno-eugenic advocate, Gregory Stock. The event signalled the kick-off of a national campaign to, in Stock's words, "make it [germline engineering] acceptable" to the American people. *The New York Times*, *The Washington Post* and other papers gave the event front-page coverage. A repeated theme was that germline engineering was all but inevitable. Stock said, "The question is not whether, but when."

After the event, Stock released a set of policy recommendations which called on the United States to "resist any effort by UNESCO or other international bodies to block the exploration of human germline engineering," and for the Federal government to rescind its 1985 germline engineering ban. Three months later, the Federal committee that oversees human genetic research, the Recombinant DNA Advisory Committee (RAC), discussed Stock's petition and agreed to review its policy on germline engineering. Simultaneously, the RAC received a proposal from W. French Anderson, the somatic therapy pioneer and a lead figure at the UCLA symposium, to begin a form of somatic therapy with a high probability of "inadvertently" modifying the human germline. It was an open secret that this proposal was a ploy. Anderson himself was quoted in the press saying that his proposal was designed to "force the debate" about germline engineering. If the RAC approves Anderson's proposal, it will establish for the first time that some forms of germline modification are permissible. Anderson hoped to be ready for human trials by 2002.

Will you speak to the challenges these issues pose for the environmental movement?

It's difficult to see how a world that accepts the germline manipulation and cloning of human beings will long be able to maintain, much less deepen, any sense of respect, reverence, and humility regarding the rest of the natural world. The techno-triumphalist vision calls for the wholesale transformation of literally everything living – plants, animals, humans, and ecosystems. It's not just a matter of putting a single pesticide gene into a corn plant or manipulating a single enzyme gene in a human zygote. What's underway is a reconfiguration of the deep structures of life. The new genetic technologies demand that the environmental movement deepen its critique if it doesn't want to be rapidly co-opted by an eco-utilitarian, technological worldview.

Have you heard of the new, transgenic EnviroPig? It's been engineered by Canadian scientists to contain both mouse genes and bacterial genes and produces manure with 20-50 percent less phosphorus than non-engineered pigs. It was developed to allow pork producers to raise more pigs per hectare and still comply with Canadian water quality regulations. Should environmentalists feel good or bad about EnviroPig? Should we oppose EnviroPig but accept EnviroHuman? Or is it the other way around? Do we accept neither? Or both?

Here's another: Michael Rose at University California, Irvine has patented human genes that some scientists suspect might be able to increase our life spans up to 150 years. Should environmentalists oppose this, support this, or isn't this an environmental issue? Students at University California, Berkeley protested research on genetically enhanced life spans, claiming that it could lead to massive overpopulation and resource degradation. But if EnviroPig can alleviate water degradation, maybe we can engineer EnviroCattle and EnviroTree to alleviate other types of resource degradation. And after that, why not EnviroPlanet: a clean, green, non-toxic, non-polluting, completely genetically engineered global ecosystem lovingly managed by genetically transformed EnviroHumans. This is exactly where we're going. Presently, environmentalists don't have a compelling way to say that this vision should be rejected. We really need to get to work.

Many are aware that the San Francisco Bay Area is now called the Biotech Capital of the world. Will you comment?

Genetic engineering proper started in San Francisco in 1973, when Herb

Boyer at University California, San Francisco and Stanley Cohen at Stanford figured out how to combine the genes of two different species. Three years later Boyer co-founded the first commercial genetic engineering firm, Genentech. Today the Bay Area has the single greatest concentration of biotech firms in the country. Besides Genentech there's Chiron, Shaman, Anergen, Clontech, SciClone and many more. University California, Berkeley just concluded a $25 million deal that gives the drug firm Novartis an unprecedented role in deciding Berkeley's research priorities. In San Francisco, Mission Bay is being developed as a 120-acre biotech theme park. Of course, much of the research going on here is beneficial and deserves support. The problem is that the biotech industry is incapable, on its own, of drawing lines between what's acceptable and what isn't, and its increasing clout is enabling it to fend off attempts at regulation.

A critical case is that of Geron Corporation, based in Menlo Park. Geron is potentially the ground-zero site for human cloning and germline manipulation, worldwide. Geron recently announced that it had acquired Roslin Bio-Med, the firm that held the patents to the technology that produced the cloned sheep in Scotland. Geron has announced its opposition to replicative human cloning, and they're probably sincere, because there's very little money in it. What they really want is the freedom to clone human embryos and use them to produce replacement tissues for a mass market. Geron claims that it wants to find a way to produce replacement tissues without having to use human embryos. That would be a good thing; I support that. But get this:a few years ago Geron established an in-house ethical advisory committee of local bio-ethicists sympathetic to human genetic manipulation and asked their advice concerning human embryo cloning. The committee concluded that embryo cloning would be acceptable so long as the embryos were "treated with respect," which Geron promptly pledged to do. So Geron appears to be hedging its bets.

Have you heard that California has established an Advisory Committee on Human Cloning? It's dominated by the biomedical and biotech community and, incredibly, seems disposed to recommend that human cloning be allowed in California as an acceptable form of reproduction. This could be explosive.

What developments with implications for human genetic engineering can we expect in mainstream media over the next few years?

Significant developments are going to appear in the press on an almost weekly basis. The sequencing of the fruit fly genome will be announced. Texas A&M hopes to announce the cloning of a pet dog, Missy, at a cost of $2.3 million dollars donated by a controversial Arizona multi-millionaire. Dr. James

Grifo of New York University hopes to announce the birth of the first baby with genes from three parents, created as part of an effort to increase fertility among older women. Richard Plomin in the UK is expected to announce the discovery of multiple genes associated with IQ scores. The big event will be the completion of the rough draft of the sequence of the human genome next spring, with the final version due 18 months later. All these developments will be interpreted by the press almost exclusively through the framework of mainstream genetic triumphalism. At this time there are few effective voices offering an alternative, critical interpretation. As a result, the scientists and the biotech industry are controlling the development of public perceptions and public policy.

What is to be done?

We can take a deep breath and remind ourselves of the beauty and mystery of human life, and of all creation besides. Then we have to get to work. Germline genetic engineering is the single most portentous technological threshold in history, and we'll need a new social movement of commensurate scope and scale to prevent ourselves from slipping, or being pushed, over it. We'll need to alert, educate, and engage the general public, policy-makers, and the press about what's at stake, and we'll need advocacy and political organizing as well. Substantively we'll need permanent global bans on germline engineering and replicative cloning, at least a moratorium on embryo cloning, and an effective system of oversight for somatic genetic applications. We need to start talking about these things with everyone we know.

Educate yourself on the issues and figure out how organizations and networks with which you're affiliated can bring their influence to bear. The great majority of people recoil at the idea of humanity divided into GenRich and Naturals. We need to make it clear that the genetic transformation of human beings is something we neither need nor want to do. If we can accomplish that, we'll have established a new foundation for using our tremendous scientific and technological gifts in the service of a truly inclusive future for life on earth.

ANDREW KIMBRELL

Andrew Kimbrell is a public-interest lawyer, activist and author. His books include The Human Body Shop: The Cloning, Engineering and Marketing of Life *(1997) and* Masculine Mystique: The Politics of Masculinity *(1993). He is the founder of the International Center for the Assessment of Technology and lives in Washington, DC.*

In The Human Body Shop, *you wrote, "Extending technology and commercialization to the living kingdom and body is among the most significant transitions in history." Will you begin by describing the importance of the larger picture, of systemic analysis, when we critique biotechnology?*

Systemic analysis of biotechnology, or any technology, is not easy and is rarely even attempted. In the past our society has failed to ask the important questions about a technology prior to its widespread use. More typically we allow a technology to become a routine part of our lives and then rely on regulatory agencies to work out the problems through so-called "cost - benefit" analysis, which usually takes place long after any rational limit to the technology is possible. This "too little-too late" approach to technology has resulted in catastrophic impacts on the environment and on our society and culture. Unfortunately this is the path corporations and government bureaucracies are currently pushing for the regulation of biotechnology.

What we fail to appreciate in our current approach to biotechnology is the extent to which technology is legislation. Deciding to use the combustion engine or nuclear power or biotechnology legislates our lives far more than most bills passed in Congress. The technologies we choose to implement determine much of who we are and what we do as a society. Technologies that destroy the natural world or encourage undemocratic and technocratic control of the basics of life should be vetoed like any other piece of pernicious legislation. Unfortunately, though we call ourselves a democracy, we do not have any mechanism by which we can vote on technology. The vast majority of Americans oppose cloning humans, the genetic engineering of foods, and much of the biotechnology revolution. But their voices are not heard.

Given that society is rarely given a role in technology decision-making, how can we change policies on biotechnology or other important technology issues?

I'm a litigator and an activist. Though I write books and articles, I'm not an academic. I'm in the trenches. Most often this means filing suits or organizing campaigns to "stop the bleeding" caused by industrial technologies. We do want to stop as many forests from being clear-cut as possible, we do want to protect wetlands, and we do want to stop as many creatures from being engineered and released into the environment as we possibly can. It's very, very important to fight these battles and I've devoted much of my adult life to it, as have many, many others. However, I also understand that this activist approach is profoundly inadequate in dealing with the problems we currently face.

Halting our indiscriminate destruction of the natural world, and the grotesque attempt of biotechnology to remake life, also requires that we change our collective consciousness and habits of perception in regard to nature. Until we change our reductionist views of nature we will continue to destroy it. A major priority for all of us, I think, is to become part of a new revolution of consciousness about life and the natural world.

Will you speak to how issues associated with biogenetic engineering should be articulated for the public?

I often say that biotechnology is taking the unthinkable, making it debatable, and then making it routine. Most people, when hearing of government researchers putting human genes into pigs, or corporate scientists cloning numbers of identical cows, instinctively are repulsed. There is great wisdom in this repulsion. It reflects an intuitive respect and empathy for the integrity of life and appropriate limits of human interference with the living kingdom. We need to affirm this popular repulsion against two powerful reductionist habits of thinking about life – modern modes of thinking which consciously or unconsciously are used by the biotech industry, academic science and the media to break down public opposition to genetic engineering.

The first is the view that the life forms of the earth are little more than biological machines. This doctrine, called "mechanism," has been around since the days of Descartes. It is a very dangerous habit of perception. It glorifies efficiency over all other values. Efficiency is, of course, the optimal trait for machines. However, making efficiency the optimal trait for living beings is a pathology. Yet this is the goal of the genetic engineers. When I have asked researchers why they are genetically engineering animals or plants, they almost always respond that the goal is to make these life forms more "efficient". Genetic engineering they say makes all of nature more efficient. What's the problem, they ask? Who's against efficiency?

I think when taken to this extreme we are all naturally repulsed by efficiency. I have never met a person who treats their children, friends, pets or any living being that they care about primarily on an efficiency basis. Only an insane person would calculate how they can put minimum time and energy into the children to get optimal results in behaviour or productivity. We don't treat the things we love efficiently. Yet the mechanistic mode of thinking has so dominated our minds that we rarely use the language of empathy or love when talking about nature, especially in the context of policy-making or in academia. But to defeat the eugenic drive of biotechnology towards making ever more efficient life forms, we are going to have to defeat the mechanistic world view and substitute one of empathy and respect for life.

Beyond the mechanistic tradition, we also have a tradition of "self-interest" that Adam Smith and the early proponents of the free market decided was the principal incentive for human activity. The drive for personal gain has become over the last two centuries the basis for capitalism. This now-global pursuit of ever more commodities has destroyed kinship, tribal relations, and spirituality. What's worse, our economic system has commodified everything. Everything is for sale as long as a profit can be made. The question that biotechnology and other advances in biology now present us with is the limits of commodification.

Are blood, organs, and foetal tissue commodities to be bought and sold? Can childbearing and children be sold through surrogate mother contracts? Can human genes and other body parts be patented by corporations? Clearly creating this human body shop of biotechnology demeans life, our respect for one another, and results in unconscionable exploitation of those who through poverty are forced to sell parts of themselves. Stopping the habit of thinking of life as a commodity is why I've been involved in litigating against surrogate motherhood and the patenting of life.

In this sense, biotechnology, with all of its perils, does offer activists the opportunity to stop the invasion of market into the body commons and, by doing so, raises the vital question of establishing limits to the market system and the commodification of nature.

Will you describe the way you look at the systemic impact of biogenetic engineering?

The biotechnology revolution now is transforming agriculture, human health and reproduction, and even military weaponry. This widespread application of the techniques of genetic engineering is creating a growing number of environmental, economic and ethical impacts. As for impacts on the environment and human health, one little discussed area of biotechnology is its use by the military. The US has spent hundreds of millions of dollars in bio-warfare research over the last two decades, without regard for the potential effects of a release of the deadly pathogens they are working with in dozens of college and corporate labs around the country. We've won several lawsuits against the Department of Defense limiting their bio-warfare research, but this aspect of genetic engineering and the potential for bio-terrorism are the kinds of scenarios that keep you up at night.

More generally, the environmental risks of genetic engineering are not widely understood because of the failure of many in the environmental community to understand the nature of biological or genetic pollution. Most environmentalists have devoted themselves to the important issue of chemical pollution. Chemical pollution is a contamination model of pollution – a variety of toxics are emitted into our air, water, and soil, causing contamination. Most environmental groups grew up in this country fighting for legislation based on the contamination model: the Clean Air Act, the Clean Water Act, and so forth. Now, many of these same environmentalists are calling genetic engineering "green technology" because it does not cause chemical contamination of the environment.

Environmentalists such as these completely miss the biological pollution paradigm, which is not a contamination model of pollution but a disease model. It's how we get sick. Right? Three people have a cold and I am exposed to them. I sit across the table from you and the bug goes to you, and so on. This is not a contamination model of pollution, it's a disease model. Some call it bio-invasion. The pollution of an ecosystem by a biological invader has of course already caused extraordinary devastation. We know how the chestnut blight and Dutch elm disease virtually wiped out those trees across the country and how kudzu vine and zebra mussels have wreaked havoc. Now, through genetic engineering, we're creating hundreds of thousands of genetically engineered microbes, plants, animals, and releasing them into the environment. This represents a real biological pollution problem. In contrast to chemical pollution, which dilutes over time, the organisms involved in biological pollution reproduce, mutate, and disseminate. There's no control of them and you can't limit their spread.

Each instance of the release of a genetically engineered organism is a kind of ecological roulette. Scientists refer to such releases as low probability-high consequence risks. We could release a thousand types of genetically engineered bacteria into the environment and only a few will create a negative effect, but that effect could be catastrophic. One graphic potential example of the devastation involved here is a genetically engineered enzyme that breaks down vegetative matter into biomass. Many environmentalists see this as a wonderfully clean new technology that could reduce our need for fossil fuels. We're trying to substitute oil and gas for biomass and here's this little enzyme that breaks down vegetative matter with amazing efficiency. Well, what if that enzyme escapes? I admit, the oil crisis would be solved, but we'd also have all our forests, crops, and vegetative life as one large bog of biomass. It would mean the end of nature. That's biological pollution by a genetically engineered organism.

A subset of biological pollution is genetic pollution. This involves a genetically engineered organism passing on a deleterious genetic trait to a native species. A classic example: the Canadian government and several corporations have taken human growth genes and put them into salmon to create super-salmon. They've also inserted chicken genes to change salmon reproduction, so the salmon don't follow their life cycles up rivers. If one of these genetically engineered salmon is released inadvertently, or not – it makes no difference – we'll have a huge salmon swimming around with human genes and chicken genes in every cell of its body. This salmon will mate with wild salmon, and some of that human and chicken genetic material will pass over to the native salmon. The native genetic pool will be contaminated forever. And assuming that the greater size of the gene-altered salmon makes them easier prey or requires that they consume more than the ecosystem can sustain, the entire species could be compromised. Over the next decades we could begin to see biological pollution matching chemical pollution as an environmental threat. It is essential that the environmental movement begin to understand biological and genetic pollution and make stopping it a top priority.

It's not difficult to see these blind spots as rooted in the difference, too, of a shallow environmentalism geared to the political wins of clean air, water, and food for humans, rather than a deep ecology with values for life itself.

Yes. And we can also see the biotechnology revolution as an extension of the pyrotechnology revolution. Since the Industrial Age, we've burned, forged, and melted the inanimate to create our metastasized nightmare of modern cities and factories. Now, from the industrial mindset, we've simply added biology to physics. The only reason you and I find that so shocking is that we, just as in almost all traditional cultures, have deep regard for living things. The idea that we're going to use the same engineering principles of abstraction, quantification, manipulation, predictability for living things as we have done on inanimate nature is wholly shocking. The devastation that we have seen with the engineering of mountains, rivers, and soils is now becoming routine for all engineered life forms, including the human body.

Then, too, over the last two hundred years of patenting, machines have long since usurped our control over them. As Mumford noted, the archway over the 1939 World's Fair carried the motto: "Science Explores, Technology Executes, Man Conforms." This was the religion of progress.

What an admission to slavery!

Yes, but initially a seductive one. When I was a kid, we thought we were going to become the Jetsons. Then suddenly, in the sixties and the seventies, it became very clear that life as we knew it was not compatible with a technological system. We had so altered the biochemistry of earth with fossil fuels and global warming, ozone and topsoil depletion, that problems weren't localized but globalized.

Yet we have a whole technological system that has become the milieu in which most of us live and from which most of us relate to "life". It is not a natural milieu, nor the social milieu of agrarian societies, but a system thoroughly mediated by TV, markets, vast information and communication networks – all of which, as it turns out, is divorced from and destructive of life. In response, many of us worked hard within the "appropriate technology" movement. We read Schumacher, saw the wisdom of simplicity and small-scale economies, and believed we could devolve technology and devolve the system so that it would comport with ecological limits and not destroy, or perhaps only minimally destroy, the world.

Suddenly we are presented with another "solution," the solution of biotechnology. Which, instead of comporting technology to benefit life, asks, why not comport life so that it becomes technology? We've now come full circle with the complete invasion of technology – life actually becomes technology. We see this quite literally in the aim to download human brains into silicon chips. We see it in more subtle ways, too, in patented chickens and turkeys without genes associated with brooding, for greater efficiency at egg laying. Quite clearly, most agricultural research is working to make fruits and animals and vegetables comport better to factory farming. We're doing it! We're working hard to create weather resistance in a number of crops so that they can survive global warming. In other words, large-scale efforts are now being made to comport all of life to the technological system. It's within that context that biotechnology can be best understood. We can all point to corporate greed, but in this larger, systemic context there's an impossible contradiction between a system of nature, or creation as it exists, and the technological system. One or the other has to give.

To a remarkable degree, we have already redefined life as machines and manufacturing under the patent system of the United States. We have done it legally. We also see a huge amount of computer literature referring to us humans as "biological machines". Our minds are software. As I mentioned earlier, this is the triumph of mechanism, the technologization, if you will, of life.

One of the greatest prides of modernity is that it is very pluralistic when it comes to religions. But, the reason the larger system can be so generous is that this religious pluralism is irrelevant. Every religious tradition is completely irrelevant to the religion of modernity, which is the religion of progress, of the mastery of nature. So there is a default religion afoot. Make no mistake about it. We live it every day. It is the complete mastery of nature through technology to create convenience and wealth. I will go so far as to say that there's a new Trinity, a secular reductionist trinity that mimics the sacred Christian Trinity. Science is God, all knowing, yet unknowable to most of us who didn't make it through reductionist college science courses; and it remains unknown, very mysterious. Science isn't too available or tempting, just like the God of the Old Testament, Yahweh. So, Science incarnates through Technology, the Son. And the Son is with us. It's not abstract. Technology is the magic that works. How do we participate in the worship of Technology? We have the ersatz Holy Spirit, the Market. People don't get up in the morning for Science, and they don't get up just for the magic of Technology. They get up in the morning with the urge to make money so they can buy things. Filled with the spirit of the Market, we pursue upward mobility, more technology in our lives, and more consumer pleasures. Belief in the secular trinity is an essential dogma of the religion of Progress. Heretics to this religion are dismissed by scientists, businessmen, and economists alike. You tell us that science is going to let us know everything, technology is going to let us do everything, and the market is going to let us buy everything. That's progress.

Do you believe our best critique of biotech and modernity in general rests on our manner and motive of knowing?

Yes. You've brought up a good point, which is the violence we commit in relationship to the "other". I see this in the environmental movement and in myself sometimes. There's this sense that to know the other is in some sense to violate it, to push the other so you can know more. This often happens in relationships when we mistakenly think we're going to figure something out by pushing at it, pulling at it, teasing it, poking it to make it come out of itself. There's very little sense that the only way to know the other is to be in loving participation with it.

Do you view biogenetic engineering as an enterprise that not only denies but destroys limits of a natural and spiritual order?

It's the whole enterprise. The whole enterprise is to do two things. One is to make limits ontologically evil and drained of all meaning. Second is to destroy any kind of sacramental imagination of life. Life can be seen as sacramental, even in, or perhaps especially in, its limits. The technological worldview views limits as ontologically evil. A recent ATT ad promised a "world without limits where everything is possible." The goal of what I call the technological imagination is to destroy all limits and boundaries. Genetic engineering is now destroying even the boundaries and limits between species. The failure of the modern mind to appreciate limits is of course destroying the environment as well as indigenous societies and cultures around the globe. Traditional societies view limits very differently. They see them as meaningful and even as sacramental. We need to regain this view of limits if we are to stop the juggernaut of biotechnology. In a sense we need to create, or revive, a new sacred understanding of limits. This does not mean that we can give up the daily battles in courts and legislatures and in the grassroots. They need to be fought. But we will also have to attack the problem at its root which is the technological imagination and counter it with a revival of the sacramental view of life.

TWO POEMS

John Burnside

THE ARGENTINE SKUNK

We had stopped the car and were out
in the wide dark of the pampas,
scanning the numberless stars for The Southern Cross,
while the driver sat at the wheel, with his mate and beads,

so my head was tipped to the sky
when I smelled it: a sour-water stink
crossing the river of highway that ran to Brazil;
the animal gone, by then, and my mind half away

in pursuit, before you told me what it was:
the skunk of the pampas, hog-nosed and quick as the wind,
vanishing into a legend of scrubland and dust
that stayed in my head for days, while the stars burned out

and the old creatures hurried away to their holts and lairs
at the edge of my mind, the creatures I never see
but scent, from time to time, in the starry dark,
brothers from somewhere near Eden, whose blood is my own.

ONE HAND CLAPPING

Heard melodies are sweet, but those unheard
Are sweeter
        John Keats

This is the tale of a man who is blind from birth:
a swaddled mind suspended in its own
momentum
        fruit falls
            mornings at the beach

the scent of oil or rain
            the perfect sound
of running water
        – what a blind man sees
by inference

        and how it fails
            one sunless afternoon
late in the year
        the pear trees shedding their leaves
a cranefly in the wash-house
            mapping a wall
like an angel at the wrong annunciation.

This is the charm we possess
in the small hours
        and the world we might create
if left to our own devices
        a purer space

where someone wakes and whispers in the dark
till nothing
        or the thought of nothing
            answers.

When I was nine years old
                         a favourite aunt
gave me a German village locked in glass
that when I shook it
                         vanished into snow.

It had a church
                         a footbridge in the distance
lights in the windows
                         cobbles
                                   painted stars.

I think I lived for months in that last house
before the bridge
                         the river at my door
phantoms and bats in the roof
                                   the smell of fir.

It made me think of order
                                   something vast
that holds us all and never lets us slip

and out of school
                         a stranger to defeat
I knew there was a word for everything
that God had spoken in the wilderness

a single word
                   hallowed and round as a pearl
for the skitter and glide of the living
                                   a proper name

for how a flock of birds is unison
swallows and terns at a breakwater
                                   hunting the light
or starlings in the dusk above a pier

how, all at once, and travelling at speed
they gather like a cloud

and come to rest

not single-minded
                    not a thoughtless skein
of instinct
            but the creatures of a mind
that knows what it intends.

What
        after all
                is the sound
of one hand clapping?
The one tree that falls in the wood
                            that nobody hears?

Remember the myth where everyone is twinned
with something in the fog
                        a lighter self
that knows its way by feel
                        and finds us out
in rainfall
        or the small hours

                        finds us out
and leads us home
                where danger never goes
to start again
                one moment at a time
grammar and kinship
                wedlock
                        collective nouns?

This is the story a man tells after he sees
and regrets his blindness
the damp leaves and whitewashed walls
                            the blood-veined wings

offensive
        as he turns back to the dark

and prays to find the old machinery:

the smell of rain and grass
                              the ghosts in snow
those better angels
                    shifting in the bone.

John Burnside lives in Fife, Scotland. He is the author of eight collections of poems, most recently The Light Trap *(Cape, 2002), and two novels. He has recently edited, with Maurice Riordan,* Wild Reckoning *(Gulbenkian Foundation, 2004), an anthology of poems on the natural world.*

TWO IRISH ADDRESSES

—

Julia Kristeva

FRENCH THEORY

The two freedoms.

It's with a certain degree of apprehension that I stand in front of you today, to address you in what is above all, for me, the language of Joyce. As you will already have noticed, my English is far from perfect, despite years of teaching in American universities. Let me confess that the reason is a double traumatism which I suffered in my childhood and which, in fact, I have never talked about in public before. Although I was successful in my studies, I was not accepted in the British school, which was generally reserved for the children of what was known as the "red bourgeoisie," because my parents did not belong to this milieu. Although they tried to keep this reason secret from me, I discovered it nonetheless, and this discovery was the cause of a feeling of bitterness which remained with me long afterwards: a bitterness at the rejection of my family by the authorities which hardened into a general rejection on my part of Anglophone culture, as symbolised by the British school. I have since that time tried to learn your language by my own means, and with the help of friends, but I suppose that the traumatic episode which I have told you about has always remained a barrier to my improvement. It's for this reason that I have particularly appreciated the wonderful hospitality that I have received in English-speaking countries, and in the first place, in the American universities where I have taught and which have translated my work into English. This has enabled other Anglophone readers and universities to discover my work and has facilitated precious contacts between them and myself, of which our meeting today is one result. The "French Theory" which is the subject of my talk today is in fact an expression first coined in the English language, in the American universities. I must therefore begin with a brief historical sketch of my relationship to the American university. This is more than a personal story, however; for, as I hope will become clear, I believe that it is impossible to define Europe today independently of our understanding of the United States.

When I arrived in Paris, the war in Vietnam was at its climax and we often protested against American bombardments. It was then that René Girard, having attended one of my first presentations of Bakhtine in Roland Barthes' seminar, invited me to teach at the University of Baltimore. I could not see myself collaborating with the "cops of the world," as we used to say at that time and, in spite of the dialectical advice that I got from my Professor, Lucien Goldmann, who used to say: "My dear, American imperialism has to be conquered from the inside," I honestly did not believe that I could do that alone. So, I remained in France. It was 1966. Several years later, in 1972, I met Professor Leon Roudiez from Columbia University, at the Cérisy conference on Artaud and Bataille. Following this contact I made my first trip to New York in 1973, and ever since I have been a Visiting Professor in the Department of French of that university, which, without improving the quality of my English, has at least helped me to make many friends in American Academia. Of all this experience, which I cannot resumé here today, and about which I have written in my first book *The Samourais* (published in English by the Columbia University Press), I would simply like to bring to you two symbolic images that have become a part of my psyche, and which will perhaps give you a sense of what my attachment to the U.S. means.

The first one is a tiny amateur photograph, in black and white, that Leon Roudiez took of me, and which shows me with my long student hair, on the ferry that took me to the skyscrapers of Manhattan. Since I do not have a picture of my arrival in Paris, this one is for me the only and the best proof of my re-naissance in the "free world".

My second image is that of my apartment at Morningside Drive which dominates Harlem Park, close to where Edward Said had an apartment and to the flat where Arendt used to live, and where I usually stay when I teach at Columbia. It's a place invaded by that unusual American light, dazzling and inviting at the same time. This is where I wrote pages that are dear to me from *Tales of Love* (1983) and *Black Sun* (1987) and *Female Genius*, a place which remains in my personal mythology, a place of happy solitude.

When Philippe Sollers and I decided to devote a whole issue of *Tel Quel* (71/73, Autumn 1977) to New York, many were surprised. What came across in that issue was a praise of American democracy, as opposed to French centralization, so hierarchical and *jacobine*. It was actually an acknowledgment of what seems to me to be the most important quality of American civilization, besides the freedom I am granted in my work there, namely, its hospitality. When I say "American" I mean to include Canada and the Canadian universities.

By hospitality I mean the ability that some have to offer a home to others who do not have one, or lack one temporarily. Running away from communism to France, I did not encounter this hospitality *there*, even though France has given me my French nationality for which I will always be grateful. Paralyzed by its administrative and cultural tradition, and at the same time trying to free itself from this, my adoptive country promotes innovations such as the artistic, philosophical and theoretical avant-gardes that have seduced me, and have contributed to its glory abroad, while, at the same time, promoting a violent rejection, if not hatred towards these innovations. On the contrary, America seems to me to be a territory that welcomes grafts and even encourages them.

Nevertheless, this is indeed a French woman that you are meeting here, or perhaps, a Gallicised European, the very "essence" of what *Frenchness* means. This often comes as a surprise to the French themselves who, obviously, do not see in *me* one of *them*. Sometimes, after listening to North American intellectuals passionately discussing my work as part of "French Theory," I am even tempted to take myself for a French intellectual. For these reasons I have at times thought about settling in America, or more precisely, in Canada which is more European and Francophone, all the more so when I feel wounded by the xenophobia of the country which has adopted me.

In this modern world of ours, in this "New World Order," we seem to lack a positive definition of what it means to be human (not in the sense of the "human species," but rather in relation to "the quality of being human"). We tend to operate with a purely negative and rather obscure notion of humanity when we talk about "crimes against humanity". My own experience, though, makes me think that the minimal definition of humanity, the degree zero of humanity, to echo an expression of Roland Barthes, is precisely hospitality. The Greeks were right when they chose the word "ethos" to designate the concept of "choice," the choice between good and bad, as well as all the other possible "choices," and that concept gave rise to the notion of ethics. Originally, the word "ethos" meant "a regular resting place, or animal shelter," finally leading to "habitat," "habit" and "character" as characteristic of an individual and of a social group that has a settlement. It was just this sense of hospitality which I found in America, which in many ways is a country which gives us a taste of *our* future, in which everyone is a foreigner, in which society consists of foreigners dealing with other foreigners.

Nevertheless, when I started teaching in America, and I've continued to do so, I tried to take with me a French and, more generally, a European cultural memory, a mixture of German, Russian and French traditions: Hegel and Freud, Russian formalism, French structuralism, the avant-gardes of the "nouveau roman," and *Tel Quel*. I hope that Americans have been able to feel that my "migrant personality" was less "French" in the sense of being somewhat rigid or even arrogant and condescending, and that through the foreigner that I am, they as foreigners could have access to this French and European culture. I must admit that at times I have had difficulty recognizing the uses to which my work has been put in the United States; since it has sometimes had a kind of politically correct bias. This is not in itself a problem since one's own work is inevitably appropriated by others in their own cultural context, as part of individual men and women's personal quests, and often in a highly original and innovative way. Nevertheless, I have not been aware of this sort of "politically correct" reading of my work by members of Irish or English universities, whom I believe are closer to my own, European sensibility. It is this particularly European sensibility which I am concerned with elaborating in my own work, and to which I will now turn.

Four Themes in My Research

There are four themes in my personal contribution to French Theory that I would like to sketch briefly: intertextuality, the distinction between the semiotic and the symbolic, the concept of the abject and abjection, and finally the idea of strangeness or foreignness.

One: The concept of *intertextuality* has enjoyed a certain degree of success internationally. This idea, which I developed starting from Bakhtine, invites the reader to interpret a text as a crossing of texts. Very often, in formalist or structuralist approaches, this has been perceived as a return to "quotation" or to "sources". For me it is principally a way of introducing *history* to structuralism: the texts that Mallarmé and Proust read, and which nourish the *Coup de Dés* and *À la recherche du temps perdu*, allow us to introduce history into the laboratory of writing. Mallarmé's interest in anarchism, for example, and Proust's interest in Zohar's Jewish mysticism and for the *Affaire Dreyfus* are useful material in this kind of approach. Also, by showing to what extent the internal dimension of the text is connected to the external context, such interpretations can reveal the inauthenticity of the writing subject. The writer becomes "*le sujet en procès*": this French expression means both a "subject in process" and a "subject on trial". As such the speaking subject is a carnival, a polyphony, forever contradictory and rebellious. The post-structuralist theme of intertextuality also gave birth to an idea that I have been trying to work on ever since, especially in my books from 1996 and 1997, namely that of the connection between "culture" and "revolt".

Two: The distinction that I have set up between the *semiotic* and the *symbolic* has no political or feminist connotation. It is simply an attempt to think of "meaning," not only as "structure," but also as "process" or "trial" in the sense I have already mentioned, by looking at the same time at syntax, logic, and what *transgresses* them, or the *trans-verbal*. I refer to this other side of "meaning" as trans-verbal because calling it *pre-verbal* could give rise to certain difficulties. The semiotic is not independent of language, but underpins language, and under the control of language, it articulates other aspects of "meaning" which are more than mere "significations," such as rhythmical and melodic inflections. Under the influence of Freudian distinctions between the *representations of things* and the *representations of words*, I try to take into consideration this double nature of the human mind, especially the constraints of biology and of instinctual drives that sustain and influence meaning and signification. This because we may indeed affirm that *in the beginning was the word*, but before the beginning there was the unconscious with its repressed content.

I am personally convinced that the future of psychoanalysis lies in this direction – that is, between the translinguistic logic of the unconscious, and biological and neurobiological constraints. At the Institut du Vivant, at the University of Paris VII, we try to bring biologists and psychoanalysts together in their work. Our basic preoccupation is the opening up of psychoanalysis to biology as well as to a more active involvement in social politics. In this connection I fully support and indeed am actively involved in President Chirac's campaign for the integration of disabled citizens in French society. We hope that this approach, along with a close rereading of Freud's texts, will revitalize contemporary psychoanalysis in the long run.

This "semiotic" trans-verbal side of our research is connected to the archaic relation between the mother and the child and allows me to investigate certain aspects of the feminine and the maternal in language, of what Freud used to call "the black continent" or Mycenaean (after the name of the Greek civilization that preceded the civilization of classical Greece.) This "other logic" of the feminine and the maternal which works against normative representation and opposes phallic representation, both masculine and feminine, is perhaps my own contribution to the effort of understanding the feminine as connected to the political via the sacred.

I am convinced that this new twenty-first century which seems to be in such need of religion is actually in need of the sacred, as opposed to fundamentalism. I understand the sacred as the desire of human beings to think, not in the sense of calculation, but rather in the sense of a need for fundamental questioning, which distinguishes us from other species and, *a contrario*, brings us closer to them. As a writer, psychoanalyst and semiotician I believe that the human characteristic that we call *the sense of the divine and of the sacred* arises at the very point of emergence of language. "The semiotic" with its maternal ties seems to be the farthest point we can reach when we try to imagine and understand the frontiers between nature, or *phusis*, and meaning. By understanding the "semiotic" as "emergence of meaning" we can overcome the dichotomies of metaphysics (soul/body, physical/psychical). My preoccupation with the sacred is, in fact, anti-metaphysical, and only feminist when we come to its consequences, namely to childbirth and the raising of children. If I am indeed passionately attached to the recognition of women in social, intellectual, and political life, this is only to the extent where we, the women, can bring a *different attitude* to the ideas of "power" and "meaning". This would be an attitude that takes into consideration the need for the survival of our species, and our need for the sacred. Women are positioned at this crossroads.

Three: The *abject* and *abjection* are concepts that I developed starting from my clinical experience when facing the symptoms that I call *New Maladies of the Soul* (Columbia University Press) where the distinction between "subject" and "object" is not clear, and where these two pseudo-entities exhaust themselves in a dialectic of attraction and repulsion. Borderline personalities, as well as some depressive personalities, can be described starting from this psychical basis which is also reminiscent of an archaic state, of the communion of maternal holding. The mother object is the first result of the process of expulsion of what is disagreeable in this archaic state, in a process which I have called abjection; the mother is then the first "abject" rather than object. Artists such as Picasso and de Kooning clearly understood something of this process.

Using the concepts of "abject" and "abjection," I first tried to understand the complex universe of a writer such as Céline, master of popular fiction, of the Parisian slang, the argot, a carrier of exceptional emotion. Instead of taking the cathartic road of abjection as religions do (and I believe any religion is in fact a way of purifying the abject), Céline insists on following imaginary abjections that he then transfers to political realities. His anti-semitism and his despicable compromises with Nazi ideology are expressed in his pamphlets that I attempted to read objectively, as an analyst, without giving in to the feelings that they inevitably arouse.

My adventures in the very dangerous territory of abjection have nevertheless brought me many alliances. Many artists from all over the world have recognized themselves in the experience of the abject, which is close to the psychotic states that they encounter in the process of artistic creation. But my research has also given rise to the sharp reaction in some academic circles and certain journals like *The Nation*, which affirmed that if I chose to analyse

Céline, it was only to excuse him, as if trying to understand means necessarily trying to forgive. That was one of the most radical rejections of my work, due to a misreading, and which I personally perceived as a form of partisan excommunication that amounted to an attack on thinking itself.

That "excommunication" now seems to me to be the tragic precursor of a more recent event, more comic than tragic, which issued from the pen of a somewhat noisy person in New York University who thought he was exposing French "impostors," (this was the name he gave to French Theorists), by rejecting our "pseudo-scientific models," when in fact, we have never tried to create scientific models, but only metaphorical transfers...

Four: The concept of *strangeness* or *foreignness*, is also, as you may know, something close to my heart. Writing my book *Strangers to Ourselves* gave me the opportunity to outline a history of foreigners, their actual destiny, and the way in which they are perceived in the West, and also to state my own position in this debate, a position which again seems to be accepted with some difficulty. First of all, I believe that in order to fight the state of national depression that we are experiencing in France (but not only in France), as a result of globalization and of the influx of immigrants, and also in order to oppose maniacal reactions to this depression (such as that of the Front National), it is important to restore national confidence. This has to be done in the same way in which we sometimes have to restore the narcissism or the ideal "ego" in a depressed patient, before proceeding to the actual "analysis," i.e., to the dissolution of his system of defence and resistance.

I am convinced that, in the next century, the cosmopolitan society that we have been dreaming of ever since the Stoics and throughout the Enlightenment, will not be possible in the utopian shape of the "melting pot," universalized and standardized by the market, the media and the Internet. At most, this will lead to a more or less conflictual cohabitation of nations and of various "social groups" which will live with and against each other. Combining a certain amount of respect for "national identity" and support for the idea of the "common good" (*l'intérêt général* as Montesquieu called it), this approach will have to replace the excesses of contemporary globalization. We have to invent a new balance between these two tendencies.

Two Types of Civilization

I have been talking about four elements of my own work: intertextuality, the distinction between the semiotic and the symbolic, abjection, and strangeness or foreignness. I would now like to distance myself from this personal research in order to understand the wider cultural and political context in which we work, and in which French Theory has been elaborated.

The collapse of the Berlin Wall in 1989 brought to light the difference between two types of culture, a European culture and a North American culture. I want to make it clear from the start, and in order to avoid any misunderstanding, that I am referring to two visions of *freedom*, that democratic societies have elaborated and which, unfortunately, we do not cherish enough. It will become clear in what I am about to say why I believe why Europe can be better understood in terms of her contrast with America. I am speaking of two visions of freedom which both rely on the Greek, Jewish and Christian traditions, and which, in spite of episodes of shame as well as of glory, remain our most important achievement. These two visions of freedom are both, nevertheless, essential. They are sometimes, as is now the case, opposed. Fundamentally, however, these two versions of freedom are complementary, and indeed I believe that they are both present in each of us, whichever side of the Atlantic we find ourselves on. If I continue to oppose them in what follows, the distinction is only a theoretical one.

Kant in his *Critique of Pure Reason* (1781) and his *Critique of Practical Reason* (1789) defines for the first time something that other people must also have experienced, but were unable to articulate, namely the fact that freedom is not, negatively speaking, an "absence of constraint," but positively speaking, the possibility of "self-beginning," *Selbstanfang*. Thus, by identifying "freedom" with the ability of spontaneously beginning, Kant opens the way to the praise of the enterprising individual, to the initiative of the "self," if I am allowed to transfer his "cosmic" thinking to a more personal level. At the same time, he subordinates the freedom of Reason, be it pure or practical, to a cause, divine or moral.

I will expand this conception by saying that, in a world more and more dominated by technology, freedom becomes the capacity to adapt to a "cause" always exterior to the "self," and which is less and less a moral cause, and more and more an economic one. In an ideal situation the two operate at the same time. In this line of thought, which is favoured by Protestantism (I'm referring here especially to Max Weber's work on the connection between capitalism and Protestantism), freedom becomes freedom to adapt to the logic of cause and effect, Hannah Arendt would say "to the calculus of consequences", the logic of production, of science, and of the economy. To be free would be then to be able to profit from adapting to this logic of causes and effects, and to the economic market.

This kind of freedom culminates in the logic of globalization and of the unrestrained free-market. The Supreme Cause (God) and the Technical Cause (the Dollar) are its two co-existing variants which guarantee the functioning of our freedom within this logic of "instrumentalisation". I am not denying here the benefits of this kind of freedom. It has the advantage of being able to adapt to the logic of "causes and effects" that culminates in a specific way of thinking, which is "thinking-as-calculus," and scientific thinking. I believe this vision to be crucial for our access to technology and automation. The American society seems to be better adapted to this kind of freedom. However, this freedom is not the only kind.

There is also another vision of freedom which emerges in the Greek world, at the very heart of its philosophy, with the Pre-Socratics, and which develops in the Socratic dialogue. This fundamental variety of freedom is not subordinate to a cause, which means that it is prior to the concatenation of Aristotelian "categories" that are already a premise for scientific and technical thinking. It relies on Being and moreover, on *the Being of Language Which is Being Delivered/ l'Etre de la Parole Qui se Livre*, a Being which delivers to itself and to the Other, and thus liberates itself, "sets itself free," liberates the Self/Other. This liberation of the Being of Language that occurs in the encounter between the Self and the Other, was emphasized in Heidegger's discussion of Kant (in a 1930 seminar "The Essence of Human Freedom," published in 1982). This approach inscribes freedom into the very essence of philosophy, as eternal questioning, before allowing it to become fixed, but also after initial fixation, in the succession of causes and effects and the ability to master it. *Poeisis* as questioning is a privileged space of French Theory, and is inseparable from style, narration, fiction. In other words, it is inseparable from poetics in a broad sense of this term embracing narrative, style, fiction (Jakobson), and the disclosure of language (Heidegger).

Do not fear, I would like to assure you that I will not go too far in this debate, that I have already over-simplified, of the two conceptions of freedom in Kant and Heidegger. What I am interested in is discussing, in the context of the modern world, this second conception of freedom. This second kind of freedom is very different from the kind of calculating logic that leads to unbridled consumerism; it is a conception that is evident in the Being of Speech in the Presencing of the Self to the Other.

I hope you understand the psychological and social connotations of this kind of freedom that constitute the essential themes of French Theory. The *poet* is its main custodian, together with the *libertine* who defies the conventions of social causes and effects in order to bring out and formulate a desire for dissidence. Not to mention the analyst in the experience of transference and counter-transference and also the revolutionary who places the liberties of the individual above any other convention. This is the foundation of Human Rights, and the slogan of the French Revolution, *Liberty-Equality-Fraternity*, which at the time reinforced the ideas of the English *Habeas Corpus*. To pay attention to these figures distances us from the abstract universalism that handicaps the legacy of the Enlightenment.

But I would like to return to our present reality. We are on our way towards building a European Community in spite of all the difficulties that we cannot ignore. In this often-chaotic European assembly, the voice of France, which sometimes finds it hard to make itself heard, still finds allies in other governments and in the public opinion of various countries, all of them deeply attached to their cultural traditions and implicitly or explicitly sharing our notion of freedom. We try to promote a "type of society" which is not exclusively that of laissez-faire capitalism, often identified as "the American model". Our requirement for this "cultural difference" which is usually referred to as the "*exception française*," is not only due to the fact that we belong to a tradition and possess a memory which may be older, "more refined" and "more sophisticated," and so on, because it originates in "The Old World". But it is due rather to the fact that we have a different vision of freedom, namely one which privileges the uniqueness of the individual over economic and scientific factors. When the French government, whether it be of the left, or of the Gaullist right, insists on our "solidarity" in opposition to "liberalism" in the classic sense of unregulated economic and social competition, we have to understand this to be a need for recognition of these different varieties of freedom.

Still, we are fully aware of the risks that may come with such an attitude: ignorance of the contemporary economic reality, excessive union demands, an inability to take part in international competition, idleness, backwardness. This is why we need to be alert and always remember the new constraints of our technological world, of the domain of "causes and effects". But, at the same time, we can easily see the advantages of this other type of freedom, which Ireland and other European nations aspire to. This is an aspiration rather than a fixed project, driven by real concern for the uniqueness and fragility of each and every human life, and not least the poor, the disabled, the retired, and those who rely on social benefits. It requires special attention to sexual and ethnic differences, to men and women considered in their unique intimacy rather than as simple groups of consumers.

From this perspective, the main characteristic of European culture, could well be its emphasis on the intimate, the particular, the art of living, taste, leisure, "idle" pleasures, grace, pure chance, playfulness, wastefulness, our "darker side" or, to put things in a nutshell, freedom as the essence of "Being-in-the-World" prior to any "Cause". (I recently tried to describe this aspect of human uniqueness when I discussed "Feminine Genius" in a trilogy on the life and work of Arendt, Klein and Colette. The notion of individual feminine genius can take us beyond mass feminism, in which the uniqueness of each woman risks being submerged, although obviously the notion of genius can be applied to both sexes.) Can we preserve this understanding of freedom as a general human value? This still remains to be seen, since we are overwhelmed by the maelstrom of our calculus-thinking and our consumerism. The only counterpoint to this seems to be the rebirth of religious sects for which the sacred is no longer "a permanent quest," as the very concept of human dignity would require, but a subordination to absolute causes and effects, here the authority of sects and fundamentalist groups. This means that today's religious alternative, to the extent that it degenerates into a clash between fundamentalisms, is not only an unreliable counterpoint to technological mastery, but even reinforces its logic of competition and conflict. It is therefore rather unlikely that this alternative vision of freedom that I'm trying to rehabilitate today can become more than an aspiration, but the die is cast, and this is the bet we have placed.

Of course, Europe is far from being homogeneous and united. In the context of the crisis in Iraq and faced with the terrorist threat, some have claimed that a rift has opened up between the countries of (to use their terminology) the "Old Europe" and those of the "New Europe". Without going too deeply into this complex set of problems, I would like to express two, highly personal, opinions on this issue. First, I believe that it is important that the "Old Europe," and France in particular, take very seriously the economic difficulties encountered by the "New Europe" which have the consequence of making these countries dependant to some degree on the United States. But we must also recognize the cultural, and in particular, religious differences which separate us from these countries, and we must respect these differences. Our famous "French arrogance" does not equip us very well for this task, and the Orthodox Christian countries in particular feel this very keenly. My second point is this: the knowledge that we in Europe have of the Arab world, after so many years of colonialism, has made us very sensitive to Islamic culture and able to soften, if not to entirely avoid, the "clash of civilizations" which I have referred to; but, at the same time, the insidious anti-semitism of our countries should make us vigilant faced with the rise of anti-semitism today, whether it come from the right or from the left.

Let me return now to the domain of the university, and in particular to the question of French Theory. I have been speaking briefly about the political implications of this European vision of freedom, a vision which is deeply ingrained in our social experience as well as in our *way of thinking*. This side of our freedom often takes the form of political contestation, but is fundamentally more than that: it is a way of being that reveals itself in the act of revolt. In fact, politics, *strictu sensu*, can also be seen as the betrayal of this freedom of thinking. This is why, in my last two books on the culture of revolt (published in a single volume in English under the title *Intimate Revolt*), I discuss the idea that "political revolution" (the French Terror of 1793 and the Russian Revolution of 1917) can be seen as the stifling of revolt in the sense of free questioning and permanent restlessness. Nevertheless, and paradoxically, the horror of totalitarianism, which took over the idea of revolt only to become a deadly dogma, hasn't managed to compromise entirely the possibility of thinking-as-revolt which is also a part of our political experience, and not only of our spiritual life.

Nevertheless, the deformation imposed by "political correctness" has hardened the political implications of philosophy which exist in the works of French theoreticians, but as an implicit dimension of our way of thinking. Some of our readers in American universities have simplified them, others have forgotten them. What was neglected by this attitude was *the working through of thought* just as Freud used to speak of the *working through of dreams*. This is "unconcealed" thinking in the sense of Heidegger, the "disclosure" of thinking according to Hannah Arendt, a kind of thinking that opposes calculus-thinking. In this way thinking finds its source in fiction and therefore in the sensitive human body, unveiling a "third type of cognition" as described by Spinoza, but also in free-association and transference in psychoanalytical experience.

I would like to think that this drive for freedom continues to grow in France. I believe that there is neither decline nor stagnation of intellectual life in contemporary France. This is visible in the ever-increasing emphasis on "the speaking subject" in the humanities. This does not mean that objective facts are ignored, but, quite the contrary, that, by taking them into consideration, the researcher is much more subjectively involved in their interpretation. In France, we will soon initiate a national debate on the role of human sciences organised around this general theme of "fact and interpretation". It goes without saying that the part played by psychoanalysis in this is crucial.

Also, and this is undoubtedly the result of the psychoanalytical perspective on human beings, the imagination is more and more perceived as an essential component of our psyche. This is the space where this other version of freedom emerges, that I am trying to rehabilitate today. We are alive precisely because we have a psychic life. This is the intimate dimension of our existence (what we call in French our *for intérieur*) which allows us to shelter from internal and external attacks on our being, i.e., psychological and biological traumas, as well as social and political external aggression. The imagination transforms them all, sublimates them, works for us and keeps us alive. Which part of our imagination? Well, for example, precisely the fantasies that psychoanalysis works with. Literature, for its part, offers a refuge for our loves and insomnia, our states of grace and crisis. Religion opposes laissez-aller capitalism and its logic of causes and effects by adding this supplement of the "human soul". In the modern state of human science, thinking is now ready for a fruitful and critical encounter with this religious imagination, and not only for its condemnation. Religion also becomes analyzable. Here, too, I believe, French Theory can make an important contribution. I recently created, along with colleagues in Paris, the Institute for Contemporary Thought, the core of which is the Roland Barthes Interdisciplinary Centre, which deals with themes situated at the interface between literature, philosophy, psychoanalysis and ethics. We try to develop those characteristics of what I believe to be essential to the French Theory I have been talking about today. Let me now move on to my conclusion.

I have placed a great deal of emphasis on the European origin of this type of freedom which, in my opinion, underpins what we call "French Theory". Still, nobody has the monopoly over this vision, neither the Catholics, nor the Protestants, on either side of the Atlantic. They both have an equal potential for dealing with these problems. Also, I believe that the idea of "being chosen" in Judaism, although different from the Greek idea of freedom that I have tried to outline here, makes a person coming from this tradition particularly capable of restoring what we lack so much, i.e., an interaction of these two versions of freedom: economic neo-liberalism and fraternal and poetic freedom, causal and "disclosing" versions of freedom.

Earlier, when criticizing the resurgence of French nationalism, I pointed out the fact that this intimate and fraternal type of freedom is indeed a difficult, if not an impossible, choice. Still, this is the challenge that France is ready to face, and, in the long run, the challenge that Europe as a whole must be willing to take. Personally, I feel highly committed to this vision.

In this context, America, the America that I love, an America which has however silenced all its opponents, risks becoming a fourth Rome, after Byzantium and Moscow. In this new economic order, and the terrorist crisis which has followed September 11, America has imposed a financial, economic and cultural oligarchy that excludes or puts at risk an important dimension of human freedom. Other civilizations, and our European civilization among these, have other visions of human freedom. They also need to be heard in this globalized world and to be allowed to bring their own correction, through diversity, to this new global vision of human destiny. The diversity of cultural models is the only guarantee for the humanity that I referred to in the beginning of my lecture, a humanity that we described as "hospitality" for lack of a better definition. But hospitality is not only the simple juxtaposition of differences with one model dominating all the others, and pretending to respect others while being indifferent to them. On the contrary, hospitality is a real attempt to understand other kinds of freedom in order to make every "way of being" more multiple, more complex. The definition of humanity that I was looking for is perhaps precisely this process of "complexification".

In this sense, understanding (or lack of understanding) on the part of the Americans for a European alternative could turn out to be a decisive step. The creed of French moralists is well-known: if God did not exist, we would have to invent Him. I would paraphrase this by saying: if Europe did not exist, the world would have to invent her. This is in the interest of our plural world, and in the interest of America. Whatever the economic and diplomatic competition between the Old and the New Worlds, our "old" Europe needs to make herself heard in the "new" America. European intellectuals have a particular responsibility here. The most urgent and the noblest mission of "French Theory" (and of European thought more generally) is, after all, that of drawing attention to human diversity in its experience of freedom. French Theory is just another term for the experience of freedom.

This address was delivered at University College, Dublin on 1 June 2004.

FEMALE GENIUS, FREEDOM AND CULTURE

On the genius of initiative.

At this moment in European history, as the enlargement of Europe allows the old continent to gradually reunite at last with the geographical limits which coincide with its cultural and historical memory, I would like to speak to you about an inheritance of which, I believe, our European culture can be proud: I will call it "the discovery and the respect of feminine genius". I have devoted a study to this theme, which is now available in English, translated by the

Columbia University Press, and which I would like to summarise today.

But first of all, and in order to allow you to better understand my point of view, which is rooted in my own personal history, let me start with some biographical details. You have in front of you today a European citizen, of Bulgarian origin, French nationality, and who considers herself a cosmopolitan intellectual: this last quality alone would have been enough to merit persecution in the Bulgaria of my childhood. Much has changed since then, and although my country of origin still struggles with various economic and political problems, the way is now open, not only for Bulgaria to become a member of NATO, but also for her to join the European Union as a full member. All of this would have been impossible to imagine thirty-nine years ago, in 1965, when I left Bulgaria to continue my studies in Paris, thanks to a grant accorded due to that visionary leader, Charles de Gaulle, who had already foreseen a Europe stretching from the Atlantic to the Urals.

In this year 2004, I still think of that time, in the not-so-distant past, and of all the efforts, sometimes discreet, but sometimes quite risky, made by many intellectuals and others during the Communist era, thanks to which Bulgaria is today a member of the society of democratic countries. It seems like a miracle, until one remembers the suffering, the never-failing hopes and the constant underground work of those whose profession is to think, which slowly ate away at the foundations of totalitarianism. It is customary on such occasions, when world history crosses one's own personal history, to evoke the memory of one's parents, and indeed I think of my father, Stoyan Kristev. This educated member of the Orthodox church wanted me to learn French from an early age, and duly registered me at the primary school run by French nuns, in order that I should absorb some of the critical spirit and taste for freedom for which France is rightly famous. I also think of my mother, Christine Kristeva, who combined a sharp scientific mind and a strong sense of duty with a gentle nature, and passed on to me that kind of rigour which is such a necessary part of one's development, especially for a woman, and even more so for a woman in exile. This was the family background, reinforced by the respect for culture and education which have developed in Bulgaria throughout its turbulent history, which was the foundation on which I received what French civilization has had to offer me subsequently. And I have a strong sense of the debt I owe to France, and feel proud, in the globalized world in which we live today, to bear the colours of the French Republic in the various countries and continents which I have occasion to visit. There's something I wrote in my book *Strangers to Ourselves* that I hope you won't mind me repeating here: I wrote that "One may feel more of a foreigner in France than in any other country, but at the same time one is *better off* being a foreigner in France than in any other country." The reason is that, although its universalism may be ambiguous, the French tradition of critical questioning, the importance attached to political debate, and the role of intellectuals – exemplified by the Enlightenment philosophers who are so emblematic of French culture – all contribute to a lively public debate which often appears dramatic but which is of a very high quality. This is a real antidote to national depression, and to its manic manifestation in nationalism. I would therefore like to pay a tribute to this culture which has adopted me, and which is never more French than when it is involved in self-criticism, to the degree that it is able to laugh about itself – and what vitality there is in this laughter! – and thus forge links with other cultures. I have absorbed this French language and this French culture to the extent that I am almost taken in by those Americans who welcome me as a French writer and intellectual.

But don't worry, I haven't forgotten that you have invited me today to talk about feminine genius. I have been working on this project, in one form or another, for a long time, in fact since my arrival in Paris at Christmas 1965, just when the movement for women's liberation was gaining momentum; but all this work finally crystallised in the form of my three-volume study entitled *Feminine Genius: Life, Madness, Words*, the three volumes being devoted respectively to Hannah Arendt, Melanie Klein and Colette. You may well wonder what the connection is with my own origins.

Well, I could speak to you at length about the intelligence and the capacity for endurance of the women of my country of origin, many of whom have distinguished themselves in literature, but also in various struggles for liberation. Nevertheless, I didn't devote my work on female genius to them, because I wanted to use examples that were known and accepted everywhere, in order to focus on the following question: "Is there a specifically feminine form of genius?" This question is not a new one, but it still retains much of its mystery. I will, then, be speaking to you about Hannah Arendt, Melanie Klein and Colette. But first I would like to reveal to you something that is not in my book.

My research led me to the discovery that the first female intellectual – and as such, necessarily a European – was neither a saint like Hildegarde of Bingen (1098-1179) or Angela of Foligno (1248-1309), nor a writer (the writers came later) such as Mme de Sévigné (1626-1696) or Mme de Staël (1766-1817) who, as a theoretician, writer and political thinker, has always been considered as the first female intellectual in the strict sense of the word – I discovered then that the first female intellectual was a Byzantine, a woman from my native region. Her name was Anne Comnena, daughter of the Emperor Alexis I, and the author of a superb history of the Crusades and of the reign of her father:

the monumental *Alexiade*, in fifteen volumes. Born in 1083, Anne Comnena began writing this work in 1138 at the age of 55, and completed it ten years later: as the first female historian, she offers us an interpretation of this period which is very different from those of the western chroniclers such as William of Tyre or Foucher de Chartres. This devotee of what will later be called Orthodox Christianity, was nevertheless raised on the Greeks and a fervent reader of Homer and Plato. She was sensitive, melancholy, and indeed romantic; a girl who was proud of her father; she was a philosopher, a politician, and her writing shows an awareness of the need for European unity, something which was such an important issue at that time.

Since I am convinced that a wider Europe will only really come into being if there is a genuine dialogue between the Eastern and Western churches, and if a bridge can be built across the abyss which still, unfortunately, separates the Orthodox and Catholic Churches in particular, I strongly believe that the exceptional work of Anne Comnena, among others, will be essential for thinking about our future Europe. That's why I made her one of the main characters in the novel that I have just published in France! I didn't do this in a chauvinistic spirit, since Anne Comnena wasn't Bulgarian, but a Byzantine princess, although her grandmother was a member of the Bulgarian nobility, and there were many marriages between Bulgarian sovereigns and the royal families of the new states which were constantly testing the borders of the Empire; and although the wars and the peace agreements followed each other in rapid succession in the Balkans, making this part of the world famous for its conflicts, but also for the ability of its inhabitants to find ways of coexisting. All of this was present, and foreseeable, in the work of Anne Comnena, a female genius who the future Europe would do well to rediscover. I am pleased, coming as I do from the Balkans, to have contributed to this rediscovery. I would like then to invite you to read, along with Arendt, Klein and Colette … Anne Comnena. Europe still reserves many surprises for us.

However, I'd now like to talk to you about the twentieth century, with the various philosophical, political and literary debates which have facilitated the liberation of men and women in our time. I would like to pose the question which is the title of this lecture: "Is there a feminine genius?" I would like to dedicate this lecture, for reasons which, I hope, will become clear, *to Simone de Beauvoir*.

For a long time now, according to the cadence of chance and necessity of intellectual life, the works of Hannah Arendt, Melanie Klein and Colette have shed light on and supported my own work and life. In addition to this past, the years I've spent writing the triptych devoted to them have enabled me to spend a lot of time with them. This leaves me now – as I complete the work – with the impression of actually having shared their lives. All these years of research have forged close bonds between us; a sisterly closeness in which affection has rivalled unconscious erotic projection, sometimes including of irritated distancing of myself from them and critical rejection of their ideas. However, it is my admiration for these three women which prevails when reading their work, and a feeling of sympathetic support prevails when I consider the winding paths of their lives. Some of my acquaintances have said that the interpretation of their work that I propose in this trilogy is a sign of generosity on my part. If readers were to confirm this impression, it would be the greatest gift that Arendt, Klein and Colette could have given me, in revealing what is often concealed by the harshness of life.

The provocative hyperbole of the term "genius" was the guiding idea which helped me to understand how these three twentieth-century women were able to surpass themselves in their respective fields (political philosophy, psychoanalysis and literature) so as to encourage each reader to surpass himself or herself in a similar way, in following the struggles of Arendt, Klein and Colette, and in working on his or her own. Because I'm convinced that the highest realisation of human rights, and of women's rights, is none other than the Scotist ideal that we are now, at this moment in history, in a position to achieve: which is a particular attention paid to the *ecceitas*, to the flourishing of the individual in his uniqueness, to what makes an individual *who* he is and raises him above ordinariness – *genius* being the most complex, the most appealing and the most fruitful form of this uniqueness at a particular moment in history, and, given that it is so, the form which is lasting and universal.

Beauvoir Between the "Situation" and "the Individual Potential of the Individual"

Insisting in this manner on the uniqueness which expresses itself in exemplary works (in particular in the humanities, which is my own field) is also a way of dissociating myself from mass feminism. Women's struggle for their emancipation has been through three stages in modern times: first, the demand for *political rights* led by the suffragettes; second, the affirmation of an ontological *equality* with men (as against the idea that women are "equal but different"), which led Simone de Beauvoir, in *The Second Sex* (1949) to demonstrate the existence, and predict the realisation of a "fraternity" between men and women, a fraternity which goes beyond their particular natural differences; and finally, in the wake of May '68 and of psychoanalysis, and this is the third stage, the search for the *difference* between men and women, which would explain a specific creativity particular to women, in the sexual domain and more generally, across the whole range of social practices, from politics to writing. At each of these stages, the liberation of all womankind has been the objective: in this respect the feminists have not departed from the totalising ambitions of the various liberation movements which arose out of Enlightenment philosophy, and, if we go further back, that was the result of the dissolution of the religious continent of which these movements struggled to realise, in this world, in all their revolted negativity, the paradisiacal teleology. Today, we know only too well the dead end which these totalising and totalitarian promises lead to. Feminism itself, whatever various currents may exist in Europe and America, has not escaped this tendency, which has resulted in it hardening into an inconsequential form of political activism which, ignorant of the uniqueness of individual subjects, believes that it can encompass all womankind, like all proletarians or the entire Third World, within a set of demands which are as passionate as they are desperate.

However, we have to recognize that its most illustrious source of inspiration, Simone de Beauvoir, was far from underestimating the "subject" in woman or the "individual" in her which "felt an undefined need to transcend itself". Faithful to this approach emanating from existentialist morality, and appropriating Marxism according to her own lights, Beauvoir the philosopher endeavoured to liberate woman from her inferior status which compels her to be the *Other* of man, who has neither the right nor the opportunity to form an *Other* herself. Denied the possibility of forming her own projects or of transcending herself, woman thus determined by the history of a society dominated by men is consigned to immanence, immobilised as an object "since her transcendence [is] perpetually transcended by another, essential and sovereign conscience." Whilst never ceasing to oppose the biological reduction of woman – "one isn't born a woman, one becomes it" – Simone de Beauvoir never lost her rage against metaphysics, because it's metaphysics which imprisons woman in her status of the *Other* consigning her to the realm of facticity and of immanence, refusing her access to the true status of humanity, that of autonomy and of freedom.

However, by putting to one side the question of difference and focussing on equality, Beauvoir denied herself the possibility of pursuing her existentialist agenda, which she had however announced, and which would, no doubt, have led her to reflect, via the consideration of women in general, upon the possibilities of freedom of each one of them as a unique human being: "The tragedy of woman consists in the conflict between the fundamental demands of each *subject* who posits herself as essential, and the demands of a situation in terms of which she is inessential. How, in the feminine condition, can a *human being* arrive at fulfilment? [...] That is to say that, by concerning ourselves with the *possibilities open to the individual*, we will not be defining these possibilities in terms of happiness, but in terms of freedom." Indeed, and although Beauvoir's thought is frequently inspired by the achievements of "individual" women, women as "subjects," examples of genius ranging from Saint Theresa or Colette to Mademoiselle de Gournay or Theroigne de Mericourt, it's less to the "human being" or to "individual possibilities" that *The Second Sex* is devoted, than to the condition of womankind. Because it was through the transformation of the condition of women in general that its author saw the possibility of individual autonomy and feminine creativity realizing itself, such "possibilities" of the individual remaining, nevertheless, in her opinion, the principal historical objective.

It would no doubt have been premature for the author of *The Second Sex* to defend the uniqueness of women while so many sexual and economic *conditions* still hampered women's liberation. Her particular style of philosophical journalism conveys her intense political commitment, coupled with her prodigious qualities as a teacher, and is tinged with a sense of irony which is as graceful as it is perceptive, and has guaranteed her book unequalled success, as we know. The issues she dealt with are still topical, to the extent that the *global era* which is emerging in the wake of *modernity* threatens to be riddled with all kinds of conservatism and archaism. Nevertheless, it's far from obvious that the "conflict" between the *condition of womankind* as a whole and the *self-realization of each individual woman* – which, according to Beauvoir, is at the root of women's suffering – can be resolved if we concern ourselves only with the "conditions" and neglect the importance of the "subject". In her thought, by focussing on the transformation of the feminine *condition*, Beauvoir herself leads us away from the essential question of individual projects, and consigns to the shadows the issue of the indeterminable possibilities arising from the *ecceitas* (or fundamental uniqueness) of each individual according to Duns Scotus. Arendt, Klein, Colette – and many others – did not wait for the "feminine condition" to be ripe in order to exercise their freedom: is not "genius" precisely the breakthrough which consists in going beyond the "situation"?

To appeal to the genius of each individual is not to underestimate the weight of History – these three women faced up to history as much and as well as any others, with courage and a sense of realism – but to attempt to free the feminine condition, and more generally the human condition, from the constraints of biology, society and destiny by placing the emphasis on the importance of the conscious or unconscious initiative of the subject faced with the programme dictated by these various determinisms.

Isn't subjective initiative, in the end, this highly personal force, tiny yet irreducible, on which the possibility of deconstructing any given "conditions" depends? By focussing on the irreducible subjectivity of these three women, on the uniqueness of the creativity of each one of them, my study has been concerned with their "individual possibilities" in "terms of [their] freedom" to use Beauvoir's own vocabulary. Moreover, leaving aside our differences, I firmly believe that I am retrieving and developing an essential question raised by *The Second Sex* which, due to historical circumstances and to her own existentialist convictions, Beauvoir had to leave unanswered, namely: *how, through the feminine condition, a woman can fulfil her being, her individual potential in terms of freedom, which is the modern meaning of happiness?* It will be seen that, in formulating my own work in these terms, I wish to express, as well as I can, my debt towards Simone de Beauvoir, that pioneer feminist who is all too often, and unjustifiably, criticized or underestimated, and dedicate my three-volume work to her.

It would be pointless drawing up a list of the qualities shared by Arendt, Klein and Colette, with the aim of defining feminine genius. Uniqueness, by its very essence, cannot be subjected to comparison: it's not something which is repeated identically from one individual to another. Nevertheless, there are some similarities in the life histories of these three women, and I'll come back to this point. But before I do, and in the absence of a real treatise on female sexuality, I should at least clarify the second term of my title, which I have left unexplained until now in the hope that its meaning would make itself clear through the various experiences of these three geniuses: namely what is the *feminine*? Is it possible to define not *woman* nor *womankind*, but a *feminine particularity* which is different in each of the sexes (thus one could speak of the feminine aspect of woman, and the feminine aspect of man), and for each individual person, if it is possible to do this, without confining the feminine in the concept of the "other" or in "that which defies representation"?

Without going so far as to propose a systematic theory, my previous work in psychoanalysis has tried to answer this question by approaching the *feminine* from the perspective of the various symptoms or psychological structures that I have been able to analyse in treating my male or female patients. Given this background of study, the existential and cultural experiences of Arendt, Klein and Colette have left their own mark and have led me to refine, and even to alter my conceptions on this question. I don't have the time now to develop this complex picture of female sexuality based on my experience as a psychoanalyst. Let me say only that it involves first a complex process of dis-identification from the mother, which results in the subject becoming a sexual object of a man (i.e., the father) but also and second in an identification with the father as a symbolic figure which allows the subject to speak, to think, and to take part in society. This theory of a (primary and a secondary Oedipus complex, which I call a) bi-facial Oedipus complex, implies that women have a stronger bisexuality than men – as Freud said. Women take part in the symbolic order, but only as outsiders, or in the words of Hegel, as the "eternal irony of the community". In addition to this the experience of maternity enables women to consider death in the light of birth, and women's experience of temporality would seem to be more like that of rebirth than the temporality of life-unto-death developed by classical philosophy, from Plato to Heidegger. Finally, the link to the other – that is, the object relation – seems to exist from early childhood, and to be stronger than the narcissistic tendencies that women are traditionally said to exhibit.

Now, what did my three geniuses have in common, and how did they differ, in terms of their feminine qualities?

Common Characteristics

Beyond the incommensurable differences and the originality of the three oeuvres that I have surveyed in my triptych, there are some common features which stand out.

One: The first one concerns the object relation. How is this expressed in the works of my three authors? Well, let me start with Hannah Arendt. Keen to defend the uniqueness of "who" an individual is (as against his various determinations, or "what" he is) which was threatened by various forms of totalitarianism, she nevertheless does not seek refuge in solipsistic incantations: against the isolation of the philosophers which she derided as a "melancholic tribe" (from Plato to Kant and to Heidegger) and against the anonymity of the crowd, the "they" (to use Heidegger's term) into which the multitude of anonymous individuals melts, our "political journalist", as she (Arendt) liked to call herself, makes an appeal for a political life in which the originality of each individual is guaranteed through the creation of a "web of human relationships" consisting of memory and narrative destined for others. This realisation of the "who" of the individual in the web of attachments which unite particular individuals is a distinctive feature of Arendtian political thought, at one and the same time intensely libertarian and eminently social –

and therefore to which, paradoxically, both the most eccentric anarchists and the most conservative spirits can subscribe. It's not simply a reversal of idealist philosophy onto the terrain of sociology, nor just a tribute to Aristotle as a counterpoint to Plato, that we should read into this transvaluation of political ties, but rather the conviction, as ontological as it is existential, that what is unique in each individual "remains hidden" to "the person himself" and does not "appear so clearly and unmistakeably [as it does] to others."

Concerning Melanie Klein, we may say that she radically transforms the Freudian hypothesis of an original narcissism, and postulates, from the very beginning of a baby's psychic life, a "self," capable of a "relationship with the object," albeit partial (to the breast), before the child becomes capable of constructing an object-relation to the "total object," following the depressive position. One consideration is prior to all others for this psychoanalyst: this is that the psyche does not exist and is inconceivable in the absence of a "self" that she postulates along with its correlate which is the relationship to the "object".

"Colette the lover", who was repeatedly betrayed in her love life – and who indeed was often herself the betrayer – finally declares herself to be beyond the passion of love: "Love, one of the great banalities of existence takes leave of mine … Once we have left it behind us, we notice that all else is gay, diverse and plentiful." Make no mistake: this comment ought not to be seen as the prologue to a melancholic report on existence: thanks to her friendships, and through the discipline of writing in which she immersed herself (forgetting herself in the act and rediscovering unity) in the pure experience of Being, Colette never renounced her participation in the plurality of this world which she celebrates in a kind of pagan mystic of self-realisation through a multitude of cosmic connections. Thus when she says "all else is gay, diverse and plentiful" this should be interpreted as a modulation of human love … beyond the love of a couple, not a love for god, but an osmosis with Being.

In these affirmations of a *self which cannot be separated from its various attachments* – political, psychical, sensory, amorous, or literary – I would be tempted to distinguish a constant of feminine psycho-sexuality. A woman is less cut-off in her erotic pleasures and more dependent on the other – whether this other is an imaginary vehicle of the psyche or of a real presence which is needed. We may venture to say, then, that a woman has a greater inclination than a man to seek and to nurture, in the context of her *attachments*, that which permits the flourishing of what is unique in her, rather than that which, in these attachments, restrains and suppresses our pleasure. And that while constantly rebelling against all kinds of fetters, constraints, prisons, camps and other concentrations of the social which reduce us to a condition of banality, woman never ceases, in spite of the obstacles, to seek in the context of an attachment to an object which is "gay, diverse and plentiful" the conditions of her political and psychical liberty.

Two: The second common characteristic of our three geniuses is their identification of thought with life. By diagnosing a radical evil in totalitarianism, which dared to announce "the superfluity of human life," Arendt set herself up as the champion of life if (and only if) *this life has a meaning*: life not as *zoé*, but as *bios* giving rise to a biography which becomes part of the memory of the city-state. Through an investigation of the meandering paths of the acts of *willing, thinking and judging* she attempts to understand the meaning of an existence such as this, in which life is coextensive with thought, and which the two versions of totalitarianism of the twentieth century started to destroy in order to annihilate, with thought, life itself. Deeply shocked, but retaining a sense of humour, she even manages to make fun of Eichmann who banalised, "trivialized evil," not by committing trivial crimes (and some have said that this is implied in what she says) but because he was "incapable of distinguishing good from evil," because he had the "sad capacity to console himself with clichés," which is "closely linked to his inability to *think* – in particular to think from another person's point of view." Arendt transformed her political struggle against totalitarianism into a philosophical struggle to defend thought: not thought in the sense of calculation (of instrumental rationality) but questioning-thought, savouring-thought, forgiving-thought.

In founding child psychoanalysis, Melanie Klein did not simply barter *eroticism*, which Freud had placed at the centre of psychic life, for the *pain* of the newly-born child which she supposes to be schizo-paranoid, and then depressive. Klein's critics have often thought that this was the case, Lacan calling her that "delightful tripe butcher". By focussing on the problems of childhood, and in particular on child psychosis, which handicaps the cognitive faculties, Klein was the first to use psychoanalysis as an art of curing the capacity to think. Bion, Winnicot and many others who followed her and often disagreed with her views, continued to innovate in terms of their practice by making it increasingly sensitive to the conditions of possibility of the human mind, so as to optimise its creative capacities.

It was not only out of vanity that Colette declared herself to be a stranger to the literary art. Was it then out of a refusal to imprison herself in a fetish of the literary object, or in the rituals of the literary milieu? No doubt it was. But she was far from having avoided the social and aesthetic traps whose perverse effects she was hardly against. However, as a writer she does not use words rhetorically, or in a quest for pure form, and still less as a means of communicating ideas. If we may say that she thinks as she writes, then it's in the sense that this written thought emerges itself as a new life which brings her, beyond a new self and a new body, a real osmosis with Being. Her writing, sensual, gustatory, and sonorous, fragrant and tactile, is thought made flesh or flesh made thought: Colette does not invent a literary form, she constructs an alphabet of the sensory world by weaving and by feeding on the fabric of the French language. Is she a novelist, a writer? Of course she is. But with an indomitable energy which never tires of reconstructing the flesh of the world in Sido's (her mother's) language.

In their different ways, none of these three women simply places thinking, or sublimation, at the centre of life: for them life is thought and thought is life, and in this way they attain this highest state of felicity in which *to live is to think-sublimate-write*. The metaphysical dichotomy between "abstract" and "concrete," "meaning" and "matter," "being" and "existence," dissolves in their experience as it does in their thought. Is this an echo of the Christian belief in reincarnation that I read into these adventures in modernity, which, however, purport to be entirely secular? Or is it not rather another instance of a resonance with female psycho-sexuality (which I sketched earlier), and which is reluctant to isolate itself in the obsessional palaces of "pure thought", in the abstractions of the superego or in the (male) phallic mastery of logical calculation? (Although many women are capable of such abstract performances, deemed as male, precisely through identification with the "male").

Doesn't the feminine prefer, on the contrary, the "poetic" regions of thought, where meaning is rooted in the world of the senses, where representations of words run alongside representations of things, and where ideas give way to instinctual drives?

Three: The third common characteristic of my three geniuses is their approach to temporality. Without having herself experienced maternity, Arendt attributed a nodal function to the temporality of birth in her ideas about freedom: it is because men are *born* "strangers" and "ephemeral" that freedom – which is the very possibility of starting anew – can be given its ontological foundation. "This freedom... is identical with the fact that men *are* because they are born, that each of them is a new beginning, begins, in a way, a new world." In contrast, Terror eliminates "the very source of freedom which man receives from the fact of his birth and which resides in the fact of his capacity of being a new beginning." Arendt did not deny that the temporality of concern and the temporality of death made an important contribution to the development of thought. But to these she adds her own reflections, inspired by St Augustine and Nietzsche, and enriched by her own experience of the twentieth century. These new conceptions are based on a new conception of time: of the time of new beginnings, of renewal.

Thanks to her analysis with Ferenczi and Abraham, the depressive Melanie Klein was born again into a new existence as a psychoanalyst. Moreover, by renouncing the German language and seeking new theoretical inspiration in English, in the context of British psychoanalysis, she reinforced the counter-transferential involvement of the analyst. This was one of her most important findings. Some accused her of using suggestion, violence, of making intrusions into the malleable psyche of her young patients. There was no lack of criticism, some of it justified. But in reality, in her infantile fantasies, Melanie puts herself at the service of the child who comes to consult her. Thanks to this unconscious projection, but nevertheless remaining sensitive to the patient's intimacy, she manages to name the unnameable trauma of the other, to name it with the child's words. Freud practised transference and counter-transference without making explicit what he was doing, and it was the female disciples of Klein, not Melanie herself, who theorised the analyst's counter-transference. But it was Melanie who revealed the need for this projection at the source of the interpretation: by allowing the child in the analyst to be reborn, she creates the possibility for the child in each of us to re-emerge. And then it was Winnicot, another attentive critic of Klein, who considers analysis itself as a perpetual rebirth of the subject: beyond biological destiny and the weight of family, rebirth becomes possible for each one of us. Freud left us a conception of the unconscious as atemporal, *zeitlos*. Through the play of transfer and counter-transfer, Klein and the post-Kleinians offer us a new conception of the temporality of analysis, as new beginning, as rebirth.

Colette avoids dwelling on the inevitability of death, and prefers to celebrate birth with Sido (and she frequently uses the image of *hatching*): "All my life, I've been interested in birth, and more so than in any other manifestation of life. That's where the essential drama of existence is situated, to a far greater degree than in death, which is no more than a banal defeat." The blooming of a cactus rose, the budding of plants and the birth of children: this woman, who was herself far from being a model mother, found in writing also, and above all in writing, this rhythm which she made her own. This is the rhythm of the infinite (in the sense of the French *in-fini*, that which is never finished), of new beginnings: "To metamorphose, to reconstruct oneself, to be born again, have never been beyond my powers."

Whether or not it is founded on the experience of menstrual cycles or of maternity, this temporality which breaks with linear time and the headlong rush of desire-unto-death also seems to resonate with female psycho-sexuality.

From the primary to the secondary Oedipus complex, as we noted, a woman follows a complex trajectory of changes of positions and of objects: passivisation, receptivity, aggression, possession – from the mother to the father, from the sensitive to the signifiable, from the anal and the vaginal and to the phallic, from the internal object to the external object. She follows this path, once again, in the perpetual Oedipus complex which never seems to end for the female subject, an episode which is never closed but which becomes calmer, less passionate through the experience of maternity, friendship, and union with nature … Might it be then that the bi-facial Oedipus complex is the source of this insistence on the rhythm of renewal, as against the linear time of the realisation of destiny?

Let me recapitulate the characteristics which are shared by our three geniuses: the permanent nature of attachments and of the object; a desire to safeguard the life of thought because life is thought; and an emphasis on the temporality of birth and rebirth. We could no doubt add other characteristics, which would be more or less convincing. The fact that we can associate them with certain constants of feminine psycho-sexuality does not mean that they cannot also be found in the works of many male authors – psychical bisexuality being common to both sexes. Besides which, in the course of my study of Arendt, Klein and Colette, we have seen the extent to which their achievements are a result of their "mental hermaphroditism" to use Colette's expression, and how it would have been impossible for them, without a sort of phallic affirmation, to express their uniqueness.

However, beyond these common features, but also in and of themselves, what has interested me during the time I have spent with these three women was, I would like to repeat, not what they have in common with all women, but how each of them, against this shared background, managed to negotiate an original and unprecedented advance.

By paying particular attention to sexual difference, my investigation of female genius has led me, in short, to go beyond the dichotomy of the sexes, to distance myself from the initial presupposition of a binary sexual system. This has been made possible not only because psychical bisexuality seemed to me to be a fact which applies to both sexes, with the dominant factor varying between sexes and between individuals. Nor is it possible just because each individually-constructed sexual identity deviates from some standard. These factors are relevant, but finally and most importantly, what allows us to overcome the traditional, binary model of sexuality is the fact that creativity, when developed to the full in genius, pushes this deviation from the standard to its furthest limit and to the highest degree of uniqueness, which is *nevertheless* something that can be shared. At the heart of the precarious solitude of their pioneering work, which was the price they paid for their unique creativity, Arendt, Klein and Colette managed to create the conditions which give rise to a necessarily public opinion, and, why not, a school, and, at best, to create an effect of seduction which solicits a communion of readings and a community of readers.

The sexual, social and political liberation of women and their entry into various intellectual and professional domains in the modern polity raises the question of their equality or their difference with regard to men. This was the central question of the twentieth century. However, the third millennium will be the millennium of individual opportunities, or it will not be (here I'm making an allusion to André Malraux, who famously said that the twentieth century would be a spiritual century, or would not be. I've tried, with my three-volume study, to go beyond the well-worn approach to these questions, which sought to define fixed sexual identities. And, beyond the sexual polymorphism which is already appearing in the global era – to the extent that it is raising questions concerning not only our identity but also the idea of the couple and of natural procreation – I would like to think that each individual invents his or her sex in the domain of intimacy: therein lies genius, which is quite simply creativity.

So, is there a feminine genius? The example of twentieth century women has made it difficult to avoid the question. And it has led us to consider that the anxiety over the feminine has been the communal experience which has allowed our civilisation to reveal, in a new way, the incommensurability of the individual. This incommensurability is rooted in sexual experience but nonetheless is realized through the risks that each of us is prepared to take by calling into question thought, language, one's own age and any identity which resides in them. You are a genius to the extent that you are able to challenge the socio-historical conditions of your identity. This is the legacy of Arendt, Klein and Colette that I'd like to share with you.

This address was delivered at Trinity College, Dublin on 31 May 2004.

Julia Kristeva was born and raised in Bulgaria and emigrated to France in 1965, when she was 24. One of her adopted country's best-known intellectuals and feminists, she is the author of nearly 30 books, mainly on semiotics, psychoanalysis and literature. Her most recent volumes are Murder in Byzantium *(2004), a detective novel, and* Female Genius *(2004), a study of Hannah Arendt, Melanie Klein and the French writer Colette. She is a professor at the Sorbonne University, Paris, and a visiting professor at Columbia University, New York.*

THE VIEW FROM THE GLEN

Cathal Ó Searcaigh

The small stream.

In the past it was customary for Irish language writers to be grumpy. They felt marginalized, left out of things. Some disorder or other in the make-up of their metabolism, perhaps, or some collapse in the set-up of their imagination made them become losers. The health food of recognition, when occasionally it came their way, only made them unhealthier. Everything around them seemed to droop and decay. If they had an artificial flower it would surely lose its lustre and die. Roger McCough in a succinct little poem titled "Missed" seems to allude to them in all their groggy hopelessness: "Out of work/divorced/usually pissed/they aimed low in life/and missed." I'm glad to be of a much more upbeat, optimistic generation of Irish language writers. As a result of our extravagant positiveness we have moved from the margins to the centre page of popularity. We are no longer the footnotes. We have become the centrefold of notoriety.

We are gods in exile. We have, I believe, the potential to empower ourselves, to be creators of our own cosmos. In the early nineties, I had a rare experience of that kind of heart-swelling ebullience at an Altan concert in Milwaukee. It was an open-air extravaganza with many great groups performing, but Altan with their predominantly Gaelic repertoire stole the show. Introducing their songs and their tunes in Gaelic they showed an unflinching belief that the Irish language was dashingly cool and daringly hip. As I cast an eye around that vast assortment of people, I could see Shamrock-clad grandmothers from Boston stomping to the thrill and throb of a *strathspey* and ageing Finn McCool hipsters from San Francisco, but with very little hair to hold the proverbial Scott McKenzie flower, all lilting that funky highway reel "The Glen Road to Carrick". I got talking to a red-headed black man from the Mississippi Delta who had a passion for "old motha Ireland and Shane-nose singin', man". Under the pull and power of Altan that huge crowd became one and I could hear a reeling chorus of heartbeats proclaiming joyously that they were Gaelic to the innermost boglands of their soul.

That swinging two-hour Gaeltacht created by Altan that night on the shores of Lake Michigan was, for me, a positive experience. It reinforced my belief that Gaelic, despite talk of its terminal decline, its low-status, marginalized existence, was still a language of awesome power. Hadn't Altan proved by their supercharged performance that they were sustained and nourished by its strength and vigour; that for them it was not an inert endowment from the past but a real source of vitality in the here and now of the present. After the concert was finished, I overheard someone use the term "ethno-futurism" to describe Altan's unabashed belief in their native tongue and their unflinching confidence in its musical culture. "Ethno-futurism" is, I suppose, about taking a spirited stance on one's own ethnic heritage; ensuring that a language and a way of life are given the chance to continue.

Over the past three decades, this corner of Gaelic-speaking Donegal, where I live, has produced an astounding wealth of musical virtuosity; artists who are affirmative about their native language. Many have become stars in the international music firmament. They blaze as brightly in California as they do in Cois Cladaigh or Caiseal na gCorr. Clannad, Altan, Enya are cherished in Detroit and Dubai as much as they are in Dore. Wherever in the world I find myself, I hear the otherworldly Gaelic music of these artists being played in public and private places. Whether it's in a ritzy restaurant on Siam Square in Bangkok, or in a goatherd's hut in a remote Himalayan Valley, that music knows no bounds, no borders, no barricades. Like light it's boundless in its capacity to cross over, to connect.

As a child growing up in the Gort a' Choirce area of North West Donegal in the fifties and sixties, the Irish language was the local community lingo but even then it was in crisis. I remember as a monolingual child of five being brought to the fair day in Falcarragh by my grandfather. Falcarragh, the commercial centre of the parish, is situated about six miles from my ancestral hill-farm in Mín a' Leá. We went there by bus. What a wondrous journey it was. My grandfather doting on me; the two of us chatting away in Irish. Strolling around in the bazaared dazzle of those fair-day streets I was baffled by my grandfather's speech. He spoke hesitantly and with great difficulty, I thought, in a strange cumbersome language. When I asked him what it was he squatted down beside me, took my small hands in his big knobbly hands, and spoke softly to me in Irish:

"Here we will have to speak English because they will think we're from the bogs."

"But aren't we from the bogs, granda," I piped up with childish innocence.

"You will have to learn English, a chroí, so that the bog can be sifted out of you."

I began to learn that day that with the colonic irrigation of English we could cleanse ourselves of the build-up of Irish in our gut. I also began to think that all Gaelic speakers were another branch of the Flintstones; a rather silly stone-age family; a goofy page right out of history. Mín a' Leá where I lived, meaning "the plain of flat stones", was, it seemed to me then, the most backward part of Bedrock. I certainly didn't want to be *yabba-dabba-doohing* in Gaelic. I didn't want to have any part in the future of our barmy Gaelic past.

I was getting the message clear and sharp that Irish was a spent force; a backward, anti-modern, parochial language, belonging to another time, another place; and to encourage in any way a widespread use of it would be a stupid isolationist act that would limit our possibilities, narrow our horizons. In the middle of the nineteenth century Daniel O'Connell, the Liberator, stated with enthusiastic assurance, "Although the Irish language is connected with many recollections that twine around the hearts of Irishmen, yet the superior utility of the English tongue as a medium of all modern communication is so great that I can witness without a sigh the gradual disuse of the Irish." Likewise the cynical post-colonial élite continued to discredit the language. For them it was an object of ridicule, the oafish tongue of the bogs. As a young boy I was picking up on all of this and getting the impression that my native language was inferior. I was conditioned to despise my language. It was the tongue of the dispossessed, the language of backwardness.

The Revivalists, many of them redneck fanatics, really added to my belief that the language was crass and dull. These smug, self-appointed defenders of language put a lot of people off Gaelic. The intimidating presence of these purists – linguistic McCarthyites who inspected your grammar, your syntax, your *blas* – made learners, especially, very self-conscious about speaking the language. Even I who was a native speaker, suffered from an acute tension in my tenses and, sometimes, a severe diarrhoea in my declensions, when these puritanical grammarians were present. When they scrutinised my vowel movements I become sexually awkward with my genitive case.

In my early teens I had a change of heart about the Irish language. The Muse of Poetry beckoned and led me back to Gaelic. She convinced me that I could be a tuned-in, cosmopolitan and still have strong roots in my *dúchas*. She opened a Gaelic doorway for me onto the world; a liberating doorway to life. She showed me a groovy, Gaelic Ireland that flourished, defiant and free, on the margins of English.

This change of heart happened in London. I became acutely aware of the word "home" while I was cruising around Piccadilly Circus, in the mid-seventies: "a hustle here, a hustle there, hey babe, take a walk on the wild side."

In the amped-up lingo of Lou Reed I was a thrill-seeking teenager, doing my best to be self-indulgently hip. But I was just a foppishly dressed yob from the backcountry.

I felt uneasy being funky and as a result I began to look into that terrible dark pool of the self; the *Duibheagán*, as I call it in Irish. At times like that, you realise you're an abyss, a pitch-black pit. There's only a deep darkness. You get dizzy looking down into the gulf, the chasm of yourself. You realise there's a deadening, deafening silence; that there are no answers. A poem became for me an act of defiance thrown in the face of that silence. I wrote in English, poems of adolescent angst, mostly. A poetry of pimples. I wrote bad poems because I didn't have the humility to read really great ones. Until one evening in the autumn of 1975 a man who worked in the storeroom of Oxford University Press walked into the pub where I worked and handed me a copy of Derek Mahon's latest collection, *The Snow Party*. That book had a profound effect on me, especially the first poem, called "Afterlives". Derek Mahon, a Belfastman, had gone to London at the beginning of the Northern Troubles and I think he felt it on his conscience that he hadn't accounted for these terrible times in his poetry. So "Afterlives" is a homecoming poem, in that Mahon came back to Belfast. The last verse was a real shock of recognition.

> But the hills are still the same
> grey blue above Belfast
> perhaps if I stayed behind
> and lived it bomb by bomb
> I might have grown up at last
> and learnt what is meant by home.

Home! The word just winged its way off the page. I felt the word as an intense desire to be reunited with something from which I felt I was cut off from. The word was a smell from another world, the last domain of my *dúchas*. *Dúchas* is a difficult word to explain in English, but briefly it means a connection, a feeling of attachment to a place, a tongue and a tradition, a belief that one belongs to a sustaining cultural and communal energy; that one has a place and a name. Suddenly I realised that I was in exile in an alien city where I neither had a face, nor a name or a place. To be an exile meant to be on my own. It meant to be without the community's sense of warmth and settledness. I had to return home to reclaim my heritage, my *dúchas*. And for me the *dúchas* is not a flight into the past, rather a rejoining of the past, the present and the future. It is a quest, perhaps for an expanded present which flows backwards and forwards with the one and same movement.

Home! The word was a discovery – but what is discovery, only what we remove the cover from. It has always been there – only hidden. I also realised that Irish was my emotional language, and not English. Intuitively, I knew more about the texture and the tone, the aura of words in Irish. The language inhabited my consciousness, perhaps, in a way that English didn't. From then on, I would write poetry in Irish. "She" would connect me to the vital creative energies of my *dúchas*. She would bring me back home.

The language linked me to a wellspring of tribal memories; an archive of ancestral experiences; a library of folk wisdom that was distinctly Gaelic. I felt that I belonged to something peculiarly enriching; something with its own irreplaceable value system. I was able to assert myself and withstand being absorbed and assimilated into whatever standard was being foisted on me from abroad. Oscar Wilde stated somewhere that "most people are other people. Their thoughts are someone else's opinions, their lives a mimicry, their passions a quotation." The Irish language enables me, I believe, to be uniquely myself. The language allows me to have a distinctively native viewpoint, my own radiant window of wonder onto the world.

I started learning English at the primary school. It was liberating becoming aware of two languages, two different ciphers to denote the same thing. How could *cnoc* be *hill*? I favoured *cnoc* because it sounded more rounded to me. It seemed to fit those bulbously plump swells that surrounded me. *Hill* seemed to me then to be slender, too blunt. It sounded more like an upthrust, a stone pillar. On the other hand I learned that fridge was called *cuisneoir* in Gaelic. We didn't have a fridge at home but I knew what it was from a shop in Gort a' Choirce. It was where they kept ice cream. *Fridge* was an ice-cold box that shut tight with a rubbery, sludgy, snap. *Cuisneoir* I'd never heard as a spoken word, a living word in the month of any local. When I asked somebody about it they said "ó sin gaeilge mhaide na leabhar". It was a school word and, because of my distaste for school, a dead word. Now I am very fond of *cuisneoir*. It's an apt evocation of the fridge in Gaeilge. It comes from the word *cuisne*, meaning frosty or cold-haze. It's the kind of linguistic adaptability I admire. Using a root word in Gaelic and extending and enlarging its meanings, its *brí*. *Brí* in Irish signifies "meaning" but also means strength and vigour. In short, having two languages enabled me to see the world through two different lenses. I came later to realise that each lens was tilted differently. It became apparent that Gaelic allowed me to see the world in emotional close-up while English provided, for me, a conceptual wide-shot of the world.

Donegal, where I live, is geographically in the North but politically in the

South. Personally I like its sort of indeterminate, borderland position. These sorts of places tend to be enigmatic and ambiguous; places where different ideas, different identities, different histories, meet and challenge each other. These places are frontiers. From here we can develop new approaches, explore unknown territories of the imagination. Donegal artists like Brian Friel, Frank McGuinness, Altán and Clannad have all drawn inspiration from the country's frontier-like location. It has conditioned how they have reshaped and renewed the tradition.

I myself live in an area where the interaction between Gaelic and English is most challenging. It's a linguistic borderland. As Gaelic-speakers we are adapting and absorbing, aligning our language to the needs and nuances of our time. We listen to sean-nós singing on ghetto-blasters made in Japan. We tell stories around our German radiators. You may be a highly esteemed traditional singer totally tapped into the *dúchas* and yet live in a mock-Tudor-thatched cottage-hacienda. A friend of mine has a libidinous tomcat called *Pangur Bán*, shaggy from too many prowling erection-packed nights. Another friend had a little soulful-looking mini-car called *An Bonnán Buí*. In my oriental draped kitchen I sometimes sing "Caoineadh na dTri Muire" to the air of "Lady Madonna". Lovely outrageous ways of repossessing the tradition and breathing new life into it. Traditionalists, who are cocooned in the past, are always fearful of the bold, risk-taking adventure of the present. As Gaelic-speakers we have to adopt new strategies for the survival of our language in a changing society – adapt ourselves to the multiple cultural realities around us. All the recent statistical studies show that the Gaeltacht, the historical heartland of Gaelic, is in a state of decline. Personally, I'm inclined nowadays to see the Gaeltacht as a fragmented entity; geographically dispersed across the globe. It is wherever people come together to speak Gaelic: a gay bar in the Greenwich Village of Gaoth Dobhair; a shopping mall in the Bay Area of San Falcarragh; a *seán-nós* singing class in the Muicíneach-Idir-Dhá-Sháile of Monte Carlo; a St. John's *tine chnámh* in the Ceathrú Thaídhg of Chicago.

Change is of course a crucial aspect of "life". We live in a flux and ferment where being is eternally in a state of becoming. Consequently, culture is never a fixed, immutable entity – something finished once and for all – that we inherit and preserve. The notion that Gaelic culture stands motionless in time, perfectly transfixed in the past, is a common belief in our country. I am not at all interested in this myopic view of culture. I'm interested in the creative and transformative possibilities of culture; its abilities to renew itself, to develop and evolve. To be fluid and dynamic, futuristic and forward-looking. Too often we become mesmerised by the past instead of paying attention to the present.

It's like driving a car and looking out the rear view mirror instead of the windshield. A deadly practice.

At present, we are expecting convulsions of change in our society; a shifting of boundaries and a reshaping of identities. With increased migration to our shores, we are living in a state of cultural multiplicity, of linguistic diversity; of inevitable hybridity. A time of wandering borders and an overlapping of cultures where it's no longer credible to believe in a single unified identify. Making claims for a pure identity can, as we know too well, create an aggressive polarity between people and lead to a vicious politics of intolerance.

Until recently the feet of many Chinese girls were bound up horrendously to hinder their natural growth. A deeply ingrained cultural perception led to the belief that deformed feet were objects of exquisite beauty. Likewise, living exclusively within a particular ethnic identify can lead to a distorted condition of the mind that skews the vision and warps the outlook. It is necessary to break out of these imposed constructs and establish more relaxed parameters for ourselves.

It is healthy to open up to uniqueness and the strangeness of other cultures, other ethnic perspectives. We are enriched by their differences, by their diversity.

As Gaelic-speakers we have to channel the potential and harness the energies of the great rainbow river of culture that is sweeping through our lives. Our great challenge is how to avail of the power of the mainstream, in order to maintain our own small stream.

This essay was written in English.

CRANN NA TEANGA

Tchím an tír sin aríst. Fearann teann na haislinge.
Tír ghlasodhar na gcnoc ansiúd idir anfa an tsaoil
   agus aghaidh na síoraíocht. Ríocht rúin m'óige.

Ansiúd bhí teangaidh feasa againn, teanga fáistíne
a tháinig anuas chugainn go beo ó bhéal gintlí na ndúl.
   Teangaidh rachtúil ó thús tintrí na cruinne.

Ansiúd tuigeadh dúinn urlabhra dúr an bhroic
agus teangaidh chábach na gcág. Labhair muid leis an lom.
   Rinne muid ár gcomhrá go binnghlórach leis na cnoic.

Ariamh anall bhí crann ann. Crann spéiriúil na sí.
Ba é an crann a bheathaigh ár dteangaidh, a deireadh na saoithe,
   a thug brí di, a chuir ag ceol i gcanúintí í.

Bhí siollaí ina nduilleoga silteacha ag fás air.
Bhláthaigh briathra síorghlasa ar a ghéaga spreagtha,
   I dtólamh bhí sé trom le toradh méith na meafar.

Sheas ár mbile buaice, crann glas an tsanais
ar an bhlár i gceartlár ár mbeatha. Sheas sé go galánta
   idir sliabh an tsolais agus mín réidh an tsuaimhnis.

Tchím an tír sin aríst. Ansiúd a saolaíodh mé
ar bhuaile gréine na bé idir an sliabh geal agus an crann glas.
   Ba iadsan a bhorr an briathar i mbéal mo chléibhe.

Ansin tháinig an anachain orainn, an doineann.
Shearg ár gcrann. Dhorchaigh an sliabh. D'fheall ar ár dteangaidh.
   Bhalbhaigh sí inár mbéal go tobann.

An teangaidh ghlanghuthach a bheathaigh gach beo
i mbithchríoch ár mbeatha; a d'anamaigh gach dúil;
   dhreoigh an smior ina cnámha craobhacha go deo.

Ní raibh mo dhaoine in ann a gcomhrá a dhéanamh
leis na feithidí ná leis na féileacáin; le hainmhithe ná le haingle.
Chúlaigh siadsan isteach i dtír an doichill, ár séanadh.

Fuaraíodh ár dteanga in oighear ré tosta.
Bhí muid caillte, conáilte. Las muid tinidh i dteach ár sinsear;
beochán beag de bhriathra dearga,

a bhí i dtaiscidh againn i gclúid na cuimhne.
Chruinnigh muid timpeall ár dtéamh féin ar chipíní gramadaí,
ar bhrosna na bhfocal go béal maidne.

Tchím an tír sin aríst. Ár gcrann gan lúth;
an bás ina sheasamh istigh ann; a theanga dhuilliúrach
titithe i dtost, an bhrí ar shiúl as a ghuth.

Don Uachtarán Máire Mhic Giolla Íosa

TREE OF THE TONGUE

I see that country again. The solid land of vision.
The greyish brown country of the hills yonder between the storm of life
and the face of eternity. The secret kingdom of my youth.

Over there we had a language of knowledge, a tongue of prophecy
that came down alive to us from the gentile mouth of the elements.
A passionate tongue from the fiery beginning of the universe.

Yonder we came to understand the surly speech of the badger
and the chattering tongue of the jackdaws. We spoke to the wilderness.
We made sweet-voiced conversation with the hills.

There had always been a tree there. The airy tree of the fairy mound.
It was the tree that nourished our tongue, the sages would say,
that gave it meaning, that sent it singing in dialects.

Syllables were dripping leaves growing on it.
Evergreen verbs blossomed on its inspired branches.
Always it was pregnant with the fertile fruit of metaphors.

Our roof-tree stood, the green tree of special learning
on the open field in the heart of our life. It stood gallantly
between the mountain of light and the smooth pasture of tranquillity.

I see that country again. Over there I was born
on the sunny pasture of the muse between the bright mountain
                                        and the green tree.
It was they that sprung the words in the mouth of my bosom.

Then the calamity came on us, the storm.
Our tree withered. The mountain darkened. Our language failed.
She became dumb suddenly in our mouth....

The clear-voiced tongue that nurtured every living thing
in the eternal region of our life; that animated every element;
the marrow in her branching bones decayed forever.

My people couldn't talk to each other
to the insects or the butterflies; to the animals or the angels.
These retreated to the land of hostility, denying us.

Our tongue was frozen in the ice of a silent age.
We were lost, perished. We lit a fire in the house of our ancestors,
a little flame of glowing words,

that we had saved in the nook of memory.
We gathered round warming ourselves with twigs of grammar,
with kindling words until break of day.

I see that country again. Our tree without vigour;
death standing inside it; its leafy tongue
fallen into silence, the strength gone from its voice.

for President Mary McAleese

Translated, from the Irish, by the Managing Editor.

Cathal Ó Searcaigh is the Irish Language Editor of this journal. His most recent volumes are Ag Trúth Leis an tSolas *(Cló Iar-Chonnachta, 2000), a collection of poems, and* Séal i Neipeal *(Cló Iar-Chonnachta, 2004), an account of his time in Nepal.*

THE Ó CADHAIN LECTURE 2003

———

Nuala Ní Dhomhnaill

Unalive beings and things that don't exist.

A few years ago when the writer and publisher, Micheál Ó Conghaile, gave this lecture, he said he was in two minds about it. He'd much prefer, he said, to write or at least attempt a short story, should it never be completed.

I am in the exact same position. Every time I'd sit down to try and write the lecture, I'd start to write a poem. Something I can't be faulted for in a way, because I well know that the Muse shouldn't be rejected, whenever she happens along. You could be quite a while longer seeking inspiration that would never come. However, a lecture has to be delivered …

In this lecture I will try to describe one of the things that has given me most enjoyment and pleasure as a person and the best literary matter as a poet – i.e., this country's folklore and, in particular, the folklore of Corca Dhuibhne.

I have always been interested in folklore, although at first I couldn't have given it such a highfalutin name. It was simply little stories interwoven as warp and woof throughout the speech when I was a little five-year-old exile over in my Aunt Máire's house in Cathair an Treanntaigh in Ventry parish in the mid-fifties.

Small things that happened from day to day that would be associated with an old story or some unusual reference. Like the day, a few years later, when I was a young girl and I happened to be walking up the Cathair road in a silk dress made of two strips of material that I had sewn together and sewn a hem around the bottom of – the only attempt, and the last one, at sewing I had ever made

"O", said John Sé, a cousin of my Grandad, whom I met on the road, "I like your dress."

"Yes," I said with sheer pride, "it's silk."

"Isn't it well I know it," said John Sé. "There was so much silk came into that cliff over there they call it Faill a' tSíoda (The Cliff of Silk), that the people of parish tied up the animals with it. 'Bhí leaincaisí síoda faoi chaoire na Cathrach (The Cathair sheep were spancelled with silk)', as the poet said" – a sentence that would stay in my head forever and would leap out at me when I'd be writing a poem years later.

Not only that but my aunt's husband Tomás Ó Murchú or Thomas Murphy as he was better known, was in our house. Here was a man very knowledgeable about his own parish, not only that but about the lore of the seven parishes west of Dingle.

I heard him one night later on in Dónal Ó Catháin's, when Breandán Mac Gearailt had assembled Oireachtas na nGael in An Buailtín. Máirtín Ó Cadhain was among those present. A dispute arose between Tomás and Art Ó Beoláin about the site and building of Carraig chapel.

"It's built on the Carraig (Rock)," said Art.

"Devil the bit," said Thomas, "it's on the Bóthar Buí (the yellow road)."

"It's built on the Carraig," said Art again.

"Who told you that?" said Thomas.

"Didn't I read it? It's written in the book."

"O," said Thomas, "whoever wrote that book, wrote the devil of a lie!"

"There's no limit," said Máirtin Ó Cadhain, "there's no limit to the real native speaker."

Around this time I gave Thomas a copy of the book *Romantic Hidden Kerry*. A few days later I went to see him.

"Well, Thomas, what do you think of the book?"

"It's not bad," said he, "it goes back two hundred years. That's not bad but I'd go four for you."

It wasn't an exaggeration entirely because he knew that it was a shot from a big gun from a vessel out in Dingle Bay that had swept the head off the Trant castle which was in the townland, instead of felling it from a boat from Ventry harbour, as one would have expected. There wasn't even a stone on top of a stone of that castle left for hundreds of years. Maybe it was in the time of Dún an Óir, or at the latest during the Cromwellian wars that the castle was destroyed. There hadn't been anyone of the Trant race on the Corca Dhuibhne peninsula for a long time, although there are three townlands in Ventry parish called after them and the name is common enough in north Kerry. Unlike their fellow Normans, the Ferriters, the Rices, the Fitzgeralds and the Husseys, they didn't survive on the peninsula.

Thomas could go back seven generations of his own ancestors; he had all their names and knew much about their lives. He used to say that his own grandfather was born in Cuan Uachtar, a townland that survived the potato blight during the Great Hunger. It was of little benefit to the tenants, however, because the townland and two other townlands on the Cuan, Cuan Íochtar and the Cúilín Bán, were cleared in the year 1867 by a land steward of Lord Ventry, a Cork man called Leahy. Thomas used always to say that his grandfather was eleven when they were put out of Cuan. Many of the tenants went to America or west to Fán or into the Great Blasket or were scattered throughout the district. Some of them came to Cathair.

"How did they manage to get possession of this place in Cathair?" said I.

"Because the place was empty," said he, "the birds had flown."

He knew how the chapel had been moved into Ventry parish from its old spot over in the east of the parish, where the school is now, to a site on Imleach Shlat bestowed by the Shea family of Imleach. His granduncle Micheál, who died tragically just after he went to America, was the last person to have public prayers said for him in the old chapel, and his aunt was the first person to be baptised in the new chapel. He knew of my own people, information you would prefer not to hear, at times. "Sulky Léan of the scaldcrow eye," he used to call my great-grandmother, Léan Ní Chearna, whom I was supposed to be like. When I was taking a further interest in Irish as a young girl, I picked up this lore mostly from him, but my memories of him and of other old-timers go back much further than that. They were full of argument and sarcasm and it was no bother to them to take you down a peg if they so wished. "Leá bumbóire, nó leá mún Móire ort" was often their prayer, or curse I should say, and "How would you know, it's not that you know the Reason for Everything", was also a saying of theirs. But my memory of them goes farther back than that, to the time I spent with them as a little five-year-old orphan across from England. I remember that at this time Johnny Long and his son Mike were looking after the farm next door and that Jacksey Sé and his sister Nell were in the house above that in the townland. John Sé's house was at the top of the townland and the pump that they had in the yard was said to always be sure not to run dry in summer. Each man of them would stand on top of his own compost heap and he'd throw backchat at the other man. I don't remember any one particular sentence they said but I well remember how poetical and intelligent their talk was. Was it any wonder, so, that when I began my first poems, it was on this level of language I set out:

MÓR ANGUISHED

Mór firmly under lock and key
in her own tiny mind
(3" x 4" x 2")
of grey, pinkish stuff

(here be the wounds
that drown the flies
while other flies survive
to make their maggots
on the carrion fringe).

"Listen, in God's name," she begs
the magpies and the crows
that come at evening
to upset their guts,
"everyone's enclosed
in their own tiny hells."

The small birds scatter and spread
when she flings up at them
a sod of earth ...

translated by Michael Hartnett

There were other people in the townland at the time who had a wonderful gift of language. As well as being native speakers they were good speakers. The best Gaelic speaker of them all, Tomás Mháiréad (Ó Sé), had been dead since 1956, just a year before I arrived in Cathair. He was the last monoglot speaker in the parish. He was reputed to have no English. I'm not saying that I ever believed that entirely:

"How could he have no English, living in this townland, where there were coastguards for over a hundred years?"

"Because he didn't consort with them. He didn't go among them."

Perhaps there was a strong hint of politics there as well. He was among those at the first meeting of the Land League during the Land Wars, a meeting held in curraghs in the middle of the harbour (some 200 of them) when Lord Ventry wouldn't allow it to be held on land. His people were called the Parnells for many a day.

But if he wasn't there, there were many others there: Fitzie and John Sé and Jacksey and his sister Nell, and Joeen, and Annie Sheehy and her brother Jackie, and Johnny Long and his son Mike Long of Cathair. They were there in profusion, and if I say it again, well-spoken.

But other things happened in my life and I cleared off out of the country as soon as I possibly could. After spending seven years overseas, especially in Holland and Turkey, I came to realise that what I wanted to do most in the world was to return to Ireland and to get down to writing full-time, if I could at all. I applied for an Arts Council bursary and got it, which brought me and my two children home and I settled into our family summer home in Cathair an Treanntaigh. The children were called the "White Turkeys" because they were so fair. "Nuala and the White Turkeys" was a common saying at the time.

I was busy with many things at the time: a novel that got the better of me, a collection of short stories that I finished but which were never published, but above all else I laid into poetry. My husband hadn't returned to us yet and I was very lonely in the house on my own when the children were asleep, looking out at Ventry shore and the tide ebbed. If I was, it was in terms of folklore that I expressed myself, drawing on the "persona" of the Mermaid:

Though I've got a fishes tail
I'm not unbeautiful.
My hair is long and yellow
and there's a shine from my scales
you won't see on landlocked women.
Their eyes are like the stones
but look into these eyes of mine
and you will see the sturgeon
and you will see fine seals
gambolling in my pupils.

Not without pain
have I landed:
I broke
the natural law.
I swapped swimming
for walking on earth,
picking my steps
like a curlew.
Believe you me
it was love, not God,
who gave the order.

You left
and took my magic cap.
It's not as easy to get back
in the roof's rafters

as it was in the fable.
I dug to the subsoil
and saw no sign of it.
The tide also fails us
and a rat
gnaws at the very sun.

translated by Michael Hartnett

It was about the same time that Seán Ó Tuama introduced me to Joe Daly and the Bab Feirtéar. I often went to see them and they were very good to me. They were great company: the Bab in her own house, a blazing fire in the hearth and cups of tea going round and Joe with his wife Peig in their house or in Dónall Ó Catháin's house in An Buailtín. I remember at the time that I recorded a few tapes of the Bab telling stories and that I'd play them to myself in bed until I'd fall asleep. It's no exaggeration to say that they influenced me greatly. Not only did they give me the titles and frame stories for my first two books of poetry but they taught me also how to express myself by changing the circumstances of my own life and transforming the raw material of feeling, to make it a thing more universal than small personal events of my own life, or too personal things concerning my own life alone. The stories helped me to tell the truth but to put a slant on it, as Emily Dickinson once suggested – "tell the truth, but tell it slant" – and to say things I couldn't say out straight. An example of this approach is the poem "Féar Suaithinseach" (Marvellous Grass), the title-poem of my second collection. The first time I recorded it, the Bab gave me a version on which I based the poem. The tape wasn't long recorded, however, when my sister destroyed it by taping pop music on it, as though it were a blank tape because there was nothing on it but talk! I went back to the Bab and got another and another version but they were all different from the version on which the poem was based. As it happens she never again told it as I first remember it: saying that the priest grasped the sacred host "go haiclí' (dextrously)". I wanted that particular expression above any other. The version I used eventually as an introduction to the book was a version I got from Professor Bo Almquist, a version recorded and then transcribed by Dr Ríonach Uí Ógáin.

By the time this happened other great changes had occurred in my life. We had just spent three years in Corca Dhuibhne. One of those years my husband was working in Dublin, returning to Corca Dhuibhne every second weekend. We appreciated that the journey was too onerous for him and that we'd have to move to Dublin. It was a horrible struggle for me to leave the western coast and for long I was very homesick for the Gaeltacht. Indeed, I was forever playing Raidió na Gaeltachta, and for a number of years after that I'd do a bit of a programme with Mike Shea on local history, especially from what I was reading in the Department of Folklore. But it was Joe Daly that directed my feet towards the Department the first day. He told me to go in there, that it would do me good, and he said to me "see all that you'll see".

First I went searching for my own people. I began of course with Thomas Murphy. And he was there. Three of his stories had been collected. A story about the greatest wonder, a story about the boy and the holy pictures, and the beginning of a certain story "an Luch is an Dreoilín" (the Mouse and the Wren). Joe had told me that that story would be there. It's a story that's in the Seanchaí Muimhneach (Munster Seanchaí), collected by Pádraig Ó Siochfhradha, better known as "An Seabhac" (The Hawk), at the beginning of the last century. By the time Joe was collecting in the thirties and forties it no longer remained in the memory or mouth of the people. He had found parts of the story here and there and no one knew the beginning. He came south to Cathair an Treanntaigh purposely to collect the story as he had heard that maybe it was there. Thomas had it. According to the account at the beginning of the story, he heard it from his mother some twenty years before that. He himself is said to be a farmer's son, twenty-eight years of age. That was true because he hadn't yet received the land from his father. But that same father, Peats Ó Murchú, was the greatest gem I discovered. I had already heard much about Peats, as he had been a very well-spoken man and phrases of his were still being recited by people during my own time. For example, his son Tomás, was born on a night of snow so that he was called ever after "Tomáisín an tSneachta" (Little Tomás of the Snow). Early next morning Peats went away off walking up over Mám na Gaoithe (The Windy Gap) towards the Leataithe road, heading north for Cathair Deargáin, where his wife, Cáit Foley, came from. It was a snowy day, Little Christmas Day, and my Gran was a little girl in Leataoibh Meánach pelting snowballs at her friends. He was accosted. "Anything new, Peats?" "Yes," says he, "I have a son since last night, the makings of a giant. Bones of a young horse under him, and he'll never catch cold." The second part of his statement was true because Thomas always had good health and he came unscathed through the Big Flu of the year '18, when three coffins – two of his uncles and a brother – were carried out of the house inside a fortnight. There wasn't the same prophetic quality in the first part of the sentence, however, for although he was fast and athletic until his old age, he was far from being a giant, so that he always thought highly of good physique. "There's nothing like it," he'd say. She little thought, my Gran would often say afterwards, that she herself would grow up, she'd have a baby daughter, and that daughter would marry that child from last night. Another utterance that stayed in people's memory was his anger with some man who began arguing with him at Dingle fair. "The cheek of you," said he, "for a man with nothing to his name but two auld broken-down knacks to be talking against a man with the grass of eight cows, and that, in a city," referring to himself and very proud of himself.

But it wasn't until I saw all the material Joe Daly collected from him that I understood how excellent a seanchaí Peats was. He had the long Fenian cycle stories: a story about Balor of the Blows, a story of Fionn and the King of Athadonáis. Not only that but he had the formulaic "runs" of the battles. The battle array of the hero, the battle array of the ship, the battle array of the sea.

For a while, then, the "runs" went to my head:

> "Which would you prefer," said the giant, "hard fierce wrestling or to strike above and below each other's ribs with sharp shining swords?"
> "I'd prefer hard fierce wrestling for that's what I practised on the playing fields along with the noble children."
> They set about each other, they struck a blow above and a blow below and a blow in the height of the wrestling on each other and the person who would come from the bottom to the top of the world to watch two wrestlers it's these two he should come to see. They'd make soft land of hard land, hollows of heights and heights of hollows. They'd bring springs of fresh water through the heart of the grey stones and up through the hard stony soil and the clods that shot from their feet, they'd take three teeth from the hag sitting in London city reddening her pipe, and those three teeth wouldn't stop through bogs and mountains until they'd knock down three castles in the Eastern World.

I learned all this by heart. A kind of madness gripped me. I went from seanchaí to seanchaí examining the different versions of the battle array. Peats a' tSaoir 'ac Loinsigh from Bhaile an tSléibhe had the best arrays. As a young man down in Ard a' Bhóthair he had given stories to the American collector, Jeremiah Curtin. The stories were in Irish but his father had put English on them for Curtin. But Peats wasn't at all happy with the English version. When he was reciting them on the Edifon later for the collector Seán Ó Dúbhda he said:

> I was telling stories to Curtin and his wife who was writing and my father was putting English on the Irish for her. And a young man, a

farmer's son, bought one of the books and my stories were there and you wouldn't believe, they weren't written down properly at all. The battle array wasn't there at all. They couldn't write the battle array.

Is it any wonder therefore that the poems I was writing at the time were full of battle arrays of different kinds? What came to my mind as I fed the baby, as I tried to describe the kind of world where the newly-born child lived – a world full of views and sounds that she couldn't yet distinguish from each other, that world of pre-symbolic sound, or the "chora" as the French feminist theorist, Julia Kristeva calls it:

Do you know day from night
that the great early ebb
announces spring tide?
That the boats
are on deep ocean,
where live the seals and fishes
and the great whales
and are coming hand over hand
each by seven oars manned?

That your small boats swims
óró in the bay
with the flippered peoples
and the small sea creatures
she slippery sleek
from stern to bow
stirring sea sand up
sinking sea foam down …
translated by Michael Hartnett

Other poems were also full of the battle arrays, poems like "The Race". What happened here was that I wanted to describe the zest and excitement of a mad session of driving up the country. I adopted the hero's battle array to express this.

Like a mad lion, like a wild bull,
a wild boar from a Fenian tale,
a hero bounding towards a giant
with a single silken crest,

I blindly drive the car
through the small towns of the west:
I drive the wind before me
and leave the wind behind.

Arrow from bow, bullet from gun.
Sparrow hawk through flock of small March birds
I scatter miles of road behind.
Figures flash on signposts –
but in kilometres or miles?
Nenagh, Roscrea, Mountmellick
(but have I travelled through these towns?)
mere things that limit speed
mere things that slow me down.

Through geographic barricades
I rush and dart from the west
I gallop towards you where you wait
I speed to where you stand.
Heights are hollows, hollows heights
dry land is marsh, marsh is dry,
all contours from the map are gone:
nothing but shriek of brakes and sparks of light.

translated by Michael Hartnett

About this same time I came on a book: *Italian Folktales Selected and Retold by Italo Calvino*. This is an English translation of a collection of fairy tales translated originally by Italo Calvino from the different local Italian languages. I took a great interest in what he had to say in the foreword about what happened to him when he got caught in this world of fairy tales:

> To me it was a sheep's leap in the ocean. An ocean into which many people before me had jumped already, over some 150 years, not seeking novelty or the unusual thing in itself, but with a deep belief that there was some dark secret element lying on the sea bed, an element that had to be rescued for the sake of the language.

From what he wrote I realised that my own disease didn't just belong to me:

I leaped into this underground world without one spark of intellectual enthusiasm for anything spontaneous or rooted or original. It was a great cause of uneasiness for me to be immersed in a non-creative element, an element that was as slow and tedious as learning by rote, an element that couldn't be controlled consciously.

By this time I had deserted the battle arrays and the Fianna stories for fairy stories and other storytellers: Tomás (Mhárthain) Mac Gearailt, Tadhg Ó Guithín, Seán 'ac Gearailt from Márthan who was married in Gorta Dubh. ("Danger" was this man's nickname). Peig Sayers and her son Mike (the Poet) Ó Guithín, Domhnall Ó Mainín from Cill Uraidh (Domhnaillín of the Smoke) who gave Joe Daly the longest story he ever wrote, a story that took twelve nights to write down. Then there was Seán Ó Grífín from Cathair Boilg. This last man wasn't renowned as a storyteller in the community as he wouldn't be telling stories in public because of a touch of stammering. But he had spent his life in the house of Peats 'ac Loinsigh, listening to him carefully and learning every story: The Black Thief, Balor of the Blows, Cuid, Céad and Céatach, Farmer Shepherd of the Weather, etc. By the time Joe Daly was collecting stories Peats was dead but he discovered Seán Ó Grífín and he got all the stories from him. Those stories are wonderful. Again, perhaps it would do no harm to listen to Italo Calvino on the same subject:

> As I pursued the work, always picking up all the material at hand, sorting and cataloguing it, a kind of madness took hold of me, an excessive eagerness with no let up, to discover every kind of version and alternative version, of certain motifs. It was as if a fever had taken over me. I felt a passion in me as in an entomologist, so that I'd have been more than happy to give up all that Proust had written for one more version of the story "Shit Gold, Little Donkey". (The most widely-known Irish version of this story is called "Cac airgead, a chapaillín bháin".)

It gave me great mental satisfaction to know that another writer had gone through the same madness as myself. Not only that but had come out on the other side. Because it was this period that he spent afloat in the unconquerable ocean of folklore that changed greatly the form of Italo Calvino's writing. He left realism behind him and set his face on what is now called "metafiction," as in his remarkable novel *Once on a Winter's Night a Traveller*. It dispersed some of my confusion to see him describing the very thing that had happened to me. It was so close to my own experience that it seemed to me he had taken the words out of my mouth:

> For two years I lived in woods and castles bewitched, torn between the urge to reflect and the urge to act … During these two years the world around me adopted features of the fairy world and everything that happened was caused by magic or by some sleep charm or by metamorphoses of one kind or another. Nests of snakes opened under the soles of my feet and just as suddenly they became streams of milk and honey. Kings whom you thought faultless until then became ruthless parents. Kingdoms that were bewitched became alive again. It seemed to me that the forgotten rules of folklore life came falling head over heels out of the little magic box I had opened.

And again, he says:

> Now that I have finished the book, I appreciate that it wasn't delirium or fantasies that had caused me to affirm completely something about which I had doubted strongly before that: that is, that there's truth in fairytales.

I had happened on the same opinion independently, and my poems had changed from bottom to top.

As I continued researching, my interest was changing from one thing to another. After indulging in the battle arrays and the international motifs, I began taking an interest in the storytellers, and especially the women storytellers, people like Peig Sayers, Cáit Ruiséal and particularly Máire Ruiséal. I suppose I fell in love with Máire Ruiséal. Her approach wasn't at all like Peig Sayers. There is something almost baroque about Peig, little twists of rhetoric about her. She likes hard words or "rocks" and a word often reminds her of a story. For instance, when potatoes called "minions" are mentioned, she says: "It was the year of the minions when my father was in the house. A woman of the roads came into the house to him" … Away she went.

Máire Ruiséal has a very straight storytelling style, although she has battle arrays in her stories just like anyone else: "and the dew and lateness of evening was coming on her and the terrier sheltering under the dock leaf, the dock running away from him, and the fox going into his own den, no harm to the honest fox." There is one place in the middle of a story that I love, where she says in an aside to Joe Daly:

> "The king's children were out on the ... Joe, can I use the Engish word here?"
>
> "Say away," says Joe.
>
> "The king's children were out on the piazza..."

I'm very pleased to note that Eilís Ní Dhuibhne chose a story of Máire Ruiséal's for the chapter on "Oral Tradition" in the *Field Day Anthology*. She gives a story called "The Story of the Little White Goat," a fine example of a "feminine fairytale". It is a version of the old tale "Psyche and Amor". Commenting on what Vladimir Propp says about this story in his essay "Historical Roots of Russian Fairy Tales," Calvino says:

> Although the customs of millennia are disregarded, the plot of the story still reflects the spirit of those laws and describes every love thwarted and forbidden by law, convention or social disparity. That is why it has been possible, from prehistory to the present, to preserve, not as a fixed formula but as a flowing element, the sensuality so often underlying this love, evident in the ecstasy and frenzy of mysterious nocturnal embraces.

This sensual love may be felt in Máire Ruiséal's version of the story and, like Peig Sayers's storytelling, there is openness of mind there about human nature that you wouldn't expect, perhaps, judging by the usual reading of the woman storyteller as a national monument:

> They went into a fine court. He spoke to her then:
>
> "Muise, well now," said he, "which would you prefer now," said he, "that I be a goat by night and a man by day or a man by night and a goat by day?"
>
> "O indeed," said she, "I prefer the night company – you to be a man by night and a goat by day."
>
> That's how it was.

I noticed as I went into the Folklore Department that my interest changed. Recently it's the little bits of *seanchas* that interest me most, the little trivial tales that happened to people. Sheehy of Baile Eaglasta telling how many houses were knocked down in every townland during the Famine. Peats Dhónail (Ó

Cíobháin) of Muiríoch talking about fishing or about Tomás na bPúcaí, a relation of my own. He had one story about Tomás and I'd have to refute it. There were three young women who were pregnant at the same time in Leataoibh Meánach. Tomás na bPúcaí had the second sight, and he said there'd be a great tragedy in the townland but he wouldn't say which of the young women would be carried off. As it happened the woman who was taken was the woman most closely related to him, the wife of his sister's son. She died of puerperal fever after bringing a baby daughter into the world. "And," said Peats Dhónaill, "the young woman died shortly after that, and the daughter died as well." Well, the daughter didn't die. How do I know that? Because she was my grandmother, and if she hadn't survived, I wouldn't be here now.

I used another story about my people as a foreword to my last collection, *Cead Aighnis* (Leave to Speak):

A Person's Three Souls

I was in bed asleep down in Baile Móir and whatever it was that brought Eoghainín Finton out he saw me going out of the house. He called his wife, Léan Ní Chearna.

"Your soul to the devil, Léan," says he, "Seán's had a stroke or something! Look at him down the side of the house. Go out," says he, "and call him." But he saw me turning again and going into the house. But Léan didn't call me at all. But people were telling me next morning but I wouldn't believe Eoghainín at all if Léan hadn't said it. I told him I didn't leave the bed since I got into it until I left it in the morning, and I fast asleep.

"That is known to happen," said Léan, "and I remembered it. If I'd called him at that time," said Léan, "he'd have stayed there forever."

But I'm forever hearing that a person is in three parts. There is the breathing soul, the feeling soul and the eternal soul. The eternal soul will stay in you until you die. I wonder was it my breathing soul or my feeling soul that was outside as I slept. I wonder was it."

(from the oral account of Seán Ó Cíobháin, IFC Mss 965, page 63)

But to return to the story I mentioned at the beginning of this talk, about "The Cathair sheep were spancelled with silk." I was in the Folklore Department the other day and happened by chance upon more information about it. I had always understood that this was a mythological incident. It was a significant example, I thought, of people's poetic prowess and of the wonderful imaginative power always to be felt strongly in the language of Corca Dhuibhne. I had never dreamed that there was any historical basis for it, but indeed there is. A big sailing boat called *The Lady Nelson* was wrecked on the Sceilg full of wine pipes along with the silk. After this ship was wrecked the lighthouse at Sceilg was built.

> It was a foggy night and the captain was saying they were three leagues from any shore. Some of the crew disagreed and they were right, because it wasn't long before she hit the Sceilg. All in her were wrecked, drowned and crushed but three who climbed unto a plank of wood. Two or three days of mist and rain from the west and south followed and the pipes of wine were moving east. Boats were searching for them. Ventry Bay was full of boats and Cathair a' Treanntaigh. There was a man called Scainlin with a boat and crew back in the bay searching for the wine when they saw the wreckage well away from them and the men on top of it. There were two of them when they got to them. The other man had fallen into the water asleep a little while before. They lifted the two and saved them. That's all that survived. The survivors sent Scainlin and his crew a mast and two sails in thanks after that.

I've arrived at the end of my journey. I hope I've given you some insight into how important the folklore of Ireland is to me and especially the Folklore Commission collection.

I believe it works on two levels: first, the Irish language level, where it reminds me of the compactness and conciseness of language I heard people tossing across the fields at each other when I was a child. Then it works on the level of imagination, when the story motifs and even the snippets of *seanchas* scattered here and there throughout the manuscripts, bring me such marvellous imagery that I can play with them, sporting and cavorting, throwing them in the air and catching them again. And of course, that sporting is one of the most important necessities in creative work. One other thing I want to mention before I come to the end of my talk tonight, and it concerns the title of the talk "unalive beings and things that don't exist". Well, until recently I'd have sworn that there was such a title on one of the sections in the general catalogue of the Irish Folklore Commission, a catalogue compiled by one of the Department's founders, the collector Seán Ó Súilleabháin. But unfortunately, when I went looking for it for this talk, I couldn't find it. I searched and searched but could find no trace of it, which suggests that maybe it never was there and that I was hallucinating from start to finish. Such a thing could happen.

Another thing I'd like to mention, that I received a book in the post this morning, which meant it was too late to work it into the body of the text. It's a book by Gearóid Ó Crualaoich, *Leabhar na Caillí – The Book of the Cailleach: Stories of the Wise-Woman Healer*. There's a piece in the chapter "Tradition and Theory" that leapt to my eye immediately because Gearóid was saying what I've have trying to express in this lecture:

> The texts of the oral narrative presented in this book and the commentaries offered with them bear witness, hopefully, to the way that traditional material, frequently seen as outmoded, naïve, parochially-bound, can constitute a rich imaginative resource for our own times and our own circumstances in a world where the local and the global are intermeshing at an increased rate for greater numbers and in ways not previously imagined.

And that's the beginning and the end of my story – how we have such a wonderful resource in the oral traditions of Ireland, whether from the Department manuscripts here, or from the plain speech of good storytellers, like the two CDs from the Bab Feirtear issued last year and that were so much in demand that I believe they've sold out twice.

I have no interest in introducing ranges of language or models of literature, *per se*, into Irish; although I'll go search for a dictionary of science, physics or chemistry if I have to, for example, when I want to describe the natural phenomenon, the Northern Lights, I saw once when I visited Fairbanks, Alaska. But what I do want to do above all else is to supply something, through the natural resources of the language, that hadn't been there before in poetry, in any language. It's for that purpose that I continue rummaging in the Department of Folklore, and with the help of gods and demons, the unalive beings and the things that don't exist, I'll do that for whatever number of days I manage to live.

Translated, from the Irish, by the Managing Editor. This address was delivered at the Merriman Summer School, Milltown Malbay, Co Clare.

Nuala Ní Dhomhnaill was born in Lancashire, England in 1952 and grew up in Co Kerry. She was Ireland Professor of Poetry from 2001 to 2004. Her most recent volume of poetry is Cead Aighnis *(2001).*

SHORT STORY

—

Máirtín Ó Cadhain

The globe arrives … from the Irish Archive.

THE YEAR 1912

– The trunk.

She said the word offhand yet there was a touch of stubbornness in her tone. She hadn't agreed to go to Brightcity with her daughter a week ago last Saturday to buy the trunk, and it irked her like a white frost the way it had been perched up on the ledge of the kitchen dresser, adored like an idol. The children having great play with it, opening, closing it, looking it all over. She hadn't the heart to vex her daughter this final week, otherwise she would have cleared it off into the room under the bed. But tonight, though the daughter might be of a different mind and anxious to show off that expensive article to the company that had gathered, the mother had followed her own inclination at nightfall and moved the trunk into the room – it might, she said, get damaged or scratched where it was.

It was like a burnt spot or a smallpox scar on the face of life, tonight especially since she seldom had a hearty gathering under her roof. It was useful and wellmade, but that was only a chimaera, a ghost from the Otherworld come to snatch away the first conception of her womb and the spring of her daily life, just when the drinking, the high spirits, the music and merrymaking were in full spate. Seven weeks ago, before the passage-money came, she had been as much on edge awaiting it as Mairin was. That their daughter should be off to America was no surprise to her, no more than the eight sisters of her own whose going was a bitter memory still. She had been schooled by the iron necessities of life to keep a grip on her feelings and throttle her motherlove – as Eve ought to have throttled the serpent of Knowledge. It was the passage money that had set the heather ablaze again. Flickers of affection, flashes of insight from shutaway feelings, were setting her sense and reason aglow with the knowledge that this going into exile was worse than the spoiling of a church or the wreck of a countryside …

But it was destiny, must be attended to. The day was agreed. Patch

Thomais was gone for the sidecar. Back in the crowded kitchen the merriment had risen to a frenzy; remnants of the wreck of a people, doomed to extinction at daybreak, bringing their ritual vigil to a hurried night's-end climax of a wild debauch .

A halfpenny candle stood on a small press by the wall in the bedroom, smeared by a breeze coming by the edge of the paper on a broken windowpane. Depth, magic, mystery of unfathomable seas, reflected by the guttering candleflame in the trunk's brass knobs. It was of pale yellow timber, the mother couldn't at once remember where she had seen that colour before – the face of a corpse after a long wake in the sultry weather. And a certain distaste kept her from looking into the trunk, that same tabu which had kept her, though she had often tried, from looking at a corpse in a coffin.

– Have you everything? She asked the daughter keeping her eyes off the dimlit thing. There were all kinds of things in it – a sod of turf, a chip off the hearthstone, tresses of hair, a bunch of shamrock though it was autumn, stockings of homespun, a handful of dulse, items of clothing, papers connected with the voyage across. The daughter took her shoes, coat, hat and dress out of the trunk and laid them on the little press to put on her. During the week she had often laid them out like that but the mother had never encouraged her, and early in the night she had implored her not to put them on till morning.

The mother shut the trunk, threw the bedquilt over it. – To keep it clean. She had long feared that her daughter once she was in the American clothes would be estranged from her, alien as the trunk. Mairin was in her stocking feet and naked except for a long white shift which she had been at great pains to fix about herself that evening and which she had no intention of taking off until she had reached the house of a relative on the other side. Seeing her like that was to see a vision, the only one which had remained clearskinned and beautiful in her memory. A vision that gave bodily shape to the dear lost Tree of Life, while it made real the delicate and deceitful skin of the Knowledge-Apple – a mother's first conception, first fruit. She had so many things on the tip of her tongue to say to her, the intimacies, the affectionate things saved up in motherlove, her life-stuff, from the moment she feels the quick seed in her womb until the flush of eternity puts out the twilight of the world.

For a month now she had said many things to the daughter, scraps scatted at long intervals … that she couldn't care if all in the house were to go so long as Mairin stayed … that the whole house would miss her, herself especially … that of all her children she was the one who had given her the least trouble … that she was fine about a house. But none of all that said was what she wanted to say. She felt like a servingwoman, the necklace she was putting about the young queen's neck had broken, in precious stones scattered here and there in danger of being crushed and broken. She felt as if some hostile force were filtering her speech, hindering her from letting loose the flow of talk that would ease the tight grip on her heart. She was aware she could never hope to express the things in her in a letter which she would have to depend on someone else to write, and in a language whose make and meaning were as unhomely to her as the make and meaning of the Ghost from the Fairymound. And a letter was a poor substitute for the living contact of speech, eyes, features. Her flowing imagination, floodtide of her love, would run thin and freeze in a niggardly writing.

She was hardly likely to see her daughter again for a very long time. Mairin would have to repay her passage, then earn the passage of one or two more of the family, as well as send a share home. It could happen that the child in her womb would set eyes on her before she did. That American coat, the graveclothes – how tell one from the other? The "God speed her" that would be said from now on had for its undermeaning "God have mercy on her soul". Children often got those two expressions mixed up. And when the time came that in actual fact would change the "God speed" into "God have mercy," it would come without a decent laying-out and a bier to be carried, and with no passionate keen. Even the graveclothes, no mother would have them awhile to shake out the folds of them from time to time as a relief to her anguish, and there would be neither name nor surname on a rough bit of board in the churchyard by the Fiord for generations to come. The voyage – that immensity, cold and sterile – would erase the name from the genealogy of the race. She would go as the wildgeese go.

But while such ideas were as a sour curd in the mother's mind, she wouldn't give in to the thought that she would never see the daughter again. Her sense and reason said no, her love, hope, determination, said yes. And it was these she listened to. Yet even if she were to see her again she knew she'd be utterly unlike the simple country girl, now nineteen years old, with a look pure as morning sun on a hillside in the Promised Land. Her lips would have been embittered by the berries from the Tree of Good and Evil. That dark weasel envy in her heart. Experience, that slimy countenance. The tone of her voice transformed by the spell of a harsh stepmother. Such were all returned Americans. She must reveal herself to her now, as the mother of the warriors in the cave used to reveal herself to her children when every sallying out in search of food was a matter of life and death. Reveal herself to her while her age and ignorance were still unmocked at, while there was yet no wall of disbelief between her daughter's mind and hers ...

The money, she thought, was the best way to begin. She took a cloth purse from her bosom, took out small change the daughter might need in Brightcity, and gave her the purse with the rest. The daughter hung it about her neck and settled it carefully in her breast under her holy scapular.

– Look now child you take good care of it. It's likely you won't need it at all, but if you fail to find work soon it would be too much to be depending on Aunt Nora who has her own children to look after. Keep the rug tucked well round you on the vessel. Make free with no one unless it happens to be someone you know. You'll be safe as soon as your reach Nora's house. Even if you have to take small pay, don't overstrain yourself working …You will make a visit home after five years. Well, at least after ten years … It can't be but you'll have a few pence put by by then. My….

She had kept her spirits up to that. But as soon as she thought to break the crust of speech she couldn't find a word to say but stood stockstill staring at her daughter. Hands fiddling with the folds of her apron. Blushing, tears and smile painfully together in her cheek. Humps and wrinkles of distress coming in her forehead like keys struggling with a lock. The daughter was almost dressed by now and asked where was the small change she'd need in Brightcity? The mother had been so eager to talk that she had forgotten to get a little purse to put in it. Turning to get it she fell into such confusion she forgot the money in her fist until it fell and scattered about the floor. Her idea had been to wait till her tongue could contrive a proper speech, then to hand over the small change to the daughter as a sacred offering, embrace and kiss her … Instead, the sacrifice had been ripped from her hand.

Putting away the little purse the daughter felt an envelope in her pocket. —A tress of your hair, mama, she said. I thought I had put it in the trunk along with the rest. She held the black tress between her and the candle, her blue eyes softened, became childlike. She felt an urge to say something to her mother, she didn't quite know what. Her thoughts went fumbling here and there as a stranger might among the blind holes of a bog on a dark night. The pair of them would have to be in the one bed, the light out, and a wand of moonlight through the small window to charm and set free the tongue. She looked her mother in the eyes to see if she might find encouragement there, but she remained unconscious of her mother's seething emotions, locked within, quite unable to crack the fixed and rigid mask of her features.

She put on the light and gaudy coat, then the wide-brimmed hat. Part of the preparations for her attack on life, she supposed, was to spend a long time fixing and refixing the set of the hat, although she had no idea which particular slant she wanted. She didn't realise that the size and the undulations of the hatbrim added nothing to her good looks, nor that the yellow dress, black hat and red coat made a devil's own trinity in conflict with her fresh and delicate features. But she was ready; hat, coat, low shoes on and lady gloves – not to be taken off again. She felt strange, surprised as a butterfly that feels for the first time that it has shed its cramped caterpillar limbs and has the endless airy spaces unimpeded to sail through on easy wings. She felt too some of the lightheaded pride of the butterfly …

The mother forgot until the trunk had been locked that she had forgotten to put a bit of hendirt in it, or somewhere among the daughter's clothing. But she wouldn't for the world unlock it again. She couldn't bear the daughter to make fun of her, this morning especially, accuse her of pishrogues and superstition. She shook a tint of holy water on her, and while she was putting the feather back in the bottle the daughter was off out to the kitchen floor to show off her American ensemble.

The sidecar hadn't come yet. There was a swirl of dancing. Tom Neile with his back to the closed door was singing *The Three Sons* in a drunken voice drowning the music –

There's many a fine spa-a-rk young hea-a-rty
Went over the wa-a-ter and ne-e-e-r return'd.

– Tone yourself down, said the mother to Tom, but she'd have given just then to have a tune like he had in order to release the load of her love in a spilling song. The girls had gathered again about the daughter, scrutinising her rig-out, although they had been a week looking at it. They gave the mother no chance of keeping her company. They thought nothing, it seemed to her, of driving a wedge into nature, one almost as inhuman as that driven in by the immense cold sterile sea. The young women were chirruping of America. Chirruping of the life they'd have together soon in South Boston. Typical of a race whose guardian angel was the American trunk, whose guiding star was the exile ship, whose Red Sea was the Atlantic. Bidin Johnny reminded her to ask her cousin to hurry with the passage-money. Judeen Sheain told her on her life not to forget to tell Liam Pheige about the fun there was at the wake of old Cait Thaidhg.

– Take care you don't forget to tell our Sean that we have the Mountain Garth under potatoes again this year, said Sorcha Phaidin. He said when he was going that after him no one would ever again be born to the race that would attempt to sow it, it was such a hardship.

– Tell my boy, Mairin, that it won't be long till I'll be over to him, Nora

Phadraig Mhurcha said in a whisper that all the girls heard.

—By cripes it won't be long till I'm knocking sparks out of the paving stones of South Boston myself, said a redhead youth whose tongue had been loosed by the drink.

—God help those that have to stay at home, said old Seamas O Currain.

The whiskey was circling again. — Here now, you ought to take a taste of it, said Peaitsin Shiubhaine who was measuring it out, heeling the glass towards Mairin with a trembling hand. He splashed some of it on her coat. — A mouthful of it will do you no harm. Devil the drop of poteen you're likely to see the rest of your life. There was an undertone to his voice, he was remembering the five daughters of his own who were "beyond" – one of them thirty-five years gone – and he had no hope of ever seeing them again... —I'll drink it myself then. Your health, Mairin, and may God bring you safe to your journey's end.

Neither Peaitsin nor anyone else in the gathering thought to add, —God send you safe home again. Such ignorance of the proper thing to say sparked off the Mother's repressed anger. —Five years from today you'll see her back home again, she said tartly.

—God grant it, said Peaitsin and Seainin Thomais Choilm together.

—And she'll marry a monied man and stay here with us for good, laughed Citin, Mairin's aunt.

—I'll have little or nothing to show after five years, said Mairin. But maybe you'd marry me yourself, Seainin, without a sixpence?

But by this time Seainin had huddled himself back against the door and was talking like a Tornado to let the mockery of the young girls pass over him.

—At all costs don't pick up an accent, said a young lad, one of her cousins, – and don't be "guessing" all round you like Micilin Eamoinn who spent only two months beyond and came home across the field with nothing to show for his voyage but half a guinea and a new waistcoat.

—Nor asking "what's that mamma?" when you see the pig.

—Anyhow, you'll send me my passage, said Mairead the next daughter to Mairin, eyes sparkling.

—And mine too, said Noirin the next sister.

The mother felt a bleak touch of her own death hearing the greedy begging voices of the pair. Years of delay were being heaped on her daughter's return, as shovelfuls of earth are heaped on a coffin. And the grace of that homecoming were receding from her – as far as Judgement Day. At that moment the children she had given birth to were her greatest enemies.

She set Mairin to drink tea again though she had just stood up from it. But she wanted to come close to her again. She must break bread, make a farewell supper with her daughter. She would tell her plain and straight that she didn't believe this parting meal to be a funeral meal as far as home was concerned: there would be an Easter to come, before the Judgement. But they weren't left to themselves. Her sister Citin with her family of daughters and some of the other girls pushed up to the table by the wall and in no time had Mairin engulfed among them.

The daughter had no wish for food. Her face burned: desire, panic, wonder, an anguish of mind, all showed in her cheek. Brightcity was the farthest from home she had ever been, but she had been nurtured on American lore from infancy. South Boston, Norwood, Butte, Montana, Minnesota, California, plucked chords in her imagination more distinctly than did Dublin, Belfast, Wexford, or even places only a few miles out on the Plain beyond Brightcity. Life and her ideas of it had been shaped and defined by the fame of America, the wealth of America, the amusements of America, the agonised longing to go to America … And though she was lonesome now at leaving home it was a lonesomeness shot through and through with hope, delight, wonder. At last she was on the threshold of the Fairy Palace … Tremendous seas, masts and yardarms, blazing lights, silvertoned streets, dark people whose skin gleamed like beetles, distorting for her already the outlines of garth, mountain, rock, fiord. Her mind tonight was nothing but a ragbag to keep the castoff shreds of memory in until she might shed them as flotsam as she sailed. She was so unguarded now that she let herself be led out to dance on the stone floor, dressed as she was for America. In any case she couldn't have found it in her heart to refuse Padraigin Phaidin.

It irked her conscience that she had so long neglected him. She began to dance in a lackadaisical way, but the pulse of the music – that music to which they were beholden even in the fairyplace – excited an impulse in herself, and soon in her dappled outfit she was like a young alien deer, fullblooded, with the common young animals of the herd prancing about her, inciting her to show what she was made of, what she could do, while the elders sat around in sage contemplation. The mother was thinking that if she was ever to see her again the hard experience of life would then be a dead weight on that lust for dancing. In place of that passion of young and eager blood that wedded her limbs to the graceful movement of the stars, the thin and watery stuff of greying age would be keeping her tired bones fixed on earth.

Nevertheless the mother was closely watching, not the daughter, but Padraigin Phaidin who was dancing with her. There and then she guessed the whole story. Easy to see. Very likely the pair had never said a word of love to each other. Very likely they hadn't said a word tonight. And they were never likely to say a word in their lives. But she realised they would be married in South Boston in a year's time, in five years' time, ten years even … She was vexed. That's what lay behind Padraigin's wild dancing fit. What she had failed to say in words he was saying in dance. Body and limbs he was enacting as perfect poem, with growing zest, abandon, vigour and precision, until a lash of his nailed boot carved a spark out of the hearthstone in time with the final beat of the music. Some might put it down to intoxication, but the mother knew better. That spark was in fact a finishing touch, a final fling of the spirit in full victory. Then hardly waiting to be asked while still breathless from the dance he began with easy power to sing. And the mother forgot the daughter listening to him:

> *The garden's a desert dear heart, and lonesome I be,*
> *No fruit on the bough, no flower on the thorn, no leaf,*
> *No harping is heard and no bird sings in the tree*
> *Since the love of my heart, white branch, went to Cashel O'Neill.*

A young spirit trying to crack the shell of the universe that shut it in, so fierce was his song. By now the mother had come to hate him. An evil being, fingering her own proper treasure …

Horses hooves and the clatter of a sidecar were heard from the cart-track outside. Music and merriment ceased suddenly. Only Seainin Tolan stretched drunk against the shut door still moaning –

> *Ora, wora, wora,*
> *It's on the southern side of New York quay*
> *That I myself will land –*

– the only snatch of a song Seainin ever raised.

–Indeed you'd be a nice gift to America! Devil drown and extinguish you, it's a pity it isn't on some quay you are, a useless hulk, instead of here, cried a youth who could stand him no longer.

The trunk was taken from the room and set like a golden calf on the table.

–Take out that and tie it up on the sidecar, said the mother.

– It might get broken, said Mairin. Leave it alone until I'm ready to go out along with it. That trunk was her licence and authority to wear an elegant hat on her head and an ostentatious coat on her back instead of a shawl. Without the trunk her lady-outfit would be an insult to God. If she let it out of her sight for as much as a second as like as not those tricksome and showy garments would wither into rags and ashes about her body.

She turned now to say goodbye to those who hadn't the strength to accompany her to as far as the king's highway. Crippled old-timers who could barely manage to shuffle across the street; for most of them this was likely the last time they'd leave their own firesides for a social occasion. This was the first link of the chain to be jerked apart, it made her feel for the first time how hard the parting was, how merciless. Whatever about the rest of the people, she would never set eyes on these again. In spite of her distress and hurry she looked closely at each one of them so as to store up in her memory their shape and features. She kept a grip on her emotion and broke down only when she came to her grandmother at the hearth. She had as much affection for her grandmother as she had for her mother, and made more free with her. And was loved in return. Never a week went by but the old women had laid aside a bit of her pension to give her, whatever else might be behindhand. The old creature was as speechless as if already turned to clay. In fact she almost was, for the best part of her was in the grip of "the One with the thin hard foot," and the rest waiting on busy death to prepare her dwelling-place. Her mouth was as dry as the timber of a new-shut coffin, and except for a faint blink of the eyelids that brought her far-off look a little closer to the here and now, Mairin would have thought that she hadn't the least notion what was going on.

–I'll never see you again, mammo, she said, her voice breaking at last in tears.

– God is good, said the mother, a shade stubborn.

Then to kiss the small children and the infant in the cradle. She felt it as a warm substantial summer after the midwinter chill. Charming her senses against the threat of the graveclothes.

The mother brought her off to the room once more. But they weren't long there till Citin and Mairead came in on them to get their shawls so as to accompany Mairin to Brightcity. The mother could have melted them. How officious they were – without them, she thought, the lump of sorrow in the throat wouldn't have hardened again. All she could say to Mairin was that she would have good earnings; that she hoped they would weather at sea; and for the life of her not to forget to have her picture taken beyond and send it home.

–My own darling girl, she said picking a speck of fluff from the shoulder of the coat and giving a hurried quirk to the hatbrim, though the daughter at once reset it her own way. And having glanced quickly around the house she was ready to go.

The sidecar went lurching down the rugged village track followed by a dense crowd, men, women and children. They had all the appearance of a sacrificial procession: the sidecare like a funeral pyre ahead, puffs of the men's tobacco-smoke hanging in the early morning air, and Mairin walking in her barbaric costume as the officiating druid.

The mother walked alongside the daughter and offered to carry her rug, but Brid Sheamais snatched it and carried it herself. She had determined to have Mairin under her own wing on this last walk, but Citin and her own Mairead thwarted her once more. Then all the young girls closed round her, some chattering and laughing, some so lonesome at her going that they hadn't the heart to say much, and others sorry that they weren't in her place or going along with her. By this time the mother had hardly any feelings of regret left so angry was she with the rabble that wished to deprive her of her daughter before she was even out of sight. She took a spleen against the sidecar too. It was moving as fast as if it was giving a corpse "the quick trot to the graveyard". It seemed to her that it was the trunk – perched up on the box of the car, its timber blond as an ear of corn in the rays of the virgin sun – that was pricking the horse to death's own scything speed. She hadn't a word left to say....

There was a mild red light from the sun just up. Field walls and piles of stone grinned bleakly. In the little pokes of fields slanting and rugged the tramped stubble was like the head of Samson having suffered the shears of Delilah. A small sailingboat just out of the harbour with a fair wind scratched a bright wake down the Fiord. Mairin looked back from the rise at Hollycliff, from then on her own house and the village houses strung around would be out of sight. Last year's new thatch joined the old black and withered roof at the ridge-strip – a line of contact between the past and the time to come. And the village seemed asleep again after a brief second of action, slight as a spit in the ocean that the sailingboat might obliterate.

The sidecar halted at the end of the track. The people formed a close group in the mouth of the highway so that the mother was cut off from the daughter. Just another stray stone in the cairn, that's all she was. The same as if she was neither kith or kin. More than ever she begrudged Citin and Mairead their going to Brightcity with Mairin.

When the kissing began the women were like a gaggle of scavengers about a prey. They pushed their way rudely up to her daughter, squeezed her hand, snatched kisses one after the other like a flock of starlings on a trash-heap. The men shook hands with her, shy, laconic, seeming to say it was all one, and if it had to be done then it were best done as quickly as might be. Padraigin Phaidin did likewise, but unlike the rest of the men he gave the slightest lift of his head and the mother caught the eyes of the couple interlocked for the nick of a second.

At last it was her turn. She hadn't kissed her daughter since she was a child. But she failed to put much yearning and anguish into the kiss, though her lips hungered for her. Hadn't she kissed all and everyone? Hadn't all and everyone got ahead of herself in the kissing, the good skimmed from it by all that had been pecking at her. Her body was cold too, cold and insubstantial as a changeling from the Liss.

But what quite spoiled the kiss for her was the sight of the trunk, she was unable to keep her eyes off it and it was all but whispering in her ear –

No mortal kiss will break the spell of the changeling, seduced by pleasure to wander and forget, whose dwelling is the golden web which young desires weave from the sunlight on green hills off from the here and now.

Mairin was now on the sidecar. Mairead sitting beside her, Citlin next to the driver on the other side, Padraigin Phaidin fixing trunk firmly between them up on the box. Damned spirits, they appeared to the mother – the accursed trunk, Mairead greedy to get her passage money, and Padraigin Phaidin on edge to get to America and marry her daughter – three damned spirits torturing her first-born and best-loved.

Padraigin had finished and the people were moving aside to make way for the horse. The women started in to sob, and the sobbing lifted into a loud wail of words, expressing no real anguish the mother thought, beyond voice and tears. They wouldn't leave her even the comfort of keening alone. And she shed no tear …

She stammered uncertainly, – I'll see you before five years are out. And couldn't raise her eyes to meet the eyes of her daughter, not if the sky fell.

The car was now moving. Sobbing the daughter whimpered, – You will. But now the mother's heart as well as her commonsense knew that she would not. Padraigin Phaidin would see her sooner and the girls of the village and her own children, even the infant then in her womb. The mother realised she was but the first of the nestlings in flight to the land of summer and joy: the wildgoose that would never again come back to its native ledge.

Translated, from the Irish, by Eoghan Ó Tuairisc(1919-1982).

This story first appeared in The Road to Brightcity, *by Máirtín Ó Cadhain, a collection of short stories selected and translated by Eoghan Ó Tuairisc (Poolbeg Press, 1981). It is republished here courtesy of the publisher and Rita Kelly.*

NOTE ON THE AUTHOR

Máirtín Ó Cadhain was born, 1906, in Cois Fharraige, that part of the Connemara littoral flanking Galway Bay. He was educated locally and a scholarship to St Patrick's Training College, Drumcondra, saved him from the exile ship. In 1926, he returned to teach in the small schools of the West, but was shocked by what he found. The new Irish State was wholly incapable of supplying the dynamic thinking necessary to save the Cois Fhairraige "American Strip" and all the other isolated Irish-speaking strips along the Atlantic. Seeing that the fight for Ireland, economic and psychological, must still continue, he joined the outlawed IRA. His republicanism had two primary objects: to check the physical erosion of a people who by then were going by whole households to America; and to check the even more terrible erosion of a culture, one of the oldest in Europe, which he saw on the brink of extinction.

In 1936, for his subversive activities, he was dismissed from his post as a National Teacher by the clerical management. During the Second World War the State had him interned in the Curragh Camp. There he conducted classes in the Irish language, culture and literature, and read widely in the Celtic languages, and in English, French, German and Russian. In the late forties, he found employment in the Translation Department of the Dáil, but still continued the economic and cultural fight as a freelance journalist. He shaped a vitriolic style, using the most shattering idioms of the living Irish speech laced with phrases from the seventeenth century and new coinages from modern thought. Trinity College, Dublin, recognising his scholarship and service to the language, appointed him lecturer in modern Irish in 1956 and professor of Irish in 1969. He died in Dublin in 1970.

Eoghan Ó Turairisc, the translator of the only collection of Ó Cadhain's stories in English, *The Road to Brightcity* (Poolbeg, 1981), remarks there of his unique literary achievement:

> Ó Cadhain the creative writer comes as a surprise. In his stories there is none of the violence and aggression which marked his public life. He is too fine an artist to attribute his own seething sense of injustice to his characters who, for the most part, are patient and long-suffering, struggling with their own immemorial way of life detached from the political world. His delineations are delicately studied and finely rounded out, grim, comic, caustic, lyrical, heroic, compassionate. With one breathtaking novel (*Cré na Cille*) and six

collections of short stories, the last published posthumously in 1977, he made an outstanding contribution to Irish writing and to its extension as a means of presenting the complexities of the human spirit in its material milieu ...

The real difficulty of the tongue, and its prime attraction for a modern writer, is its unique mixture of the muck-and-tangle of earth existence with a cosmic view and sense of the "otherworld". This otherworld sense as Ó Cadhain presents it is a very complex combination of a fundamentalist Christianity, emphasizing the Fall of Man, with a large share of the old pagan nature religion. "Ghost," "phantom," "fairy," "the dead," "the changeling," are practically identical terms, and all of them, along with the living, are implicated in a conflict of good and evil, light and dark. Such a worldview is the opposite of romantic, for in it almost all aspects of wild nature – not only sea and storm, but the blue sky, the butterfly, the fine-weather sparkles on water, the hazelnuts – are felt as hostile, always inhuman, at times malicious. Among the few friendly forces are eggs, fire, greying hair and, oddly enough, hendirt ... It is like being confronted with a Rouault *Christ* where one had expected a Jack B. Yeats *Blackbird Bathing in Tir-na-nOg*.

SPECKLED PEOPLE

———

Gerald Dawe

Breaking the closed shop of Irish Writing.

Hugo Hamilton was born in Dublin in 1953 of Irish-German parentage. His home languages were Irish (on his father's instructions) and German (his mother's first language). He is the author of five novels: *Surrogate City*, *The Last Shot* and *The Love Test*, all three set in Germany, and *Head Banger* and *Sad Bastard*, the Coyne thrillers set in Dublin. Hamilton has also published a collection of short stories, *Dublin Where the Palm Trees Grow* in which appears "Nazi Christmas," a first outing of the idea which was to blossom into *The Speckled People*. All this work was published during the 1990s.

In 2003 he published *The Speckled People*. It is in my opinion one of the most significant works by an Irish writer for some time – a fictionalised memoir which will have (or maybe, that is, *should* have) the kind of popular and critical impact as *Reading in the Dark* by Seamus Deane or Joseph O Neill's *Blood-Dark Track* – a book which Hamilton has cited as a significant example for his own work. Hamilton has also alluded to the influence of the Central European tradition in Elias Canetti; the first volume of whose autobiography *The Tongue Set Free* provides *The Speckled People* with its epigraph. There are tentative parallels to be drawn between the narrative voice of *The Speckled People* – a young boy's – and the mesmeric tone of Oskar in Günter Grass's masterpiece, *The Tin Drum*.

To put it at its simplest, *The Speckled People* is a story about finding a home in language; a cultural "locatedness" in the place where one lives, even though there are other powerful and countervailing influences pulling one away to somewhere else. What those influences may be are varied. In Hamilton's account, they are immediate and pervasive.

His Irish-language-speaking, activist father is an authoritarian figure who represses certain elements of his own English-speaking upbringing in Cork – his own father, for instance, had served in the British Navy. He has instead opted for a particular form of nationalism that passionately – and on occasion brutally – believes in the strict faith of an imagined Ireland, its religion and its Gaelic roots. A sort of fundamentalism, in fact: simultaneously understandable, grim and grotesque.

The propagandist father (along with his close circle of friends) yearns for a distinctive, independent Irish culture that shuns the materialistic and heathen superficiality of mid-twentieth century Anglo-America – a worldview that threatens to contaminate his "Ireland". The radio threatens with its popular music; and singing of any "English" songs (even entertaining such thoughts the father considers transgressive of his priorities) leads to punishment. Yet the father is no narrow-minded or stereotypical chauvinist. His idealism and passionate beliefs are revealed in Hamilton's writing with real understanding; indeed, a shocking kind of realization of the father's emblematic "lost-ness" closes the memoir. (In deference to those who have not yet read *The Speckled People*, I think it best if I leave the particular ending of the father's story undisclosed).

The mother survived the Second World War in Germany. Her middle-class Catholic German family has survived not only the horrendous violence of war; she also has overcome the particularly gruesome aspect of her German life at the hands of her boss, a Nazi creep. Her story runs like a geological seam through *The Speckled People*, as a kind of counterforce to the often-ludicrous antics of the father. One history of past epic and colonized grievance (the Irish) is set alongside another history of recent and intensely apocalyptic destructiveness (the German).

The crosscutting of these contrasting time zones and geopolitical sensibilities is the bedrock upon which the master narrative unfolds. Because in the mid-fifties and early sixties, with Europe in recovery and Ireland in denial, the family of boys and girls are taken out of their here and now. Instead, they live at the intersection between their father's messianic hope for the future and their mother's keenly private, yet haunting, sense of her own dislodged, lost past.

Speaking Irish to the father, German to the mother and conceding to English only when the public occasion requires it, the young narrator is caught between the life lived indoors in the family home in south County Dublin and the expectations, misunderstandings and changes taking place outside their front door. A door which repeatedly (and symbolically) slams – as do other doors throughout the house, in the increasingly desperate drama of the father as he struggles to preserve his Little Ireland by keeping out the world beyond. The children are seen as "soldiers" in a language war – and they pay for it. Local lads turn on the young narrator, his brother and sister, calling them "Nazis" and subjecting them to a mock execution. The growing personalities are split between loyalty to their father and mother and bewilderment at the treatment meted out to them by their own peers.

"As a child," Hamilton has observed, "the overwhelming predicament for me was the linguistic predicament – but the clash of histories also preoccupied me. When you're called a Nazi on the street, you tend to become aware of history very quickly." The clash exists at literally every level of *The Speckled People*. Counting the stairs in German, English and Irish, Hamilton portrays the home as both a refuge and a prison-house of language. His brother's nose is broken for using English, outside "is a different place," "not even one of their [English] words enters the hall."

It seems that at every turn the maturing children are caught in a web within which they struggle to become conscious of their individual selves while the complexities of the past are seemingly reduced to one overarching story in which they are actors.

On a trip to their mother's family in Germany, the in-laws remark how the German the children speak "was different, softer, more like the old days". After the mandatory holidays in the Connemara Gaeltacht and the concentration on speaking Irish within the home, the teenage narrator is applauded at school for the quality of his Irish. A true Gael. The father's realization ultimately becomes a parable in itself:

> We are the new Irish. Partly from Ireland and partly from somewhere
> else, half-Irish and half-German. We're the speckled people, he says,
> the "brack" people, which is a word that comes from the Irish
> language…[it] means speckled, dappled, flecked, spotted, coloured.

The dog on the shoreline that barks until it is hoarse; the marvelous comic scene of the family sitting down to eat a cow's tongue; the liberating silence of swimming, when the outside world is closed off and one hears nothing; the tap-tapping of the mother at her typewriter as she records her own story for her children – bring the reader back to the core theme of this brave book.

What is it that makes us who we are? How is "identity" generated if not from the inherited codicils of the past – of what has been honestly faced and revealed, repressed or wisely forgotten, unceremoniously dumped or lost sight of, in the wider familial, political or cultural exigencies of private and civic life? These are the issues that *The Speckled People* dramatizes with such unsolemn energy.

The ghostly presences in *The Speckled People* of the old Gaelic traditions and legends, and the recurring image of the dead talking, of a culture vanishing, remind us of how ancestral voices play their own totally unpredictable role in contemporary self-projection. That, if you like, the past never dies, even though in *The Speckled People* the father's death implies the death of his vision. Yet there is also the mother's release and the almost Lawrentian gesture of the young narrator who heads for home, having faced down his aggressive accusatory peers, seekers of their own conforming kind of orthodoxy:

> When I looked into the shadows under the trees it was so dark that I could see nothing…When you're small you know nothing. I know the sea is like a piece of silver paper in the sun. I can see people walking along the seafront with ice cream cones. I can hear the bells and I'm not afraid any more of being German or Irish, or anywhere in between. Maybe your country is only a place you make up in your own mind. Something you dream about and sing about. Maybe it's not a place on the map at all, but just a story full of people you meet and places you visit, full of books and films you've been to. I'm not afraid of being homesick and having no language to live in. I don't have to be like anyone else. I'm walking on the wall and nobody can stop me.

The politics that subsists within this splendid book is a topic all to itself, as is the fine imaginative recreation of different times and places. And the remarkable sleight-of-hand that Hamilton achieves in *The Speckled People* (and in his three German-based novels) of convincing us that we are hearing a foreign language while reading English is a form of Friel-like trickery.

The Speckled People is a tragicomic work of fiction and a memoir of often heart-rending simplicity. It is also a powerfully liberating challenge to the standard critical categories which operate, both internally and externally, when the phrase *Irish Writing* is brought to mind. Critical expectations, that is, which can stunt a writer and narrow the scope of "our" literature.

For Hamilton reminds us that *Irish* is no monolithic, self-evident cultural or political entity. That the emigrant, refugee and diverse ethnic, religious and cultural roots of this island are a vital and necessary part of the historical narrative of the country. All too often these stories have been marginalized, or self-repressed, since individuals felt either ashamed or embarrassed by their family's "non-Irish" past. As the more visible and predominant Anglo-American realities on this island – as well as the enabling values of the traditional Gaelic past, Scottish as much as Irish – come into greater critical scrutiny, it is important that the multiculturalism of Ireland's own past (limited as it may be) is brought into view along with the developing diversity of today.

In this sense Hugo Hamilton's *The Speckled People*, along with the work of other poets and playwrights of his generation based in Ireland (including those born and raised overseas), or now further afield, points out possibilities for a fresh, critically open engagement with the meanings of "Irish Writing". His memoir might well mark a significant step for those of us who wish to see, not only Irish writing, but Irish life, interpreted in a much more radical way than the time-warped comfort zone of Anglo-centric familiarities and introverted two-way stereotypes. In this way, the cultural diversity of Irish society, reflected by multifaceted imaginative voices, both today and historically, would find an adequate critical recognition and pedagogical response.

Unless I am completely off-track, buried deep in *The Speckled People* there is a kind of echoing parable. Listening to the story of his mother's family's experience of war and her sister Marianne's bravery in the face of totalitarianism, the young narrator reaches a clarifying point of self-awareness, a breakthrough in consciousness.

While Hamilton's reconciliation with his father and what he stood for is clear from the altering, distancing images of the man, it is this conclusive resolution vis-à-vis his mother which strikes me as the most potent in the entire book:

My mother says you can only really be brave if you know you will lose. And the silent negative is not like any other silence either, because one day you will say what you're thinking out loud with your arms folded, like Marianne. You can't be afraid of saying the opposite, even if you look like a fool and everybody thinks you're in the wrong country, speaking the wrong language.

Gerald Dawe's most recent collection of poetry is Lake Geneva *(Gallery, 2003). He is the Director of the Oscar Wilde Centre for Irish Writing, Trinity College, Dublin.*